DICK KIRBY
has also written

Rough Justice – Memoirs of a Flying Squad Detective

'Real Boys' Own stuff, this. Tinged with a wry sense of humour which makes this an excellent read.' METROPOLITAN POLICE HISTORY SOCIETY

The Real Sweeney

'These are the real-life accounts of a tough London cop.' DAILY EXPRESS

You're Nicked!

'It's full of dark humour, tense busts and stand-offs. As crime rates rocket, this book will go down well.' DAILY SPORT

Villains

'All of the stories are told with Dick Kirby's acerbic, black humour in a compelling style, by a detective who was there.' AMERICAN POLICE BEAT

The Guv'nors – Ten of Scotland Yard's Greatest Detectives

'Scotland Yard legends are vividly brought to life by a man who has walked the walk, the Flying Squad's own Dick Kirby. What a brilliant TV series this would make!' JOSEPH WAMBAUGH, AUTHOR OF THE CHOIRBOYS

The Sweeney – The First Sixty Years of Scotland Yard's Crimebusting Flying Squad

'This thoroughly researched and enjoyable history, crammed with vivid descriptions … races along like an Invicta Tourer at full throttle.' DAILY EXPRESS

Scotland Yard's Ghost Squad

'A superb description of crime-busting at the front end.' BERTRAMS – THE HEART OF THE BOOK TRADE

The Brave Blue Line

'This is simply the best book about police gallantry ever written.' HISTORY BY THE YARD

DEATH ON THE BEAT

POLICE OFFICERS KILLED IN THE LINE OF DUTY

DICK KIRBY

First published in Great Britain in 2012 by
Wharncliffe Local History
an imprint of
Pen & Sword Books Ltd
47 Church Street
Barnsley
South Yorkshire
S70 2AS

Hardback ISBN 978 1 84884 620 3
Trade Pbk ISBN 978 1 84563 161 1

Typeset in 11/13pt Plantin by
Mac Style, Beverley, East Yorkshire

Printed and bound in the UK
by CPI Group (UK) Ltd, Croydon, CRO 4YY

Pen & Sword Books Ltd incorporates the Imprints of
Pen & Sword Aviation, Pen & Sword Family History,
Pen & Sword Maritime, Pen & Sword Military, Pen & Sword
Discovery, Wharncliffe Local History, Wharncliffe True Crime,
Wharncliffe Transport, Pen & Sword Select, Pen & Sword
Military Classics, Leo Cooper, The Praetorian Press,
Remember When, Seaforth Publishing and
Frontline Publishing

For a complete list of Pen & Sword titles please contact
PEN & SWORD BOOKS LIMITED
47 Church Street, Barnsley, South Yorkshire, S70 2AS, England
E-mail: enquiries@pen-and-sword.co.uk
Website: www.pen-and-sword.co.uk

Contents

This book is dedicated to
the late Detective Constable Ray Wood OBE –
a true hero who looked death and danger in the face, not once
but many times;
also to the men and women of
the Metropolitan Police,
who provide the front line of policing.
Remember those who fell;
there, but for the grace of God, goes every single one of you.

Acknowledgements

Firstly, I would like to express my grateful thanks to Michael Winner for kindly supplying the foreword to this book.

I am indebted to the staff at Pen & Sword Books for their hard work, especially my publishing manager, Brigadier Henry Wilson, for his wisdom and enthusiasm, and my editors, George and Jan Chamier; when I falter, they pounce. I am also indebted to Alan Moss of *History by the Yard*, Keith Skinner, Bob Fenton QGM, Association of Ex-CID Officers, Pam Pappé and Katie Hamilton from the Peel Centre Library, Susi Rogol, editor of the *London Police Pensioner* magazine, Andrew Brown, Directorate of Information, Metropolitan Police Service, Tony Rae and Keith Foster from the Police Roll of Honour Trust, Phillip Barnes-Warden, Neil Paterson and Paul Dew from the Met Collection and my son, Mark Kirby, for his enthusiastic research.

My thanks go to the Metropolitan Police Service, Adrian Blackledge, Dick Bowen, Gillian Bull, Joanna Chambers, Harry Clement, Irene Dodd, Ivan Dunne, Alan Fairfax, Gerry Gallagher, Maurice Marshall, Morgan O'Grady and Gary Parkins for use of the photographs. Every effort has been made to contact copyright holders; the author and the publishers apologize for any inadvertent omissions.

And in alphabetical order, my thanks also go to the following, who contributed to the content of the book: Terry Allen, Geoffrey E. Anderson, Dave Ayling, Adrian Blackledge, Dick Bowen, Bernie Brown, Gillian Bull, Chris Burke, John Cann, Alan Clarke MBE, Harry Clement BEM, Michael Cookson, Terry Corbett, Charlie Cox GM, Jean Cox, Fred Cutts LL.B, Bernie Davis, John Davis, Reg Davis BA (Hons), John Day, Jim Diplock, Ivan Dunne, Alec Edwards, the late Dick Elsey, Peter Elston, Alan Fairfax, Jim Farrell, Alex Fish, Kenneth Foskett, Peter Francis, Gerry Gallagher, Derek Godfrey, Harry Greig, John Grey, John Hall, Ted Harrington, Bob Hayday, Mike Hames, Martin Hampton, Pat Hastings, Tony Holt, William Hucklesby QPM, FRGS, Reg Humphries, Gordon Hunter, Gerald Hyder, David

Jenkinson, Ted Jolly, John Jones, Peter Johnstone, Brian King, Alan Lewis, Doug MacDonald, Susan Mansell, Maurice Marshall, Michael Masson, Jeff Maund, Anne McDaid, John Merry, Chris Mikellides, Morgan O'Grady, Colin Osborn, Ken 'Pedlar' Palmer, Gary Parkins, Geoff Parratt, Dave Patrick, Paul Phillips, Alexandra Porter, Michael Rawson, Steve Richardson, Bob Roach, Pete Rogers, Tony Roots, Peter Rowling, Peter Ryan, David 'Sandy' Sanderson, Peter Sheldrick, John Simmonds, Richard Slater, the late Jack Slipper, Stephanie Smith, Richard Swarbrick, Harry Tester, Peter Thompson, Bob Thorn, Mick Thwaites, Brian Tomkins, Ken Van-Thal, Ken Walker, Dennis Walland, Alfie Wells, Peter Westley, Allan Willcox, Gillian Wombwell and Laurie Young. Any faults or imperfections in this book are mine alone.

As always, I want to express my thanks to my family: Sue and Steve Cowper and their children, Emma, Jessica and Harry; Barbara and Rich Jerreat and their children, Samuel and Annie Grace; and my sons, Mark and Robert Kirby. It is only through their love and encouragement that I successfully manage to scribble.

Lastly, my thanks to my wife Ann, who always says the right thing at the right time and has all my love and admiration.

Dick Kirby
Suffolk, 2012

Author's Note

WPC Yvonne Fletcher was senselessly, brutally murdered on 17 April 1984 while she was on duty outside the Libyan Embassy in London. Those responsible were Middle Eastern terrorists who masqueraded as diplomats, and they were permitted to return home to Libya, where a hero's welcome awaited them.

Meanwhile, the rest of the world was profoundly shocked by this cruel killing. While politicians whimpered platitudes, Yvonne's loved ones and her close colleagues grieved and wept, and there was a sense of rage and injustice that her killers had walked away scot-free. The Metropolitan Police was utterly demoralized. One man did more than any other to raise their morale, and his name is Michael Winner.

Commencing his career as a newspaper columnist, later an acclaimed director of films on both sides of the Atlantic, Winner is a no-nonsense character, sometimes rude, often abrasive; restaurateurs have been known to tremble at the thought of receiving a savaging in his *Winner's Dinners* column in *The Sunday Times*. But what he wants, he gets, and the Metropolitan Police rank and file adore him; within four days of Yvonne's murder, *The Times* published a letter from him suggesting that memorials should be erected to police officers killed in the line of duty. In part, the letter read:

> It would serve to indicate that not everyone in this country takes seeming pleasure in attacking the police in the execution of their difficult duties, but that most of us regard their conduct and bravery under a whole series of endless and varied provocations as demonstrably noble and worthy of our thanks.

Letters of support and donations poured in, and within two weeks of the murder Michael Winner formed the Police Memorial Trust on 3 May 1984. These were its aims:

> The promotion of good citizenship through the provision of memorials to police officers killed in the execution of their hazardous duty, and through these memorials also to honour

the Police Service in general and subject thereto to relieve the need of police officers or their dependants arising from the special hazards of police duty.

It was intended that these memorials should be erected as close as possible to the spot where the officers had met their death; the concept caught the imagination of the great and the good, the heads of large corporations and the general public, and now the money poured in to the Trust. Since that time, memorials have been unveiled as tributes to almost fifty officers killed in the line of duty. The Police Roll of Honour Trust was formed in 2000 and it provided details of Metropolitan Police officers killed in the line of duty; it was opened by Her Majesty the Queen at Peel Training Centre in 2001. A National Police Memorial was similarly dedicated by Her Majesty in 2005.

What follows are the stories of some of those police officers, men and women, who died in the line of duty. I have described the investigations into their deaths and how their murder affected their colleagues and loved ones; I hope I have done them proud.

Dick Kirby

Foreword

When Yvonne Fletcher was killed it dawned on my rather befuddled mind that it was grossly unfair there should be memorials to services who fight and die on our behalf – the army, the navy and the air force – but none to the police who also fight and die for us. Theirs is a war with no beginning and no end. Brave men and women go forward unarmed and not infrequently pay the price by being shot, beaten to death, knifed, thrown from roofs, run down by cars etc.

My letter to *The Times* about this follow-up article in the *Daily Mail* produced a number of donations from the public. I had not the slightest intention of doing anything about it. I was simply writing. So I wrote to the Charity Commissioners, asking how to start a charity for police memorials. I intended to send their reply to the people who sent money, saying, "You form the charity, count me in for £5,000!" A charity commissioner, Mr Rao, rang me and said, "I have your letter in front of me, Mr Winner. Are you seriously telling me you want to put up memorials to mere policemen?" When he said that I put my hand over the phone and said to my assistant, "Fuck it, I'll have to do this." Thus the Police Memorial Trust was rather unceremoniously born.

We have some 43 memorials up all over the land. After ten years of frustration, hard work and massive energy I managed to get the first memorial placed in the Mall for over 100 years. The National Police Memorial is on the corner of Horse Guards and the Mall. It was unveiled by Her Majesty the Queen and represents what, I firmly believe, the police deserve. Namely, recognition. It is a national pastime to attack the police. It's about time somebody dealt with appreciating their valour and service.

I am delighted that Dick Kirby has written this book. I am sure those who read it will realize how very hazardous the life of a policeman is. One day they may be giving advice to citizens on road directions, another filling in forms, another attempting to contain riots, and on other days they will quite simply be killed. Such heroes should be remembered.

Michael Winner MA (Cantab), OBE (offered but rejected)
Chairman and Founder, the Police Memorial Trust

CHAPTER 1

Shot in the Back

Before Metropolitan Police districts, divisions and beats became 'boroughs' and 'neighbourhoods', what was known as 'Y' Division covered a very large area of North London, including Tottenham, Wood Green, Southgate and Winchmore Hill, and the northern boundaries of the division flanked those of the Hertfordshire Constabulary. In 1948 criminality had slightly stabilized, with 126,597 indictable offences being recorded in the Metropolitan Police Area, after a dramatic rise in crime – to 128,954 offences – following the end of the Second World War.

Rationing was still in place, and although Scotland Yard's secret post-war Ghost Squad was having 'its best year ever' in its fight against the black marketeers and lorry hijackers, the number of police officers patrolling the streets was far smaller than was considered desirable. Recruitment had recommenced following the end of the war, but although the authorized establishment of 'Y' Division should have been 831, the actual figure was 646. Much of the housing in 'Y' Division in 1948 was situated in smart commuter land and as such it attracted the attention of housebreakers. Apart from burglary, problems were also being experienced with desertion from the armed services – and sometimes the two crimes coincided.

In February 1948 there had been a spate of twenty-nine burglaries in and around the areas of Winchmore Hill and Southgate, and therefore, whilst all police personnel were expected to keep their eyes peeled, it fell to the aids to CID to go out and patrol, keep observations, press their informants for details as to who was responsible and, ideally, make arrests. These fledgling CID men were uniformed officers in plain clothes, and for an aid to CID to arrest a burglar – i.e. one who broke into dwelling houses during the hours of darkness – more or less guaranteed his acceptance into the CID proper. The aids patrolled in pairs – their partners were known as 'bucks' – and quite often, especially in an area as big as 'Y' Division, on bicycles, meeting up at previously agreed locations or giving hand signals if something occurred which would necessitate the assistance of the other.

But at one o'clock on the afternoon of Friday 13 February, the pair of aids who booked on duty to commence their patrol decided to work the area on foot. Police Constable 559 'Y' John McPartlan had joined the police in 1931 and his entire career had been spent on 'Y' Division. Just under five feet ten, McPartlan, a native of Haywood, Lanarkshire, aspired to promotion but had only passed his Civil Servants Examination (Second Class) – necessary before sitting the police examination for sergeant – on the fifth occasion. He fared little better with the sergeant's examination, only passing the qualifying examination for detective sergeant (second class) at the fourth attempt in 1940. However, there was first the matter of being selected for the rank of detective constable. He was better at being a thief catcher; in 1938 he had been commended by the commissioner, the Justices at Wood Green Petty Sessions and the Deputy Chairman of the Middlesex Sessions for his actions in effecting an arrest in a case of shopbreaking and larceny. McPartlan was now thirty-nine years of age – quite old for an aid – and was married with two children, a boy and a girl, both born in 1947.

McPartlan's partner was Police Constable 807 'Y' Nathanael – but always known as 'Nat' – Edgar, a fellow Scot from Leslie, Fife. Edgar was one of 238 candidates who joined the police on 2 September 1939, and he was posted to 'Y' Division. Nine months later, he married Florence at the Holy Trinity Church, Islington, and they moved into 231 Falloden Way (on the A1 trunk road), Golders Green. Two sons were born to them: Thomas Leslie in 1943 and Neil Henry two years later.

In 1943, Edgar had volunteered for service with the Royal Navy, and following his demobilization in 1946 he returned to 'Y' Division. He passed his Civil Servants Examination in 1941 but failed the sergeant's exam in 1946. Edgar had been commended twice in 1947, once for the arrest of a thief before he could climb into a getaway car, and secondly for arresting a housebreaker. And so thirty-three-year-old Edgar set off on patrol that Friday afternoon with his 'buck', hopeful of catching a burglar.

★   ★   ★

For the next four and a half hours the two aids patrolled Southgate, meticulously quartering the area, but without any success; after a refreshment break at six o'clock they decided to patrol the area of Winchmore Hill and the Oakwood Estate.

At seven o'clock they saw a suspect with a slight limp, a hatless man in a dark overcoat, in Wychgate and followed him into Park

View; but by now it was quite dark, and after twenty minutes the man disappeared in the vicinity of Grovelands Park, which bordered those thoroughfares to the south. The officers decided to separate and patrol the area of the Oakwood Estate individually, then, if nothing happened, to meet up in Winchmore Hill Road at eight o'clock. And nothing did transpire; so they decided to continue their lone patrols and meet up at Southgate Tube Station an hour later.

Edgar walked off along Winchmore Hill Road and then cut through to Park View, where he and McPartlan had originally seen the suspect. Then, just before 8.30, he found him. The man appeared to be just about to climb the drainpipe of a house in Wades Hill, but as Edgar walked up to the premises, so the man left by the front gate. Edgar stopped him and asked for an explanation; the man told him that he had intended to visit a house further along the road, but there was nobody at home. Not unnaturally, Edgar demanded the suspect's name and address. The man produced his identity card and Edgar recorded the details: his identity number, BEAH 257/2, and his name and address – Thomas, Donald, 247 Cambridge Road, Enfield.

Thomas offered to show Edgar the house which he had intended to visit, and the two men walked down Wades Hill to No. 112, which Thomas indicated. But just at that moment, a light came on in the house – which rather spoilt Thomas' claim that the premises were unoccupied.

Edgar may have turned to look down the road and see if he could spot his colleague, McPartlan. It was then that Thomas took the opportunity to draw a Luger pistol. With Edgar's back turned, he fired three shots which hit Edgar in the base of his spine, his buttock and his right thigh.

The shots were heard by Mrs Mary Laing, who was walking along Broadlands Avenue with her brother, Mr James Baillie, and she then saw a man run along Broadlands Avenue from the direction of Wades Hill. As they entered the junction they could see the collapsed PC Edgar lying face down, groaning and bleeding on the driveway. Mrs Laing called the police. Mr and Mrs John Hansen, who lived next door, also heard the shots but although they looked outside they were unable to see Edgar's body in the darkness, lying in next door's driveway.

Dr Edward Soloman Samuels, who lived nearby, also heard the shots and the sound of running footsteps, and when he found Edgar, obviously grievously wounded, he tended his wounds, administered two injections of morphine and called for an ambulance. At the same time, the area car drew up and Police

Constable 733 'Y' William Crow and Police Constable 538 'Y' Yves Jennings saw immediately that the wounded man was one of their colleagues.

With enormous willpower, Edgar provided a description of the gunman and told the area car crew, "The man was by the door. I got his identity card and name. I do not know if it is right. He shot me in the legs with three shots. The pocket book is in my inside pocket." With that, he sank into unconsciousness and was conveyed to North Middlesex Hospital, Edmonton.

Police Constable 452 'Y' Allan Willcox was a young probationer with five months' service at Wood Green police station, and he and his wife were on their way to a social function at her company on the North Circular Road, Palmers Green, when a police car and an ambulance, sirens wailing, passed them en route to the hospital. Despite the surgeons' most determined efforts to save him, Edgar died without regaining consciousness at 9.30 that evening. As Wilcox told me, "The following morning, the news broke and the whole of the area was in shock."

* * *

Donald George Thomas had been responsible for sixteen of the burglaries in that area and had just been attempting his seventeenth when he was stopped by PC Edgar. Twenty-three years of age, he had been brought up in Edmonton, was among the brightest half-dozen boys in his school, captain of the cricket team and a member of the Boys' Brigade, before going off the rails in his teens. He was placed on probation twice. His mother had found a pound note missing from her purse and called the police, who were more interested in the two stolen bicycles at the family address. He stole another bicycle and was sent to an Approved School. In January 1945 he was called up for military service, and within a fortnight he had deserted from the General Service Corps. After two years on the run, he surrendered to the Military Police and was sentenced to 160 days' detention; almost immediately after being returned to his unit, on 13 October 1947 he deserted once more. Since that time he had secured an income, sometimes with an associate, sometimes alone, by breaking into houses.

* * *

The crew of the area car, together with PC McPartlan, rushed to the divisional headquarters at Wood Green police station and handed over Edgar's pocket book. McPartlan had been several streets away at the time of the shooting but was able to provide a description of the suspect that he and Edgar had seen previously: aged about twenty-five and five feet eight tall. Furthermore, he had seen Edgar's pocket book earlier in the day; Thomas' details had not been written down then and no entry had been made the last time they had met at eight o'clock. Therefore, when Edgar had murmured to PC Crow that he had written down the gunman's details from his identity card, it appeared that that man concerned was the killer.

The officer in charge of the murder investigation was Divisional Detective Inspector Thomas Owen Harry Stinton. He was then forty-two years of age and had been a police officer since 1925. Stinton had spent several years at C1 Department at the Yard, and the complicated cases he had dealt with there had materially helped the investigations which he had solved on divisional duties – on 'C', 'X' and now 'Y' Division. He had been commended on nineteen occasions, mainly for solving white-collar crimes, including a number of frauds, bribery, a rather odd offence in contravention of the Coal Mines Act and an even stranger one, where he was commended for 'ability in a difficult case of a mysterious death'.

Not that there was anything mysterious regarding Edgar's death; it was cold-blooded murder, pure and simple. The investigation commenced with Stinton telephoning the details contained in Edgar's pocket book to Criminal Records Office at the Yard; within seconds, it was revealed that Thomas was circulated as being wanted for desertion and that the address in Cambridge Road, Enfield was his last known address. Armed police raided the premises, which were occupied by his mother, but Thomas had long since vanished from there. Nevertheless, a twenty-four-hour watch was maintained on the property in case he did return.

The head of the CID at No. 2 District Headquarters, Detective Superintendent Peter Henderson Beveridge MBE, a very tough, red-haired Scot who had led the Flying Squad through the war years, was apprised of the situation and went straight to the Yard. He, like Edgar, came from Fife, and there was another bond, because he knew that Edgar's younger brother had been captured with the 51st Highland Division at St Valéry in 1940 and had made a daring escape through France and into Spain. There was public (as well as police) outrage at the crime; it was the first time in almost thirty years that a Metropolitan Police officer had been fatally shot, and he wanted the case cleared up before anybody else could be murdered. Beveridge insisted that Thomas' photograph be published in the newspapers, and although his request was initially rejected, the Assistant Commissioner (Crime) Ronald Howe MVO, MC, and the Commissioner, Sir Harold Scott GCVO, KCB, KBE, finally agreed to permit publication of the photograph. It was a wise choice. Two years previously, Sir Harold had decided not to allow publication of the photograph of Neville George Clevely Heath, who was wanted for a sickening, degrading sex murder. No one knew where Heath was, he had no known associates, he was renowned for using a string of aliases; when he was finally arrested, it was discovered that, during the intervening period, he had committed a second murder, just as savage and depraved as the first. There had been some unwelcome publicity following Sir Harold's lamentably irrational decision, but, like the true civil servant which he was at heart, he survived the ordeal. However, he was probably astute enough to know that if the same thing happened again, adverse public opinion would ensure that he did not complete his tenure as commissioner; therefore, the following day (and this was the first time a wanted person's picture had been published), a photograph of Thomas appeared in the newspapers with the bland statement that this man could assist the police with their enquiries into the murder of PC Edgar. Fortunately, the item was seen by a certain Stanley J. Winkless of Camberwell.

Winkless recognized Thomas as being a man whom he had known for about three months and with whom his wife, Noreen, a twenty-seven-year-old usherette at the New Victoria Cinema, had fallen passionately in love. Three weeks previously, she had run off with Thomas, leaving her husband and their three children. Winkless produced a photograph of his faithless wife, and on the morning of Tuesday, 17 February the faces of Donald Thomas and Noreen Winkless featured prominently in the morning newspapers. This photograph was seen by Mrs Connie Smeed, the landlady of a house which had been converted into bedsits at 16 Mayflower Road, Stockwell, South London. She realized that she was looking at photographs of two of her tenants, whom she knew as Don and Noreen Winkless, currently resident on the top floor. Mrs Smeed ran out into the street and stopped fifty-three-year-old ex-War Reserve Police Constable 103 'L' George Charles Searle, who contacted the local station and then kept watch to ensure the suspects did not abscond.

Meanwhile, Mrs Smeed's 'ideal couple' were languishing in bed. The star-crossed lovers had been staying in their thirty-shillings-a-week accommodation since 24 January, the date of their flight from nearby Camberwell. On the day of the murder, Thomas had gone out at 6.30 in the evening to travel to Winchmore Hill and find a house to burgle. When he returned the following morning, he admitted to his paramour that he had shot a police officer but stressed that he had "only intended to maim him." Reassured by this apparently acceptable explanation, Noreen Winkless resolved to 'stand by her man'.

While he waited for his landlady to bring up the breakfast tray, Thomas was in good company. As well as having the glamorous Mrs Winkless for companionship, he also had a jemmy, a rubber cosh and half a dozen other identity cards; to pass the time, his reading material included *Shooting to Live, with the One-handed Gun* by Captain W. E. Fairburn and Captain E. A. Sykes, both of whom had been very tough instructors to the wartime Special Forces. For extra reassurance, underneath the pillow he had his 9mm Luger pistol, fully loaded with a clip of eight rounds, plus one in the breech; in addition, he had a further seventeen rounds of ammunition.

* * *

There was absolutely no time to contact the investigating officers far north of the Thames; action had to be taken immediately, and Inspector William Arthur Moody from Brixton police station took charge of the situation. At five feet eleven and weighing almost sixteen stone, the forty-year-old former goalkeeper for the Metropolitan Police's first eleven had been a police officer for twenty years, and the previous year he had been commended by the commissioner for displaying initiative in a case of shopbreaking. Now, Moody, a married man with a son aged nine and two daughters, aged ten and twelve months, assembled his men. The first was Police Constable 98 'L' Dennis Edward Wheeler, who had spent seventeen years in the police and two years previously had been commended in a case of robbery. The second was Police Constable 359 'L' Robert Henry Hide, who was forty-one years of age. He had joined the police in 1926 and made his career in the CID on 'C' and 'G' Divisions, passing the examination for detective sergeant (second class) in 1931. He was a successful CID officer, having been commended by the commissioner on six occasions until in 1937 he returned to uniform at his own request. Six feet tall, and a single man, the last ten years of his service had been spent at Brixton police station.

* * *

Arriving at Mayflower Road at 8.15, Inspector Moody saw Mrs Smeed in her kitchen; she told him that she was supposed to take a breakfast tray up to her lodgers at 8.30. Moody asked her to do just that, and he and his men followed her silently up the stairs. Mrs Smeed set down the tray containing toast, marmalade and tea and knocked on the door; a man's voice from within the room called out, "Okay." As Mrs Smeed descended the stairs, Moody and Wheeler (who was in plain clothes) waited at either side of the door; PC Hyde was on the landing and PC Searle a few steps down on the stairs.

They heard the sound of the key being turned in the lock, and then Thomas, dressed only in vest and pants, opened the door an inch and peered out at the landing – enough to see at least one officer outside, whereupon he slammed the door shut. Before he had a chance to lock it, Moody and Wheeler launched themselves at the door, which flew open, in time for them to see Thomas rush towards the bed. Wheeler dived for his legs and brought him down in a rugby tackle, but as he fell, so Thomas reached the bed and seized the pistol under the pillow. At the same moment, Moody leapt on top of him and flattened him with his bulk, and as Thomas turned the pistol towards him, Moody grabbed Thomas' gun-hand with both of his hands and wrenched the pistol from his grasp. The two officers were assisted by PCs Hide and Searle who then managed to overpower Thomas. From underneath the bedclothes came a muffled voice: "What's going on? Let me get up!" – and out crawled Mrs Winkless.

Moody told Thomas he was under arrest and asked if the Luger was loaded. "Yes, full up," replied Thomas, adding, "and they were all for you!" As he was driven to Brixton police station, Thomas told Moody, "You were lucky; I might as well be hung for a sheep as a lamb."

At 11.15 that morning DDI Stinton arrived at Brixton, and having been told of Thomas' remarks regarding the pistol, examined it, to find that it was indeed "full up" and, in addition, that the safety catch was off. Thomas later told the jury at the Old Bailey that when Stinton saw him he exclaimed, "You bastard! You're just the right build to string up and I'm going to make sure you go!" But it mattered little whether the jury believed that a highly respected senior CID officer who had spent his career meticulously investigating fraud cases was capable of such an outburst. Public opinion was firmly against a man like Thomas – a double deserter, a housebreaker, an adulterer and a police murderer – and there were angry scenes from the public as he arrived at Wood Green police station to be charged with the murder of PC Nat Edgar.

Apart from his boastful utterances to the arresting officers, Thomas appeared truculent but had little to say for himself. Others, however, had a great deal more to say. Mrs Winkless may have initially been swept away by the hot, lustful blood rushing through her veins and by romantic notions of being a gangster's moll on the run with her younger paramour ("When love speaks," says Berowne in *Love's Labour's Lost*, "the voice of all the gods makes heaven drowsy with the harmony"). However, these delightful feelings quickly evaporated as the gravity of the situation became apparent, and Mrs Winkless came down to earth with a bump. Discovering that Donald Thomas was not quite as enthralling as she had first thought, she made a statement to police in which she recounted all of their conversations regarding the shooting of PC Edgar, and this became a template for the prosecution. In addition, ballistic tests revealed that the three bullets which had murdered PC Edgar had been fired from the pistol which was found in his possession.

The evidence was therefore so compelling that when the sub-divisional inspector informed the clientele of Wood Green police station's canteen, "I'll bet a thousand pound he'll swing for it" there were no takers; but as former PC Allan Willcox told me, "I wish I'd taken him on," because Sidney Silverman MP, a capital punishment abolitionist, was making himself extremely busy in Parliament.

At his trial at the Old Bailey, Thomas pleaded not guilty to murdering PC Edgar, and, given the weight of the evidence against him, he had to come up with a fairly persuasive defence. Unfortunately for him, he was unable to do so. Thomas told the court that he was desperate to get away because if he had been caught as a deserter from the army he could have expected three years' imprisonment. Telling the jury he had purchased the pistol from a man in Soho for £5, Thomas stated that PC Edgar had grappled with him for possession of the weapon, which went off accidentally. "I had no intention of killing PC Edgar," stated Thomas. "I pulled the gun to scare him." This was firmly contradicted by the witnesses who informed the court that there had been three deliberate shots, as opposed to randomly spaced or panicky ones, and also by the pathologist, who gave evidence that Edgar was shot in the back.

On 20 April Thomas was found guilty of the murder and Mr Justice Hilbery, the black cap on his head, pronounced the sentence of death. But as he did so, he knew that this sentence would not be carried out. Four days previously, there had been a parliamentary vote by which it was decided that capital punishment be held in abeyance. It was smartly reintroduced on 10 June, courtesy of Lord Goddard's maiden speech in the House of Lords and by 181 votes to 28; but although it was reported that Thomas nervously asked the warders, "What do you think? They won't hang me, will they?", there was never any chance that 'they' would.

★ ★ ★

Inspector Moody and Police Constables Wheeler, Hide and Searle were all highly commended by the commissioner and awarded £15 each from the Bow Street Reward Fund; unfortunately, payment had to be deferred due to the post-war lack of public funds. But on 26 July 1949 the four officers were invited to Buckingham Palace, where each of them was awarded the King's Police and Fire Services Medal for gallantry (in fact, Searle accepted his award as a civilian; he had resigned from the police on New Year's Eve, 1948).

Hide never resumed his former career as a CID officer (although no doubt he was asked to), and two years later he was commended by the commissioner for alertness in arresting two men for larceny. He retired in 1955, having completed just over twenty-nine years' service, and died twenty-three years later at the age of seventy-two.

Wheeler was granted a divorce three months after receiving his medal, and six months later he was transferred to 'Y' Division. He had completed twenty-five years' service when he resigned, six months after Hide.

Moody, whose police career had been interrupted by war service in the army, where he attained the rank of major, was worshipped by his men. He was promoted to chief inspector in 1951 and posted to Hendon. In 1953 he passed the senior course at Ryton-on-Dunsmore Police College and the following year he was promoted to superintendent. He retired after thirty-one years' service and died aged sixty-nine.

In 1950, McPartlan, Edgar's erstwhile partner, re-took his examination, was promoted to uniformed sergeant and was posted to 'S' Division, where once again he would have encountered Moody. McPartlan served on the division for nine years, and eight years after retirement he died, at the early age of fifty-eight.

A year after the Old Bailey case, DDI Stinton was promoted to detective chief inspector and was posted to C1 Department at the Yard for the third time, where, in all, he served a total of eight years. He retired after twenty-six years' service and enjoyed a long retirement, dying at the age of eighty.

★   ★   ★

Edgar's funeral took place two days after Thomas' arrest. He was laid to rest in St Marylebone Cemetery, Finchley, with the ceremony commensurate for an officer who was known locally as 'Gentleman Edgar'. The Home Secretary, Mr J. Chuter Ede, attended, as did the Commissioner, the Deputy Commissioner, John Nott-Bower KPM, and a number of senior officers, including DDI Stinton and the arresting officer, Inspector Moody. The Metropolitan Police Band attended, as did representatives from provincial police forces; and although the weather was bitterly cold with snow flurries, it did not prevent the attendance of hundreds of other friends and colleagues.

The Mayor of Southgate, together with local residents and businessmen, started a fund for Edgar's widow that realized £600, and the *News of the World* also made a contribution of £250. Mrs Edgar's widow's pension from the police amounted to just £109 4s 0d per year, plus annual allowances of £21 16s 10d each in respect of her two sons. The paltriness of this sum resulted in a demand for higher pensions for the widows of murdered police officers. The boys were later educated at Reed's School, Cobham, Surrey, with assistance from police funds. On the fiftieth anniversary of the murder, a plaque was unveiled at Muswell Hill police station to the memory of PC Edgar. It was at the initiative of his brother, David Edgar, who as part of the Greenwich Police Consultative Group was a strong supporter of the police. Although Mr Edgar was quite prepared to pay for the plaque himself, the money was raised after an appeal to the Police Federation and the Friends of the Metropolitan Police Museum.

★   ★   ★

Donald Thomas' sentence was commuted to one of life imprisonment. He was released from Parkhurst Prison in April 1962, having served thirteen years. His behaviour during incarceration had been said to be 'indifferent'. His jemmy, book on shooting skills, bullets and bullet cases were sent, together with PC Edgar's pocket book containing his details, to the Yard's Black Museum. But there were two additional memorials to PC Edgar's memory.

The fact that at the time of his death at the hands of a young tearaway PC Edgar was in plain clothes detracted nothing from his persona as a popular 'Bobby on the Beat'. It inspired the PC Dixon character in Basil Dearden's 1949 film, *The Blue Lamp*, who was similarly shot dead by a young thug. The film, which was shot in a revolutionary semi-documentary style, was made with the backing of the commissioner of police, and because the police were held in high regard by the general public, it was an enormous success. Now, over sixty years later, it still stands the test of time.

And there was a second, little-known memorial. Dr Samuels, who had administered first aid to PC Edgar as he lay on the driveway in Wades Hill, had his gates and garage door repainted in police-box blue. It was his own, private way of saluting the courage of a fine community police officer.

Chapter 2

Death on the Rooftop

The George Cross was struck in 1940 'for acts of the greatest heroism or of the most conspicuous courage in circumstances of extreme danger', and it is the highest award for bravery which can be given to members of the civilian population. Quite properly, it is sparingly presented; in its seventy-year history only 160 have been awarded, and out of that number, just four have gone to Metropolitan Police officers, the first such award being in 1953. The recipient thoroughly deserved the honour, but the contentious aspects of the circumstances which led to the award continued to be controversial for another forty-five years.

★   ★   ★

Many people believe that what became known as 'The Craig and Bentley Case' commenced on the roof of a Croydon warehouse on the evening of 2 November 1952; in fact, it began three days before that.

Niven Scott Craig was a thoroughly dangerous career criminal, with convictions for armed robbery. Inexplicably nicknamed 'The Velvet Kid', Craig was convicted first as a juvenile aged fourteen, and in 1940 for an offence of storebreaking he was sent to an Approved School. He escaped and went on the run with another absconder, having broken into a Home Guard store in order to obtain firearms. Both boys acquired hero-like status in the popular press after they were arrested in a rowing boat in which, they stated, they intended to cross the English Channel in order to 'have a crack at the Germans'. During Craig's army service with the Gordon Highlanders a few years later, he had a crack at the Allies instead, which resulted in a five-year sentence for armed robbery. Escaping from his escort, Craig carried out four more robberies at gunpoint of army vehicles and their contents before his recapture. During his time in the army, he had been convicted on no fewer than twelve occasions. Following Craig's release from military prison in 1950 and his dishonourable discharge, he had been arrested by the Flying Squad in 1952 in possession of a loaded and cocked pistol, after having spent six months on the run following an armed robbery at Waltham Abbey. Craig told the jury at the Old Bailey that on the night of the robbery he had been staying at an address at Wells-next-the-Sea in Norfolk, and although this was confirmed by his younger brother and a friend, they were not believed. On 30 October 1952 the trial judge, Mr Justice Hilbery, told twenty-six-year-old Craig, "I believe that you would shoot down, if you had the opportunity to do so, any police officer who was attempting to arrest you," and sentenced him to twelve years' imprisonment. "At least we've put that bastard away for a few years," a detective allegedly said, within hearing of one of Craig's disbelieved alibi witnesses, and it is suggested that this remark prompted sixteen-year-old Christopher Craig to take revenge. It may or may not be true; the younger Craig – a devotee of gangster films, sometimes visiting the cinema two or three times per week – was by now almost as dangerous as his elder sibling. Even before his brother's trial had started, Christopher Craig and Norman Parsley (also aged sixteen) had robbed an elderly couple at gunpoint on 18 October. Knocking on the front door of Mr and Mrs Christopher Howes' home at Avon Path, Croydon, the teenagers, both masked and carrying handguns, pushed Mrs Howes to the floor and demanded money. Mr Howes gave them a bag containing £4 in coins, but when the boys told the couple they intended to tie them up, Mr Howes bravely ordered them out of his house, and they went.

Christopher Craig was the youngest of eight children, and apart from him and his brother Niven, the rest of the siblings were eminently respectable, as were both parents. The family lived in Norbury Court Road, and their father, Niven Matthew Craig, had served with distinction as a captain in the London Scottish Brigade in the First World War and had been a member of the Home Guard during the Second. He was now a cashier in a bank in London's Victoria Street. Christopher Craig had not distinguished himself at school – he suffered from dyslexia – and comics appeared to be his staple reading diet. He was now working in a garage. Eighteen months previously, he and another boy had run away from home. When they were caught in Hove, Sussex, the local juvenile court fined him for being in possession of a .45 Webley revolver. His companion had been carrying a Luger automatic. In an act oddly reminiscent of his elder brother's exploit some ten years earlier, Craig was discovered sheltering under a boat in Brighton which he intended to use for his flight to France, which by then had been vacated by the German armed forces.

Firearms fascinated Craig – coincidentally, his father had been rated the fourth best shot in the Army, but Craig senior was unaware that his youngest son had possessed anything between forty to fifty guns of his own (although not simultaneously) which he took to school, showed to his friends and swapped for others.

During the afternoon of Sunday 2 November, Craig had gone to the cinema with a girlfriend to watch Anthony Young's 1952 British thriller, *My Death is a Mockery*, in which a man is killed and a smuggler is convicted and hanged. That evening, Craig went out with Derek William Bentley, who was aged nineteen. At the age of five, Bentley had landed on his head after a fall from a lorry which had caused epilepsy, and during the Second World War he had again suffered head injuries when the house in which he was living was bombed. He had learning difficulties and had twice been convicted, firstly for attempted shopbreaking and attempted larceny, for which he was bound over, and secondly for stealing tools, for which he was sentenced to three years at Kingswood Approved School, Bristol (he was released after two). Bentley's disabilities were severe enough for him to be excluded from National Service. He had had a number of menial, low-paid jobs, and at the time of his excursion with Craig he was unemployed and living with his parents at 1 Fairview Road, Norbury.

As they made their way to Croydon that evening, both Bentley and Craig were armed, Bentley with a knuckleduster, which Craig had given him, and a small knife, and Craig with a larger sheath knife and a First World War standard issue .455 Eley service revolver, together with ammunition. The gun had been stolen from a house in Purley, and Craig had sawn off the end of the barrel so that it might be more easily concealed.

The reason for their outing was this: the previous day, Bentley had stolen a set of keys to a butcher's shop in Tamworth Road, Croydon. Working on the assumption that the week's takings would still be on the premises, the youths decided to use the keys to break in and help themselves; however, upon arrival at the shop they saw a light and could hear movements inside. They waited to see if the light would be extinguished and the occupants would leave, but when nothing of the kind happened the duo moved on, looking for another target. An electrical shop might have held promise, but a courting couple were lingering outside it, and the youths continued walking.

At 9.20 in Tamworth Road, Croydon, they were spotted by Mrs Edith Ware, who was about to put her nine-year-old daughter Pearl to bed, after the child drew her attention to Craig and Bentley in the street below. Both were acting suspiciously by a warehouse belonging to Barlow & Parker, a wholesale confectioners' company, because they felt that here too might be substantial sums of money waiting to be banked the following day. Entry at ground level presented the pair with insurmountable difficulties, but access via the roof might well be an option. They had climbed over a spiked iron gate by the time that Mr Ware slipped out of the house to call the police from a telephone kiosk. Officers from Croydon police station arrived five minutes later; Detective Constable Frederick William Fairfax together with Police Constable 192 'Z' Norman Harrison and other officers arrived in a police van, whilst Police Constable 528 'Z' James Christie McDonald turned up in a wireless car. This had been driven by Police Constable Leslie Miles – not PC Sidney Miles, as many writers believe.

Fairfax took charge of the operation and, seeing a footprint on the windowsill of the warehouse, he correctly assumed that that was the route the intruders had taken; he therefore commenced climbing the adjoining drainpipe. It was a feat which presented little difficulty for Fairfax; joining the police in 1936, he had volunteered for the army after hostilities broke out and, as a captain with the Royal Berkshire Regiment and a skilled boxer, had been seconded to train the newly formed commandos in Scotland. Following demobilization, he had returned to the police and had been commended on six occasions, mainly for the arrest of housebreakers who were variously described as being 'persistent', 'troublesome' and 'active'.

Now, the balding, thirty-five-year-old detective quickly scaled the drainpipe, which led to a flat asphalt roof twenty-two feet above ground; not so PC McDonald, who followed him but was unable to complete the climb and had to return to the ground. As Fairfax pulled himself on to the roof, he quickly took stock of his surroundings. The roof area measured ninety by fifty-four feet and encircling it was a guard rail two feet six inches high. Four glass roof lights, each four and a half feet high were at the centre; at the rear was the head of the lift-shaft, almost twelve feet high. Forty feet away from the lift-shaft was the door to an interior staircase, and it was here that Fairfax first set foot on the roof. Fifty feet to Fairfax's right was the front of the building, overlooking Tamworth Road; straight ahead of him were the roof lights and to his left the brick stack enclosing the lift-shaft.

He instantly became aware of two figures on the roof, both of whom made for the sanctuary of the lift-shaft. "I'm a police officer," shouted Fairfax. "Come out from behind that stack!"

This brought the response from Craig, "If you want us, fucking-well come and get us!"

"All right," replied Fairfax, who advanced, ducked behind the stack, grabbed hold of Bentley and then went for Craig. But Bentley broke free and then Fairfax heard the words which would cause so much controversy: "Let him have it, Chris!" With that, from a distance of six feet, Craig fired the first of eleven shots (nine, according to Craig), hitting Fairfax in the shoulder. As he fell to the ground Craig and Bentley ran past him, but Fairfax with extraordinary fortitude got to his feet, chased them, grabbed hold of Bentley and flattened him with one punch. As he did so, Craig fired again, fortunately missing Fairfax.

Searching Bentley's pockets from behind a roof-light and finding and removing the knuckleduster and knife, Fairfax pulled his captive away until he reached the head of the staircase. There he discovered PC McDonald, who upon hearing the shots had made a further creditable attempt to scale the drainpipe; and despite his injury, Fairfax pulled him on to the roof. McDonald, a former labourer (and just three-quarters of an inch over the minimum height for police of five feet eight), was a native of Perthshire. Within two years of joining the police, he had volunteered for wartime service with the army and during that time had married. With three children, two boys now aged four and eighteen months and a girl aged nine months, McDonald had proved a resourceful officer, having already been commended for vigilance in the arrest of two men for receiving.

By now, Craig had retreated to the area of the lift-shaft, about forty feet away from the officers. "Drop your gun!" shouted Fairfax, and Craig responded by firing another shot, at the same time jeering, "Come and get it!" Fairfax revealed to McDonald, "He got me in the shoulder," and Bentley said, "I told the silly bugger not to use it."

Meanwhile, PC Harrison, a married twenty-four-year-old former bus conductor who had joined the police in 1950 and had spent his National Service with the East Surrey Regiment, had climbed on to an adjacent roof and edged his way towards Craig. It was an extraordinarily awkward and dangerous manoeuvre, because Harrison had to lean back on the sloping roof with his heels in the guttering in order to get close to the gunman. Craig fired two shots at him, both of which missed, and Harrison reached the comparative safety of a chimney stack and managed to make his way down to the ground.

There he met up with forty-two-year-old Police Constable 550 'Z' Sidney George Miles, who had obtained the warehouse keys from the manager, and both officers climbed the interior staircase leading to the roof. The door to the roof was fastened with a bar to prevent unauthorized entry; Miles pushed up the bar and had to kick open the door. Fairfax shouted out that they were to one side of the staircase. He did not have to tell him that a gunman was on the roof – Miles would have known this, since Harrison would have told him that he had been fired at twice, and in any event he would have heard the shots himself. Nevertheless, he stepped from the doorway, Craig fired and Miles crashed to the ground. Fairfax and McDonald broke cover and pulled Miles' body behind the stair-head; as they did so, Craig fired again, missing them but hitting the door frame. For Miles, however, their attempt to save his life was too late. Craig had shot him just above the left eyebrow, killing him instantly.

Further police reinforcements now arrived, bringing with them some service side-arms. One of the officers, Police Constable 463 'Z' Robert James William Jaggs, who climbed the drainpipe, was also fired at and joined his colleagues. Twenty-eight-year-old Jaggs had seen wartime service in both the Merchant and Royal Navy and following demobilization had joined the Fire Service. He became a member of the Metropolitan Police in 1950 and was married with two daughters, aged two and twelve months.

One of the residents of Tamworth Road, attracted by the commotion, later stated that she heard a voice from the roof shout, "Come on – I'm enjoying myself!" It was not Bentley's voice and it was certainly none of the police officers.

"Come on you brave coppers!" shouted Craig. "Think of your wives!" No doubt many of them did. Nevertheless, Harrison emerged from the doorway directly into the line of fire for a second time and hurled his truncheon, a milk bottle and a lump of wood in Craig's direction, and as Craig fired at him, shouting, "I'm Craig! You've just given my brother twelve years! Come on, you coppers – I'm only sixteen!" McDonald managed to reach his three colleagues. Craig was now shouting, illogically, "It's a Colt .45 ... are you hiding behind a shield? Is it bullet-proof? Are we going to have a shooting match? It's just what I'd like ... have they hurt you, Derek?" The officers then pulled and pushed Bentley through the doorway. "Look out, Chris!" shouted Bentley. "They're taking me down!" The three officers dragged Bentley down the stairs, where he was held by other officers, but Fairfax, now having been handed a police issue Webley & Scott .32 automatic pistol[1] and displaying astonishing bravery, returned to the roof. "Drop your gun!" he shouted. "I also have a gun!"

---

1. Six months later, a review of many of these types of weapon described their condition as 'wretched'.

"Come on, copper!" yelled Craig. "Let's have it out!" and as Fairfax rushed forwards, Craig fired a shot and Fairfax returned fire, letting off two shots in Craig's direction. There were a series of 'clicks' from Craig's revolver, and he shouted, "See? It's empty." With that, he stood on the edge of the parapet, shouted, "Well, here we go – give my love to Pam," dived off the roof and landed, fracturing his spine, breastbone and forearm. As he lay on the ground, he gasped, "I wish I was fucking dead! I hope I've killed the fucking lot!" Ironically, Fairfax and Craig shared the same ambulance, which took them both to Croydon General Hospital, where they spent the night a few feet from each other. Fairfax was treated by the casualty officer, Dr Nicholas Jazwon, and was found to be badly shocked and with a grazed shoulder; the bullet which had caused the wound was found lodged in his braces.

Detective Sergeant Stanley Edward Shepherd was tasked to stay with Craig and record any comments he might make. Having served five years in the Royal Navy, Shepherd had joined the police in 1931. He had been posted to 'Z' Division in 1948 where he would spend ten years of his service. An industrious officer, he had been awarded his ninth commendation two months earlier, for valuable assistance in a case of murder.

"Is the copper dead?" Craig asked him. "How about the others? We ought to have shot them all."

Half an hour later, the senior investigating officer arrived, having made a formal identification of PC Miles at the Mayday Mortuary. Detective Chief Inspector John Leslie Smith had joined the Metropolitan Police in 1924 and spent a total of thirteen years on 'Z' Division. He had been commended on fourteen occasions for conscientious and courageous police work and was a good, solid all-round detective. When he told Craig that he and Derek Bentley would be charged with PC Miles' murder, Craig replied, "He's dead, is he? What about the others?"

Later, Smith and Shepherd saw Bentley at Croydon police station. "Are you in charge of this, Guv'nor?" Bentley asked Smith, who replied, "Yes."

"I didn't kill him, Guv; Chris did it," said Bentley and volunteered a written statement. It was taken down by Shepherd, and because Bentley was unable to do so, it was read over to him by Shepherd. Bentley then signed his name to it.

Upon being formally charged and cautioned, Bentley replied, "Craig shot him. I hadn't got a gun. He was with me on the roof and then shot him between the eyes."

Later the same morning, Woman Police Constable 325 'Z' Kathleen Parrott (who two years later would be awarded the

George Medal for her astonishing bravery at decoy work) came on duty for the early shift at Croydon. "You can imagine what the atmosphere was like," she told me, fifty-seven years after the event. "It was awful."

The Commissioner, Sir Harold Scott, visited the police station, saw Police Constables Harrison, McDonald and Jaggs, and later stated, "These three men ... were less interested in the night's events than concerned for the widow of the shot policeman, Miles. My impression, indeed, was that I had gone into a family home where one of the family had suddenly died." He later saw Fairfax who, he said, "minimised his part in the affair, giving me a straightforward account of his actions on the roof, with no attempt at dramatisation."

Craig was still under police guard in hospital and made a number of damaging remarks, one of which was, "If I hadn't cut a bit off the barrel of my gun, I would probably have killed a lot more policemen ... I shot the policeman in the head with my .45. If it had been the .22 he might not have died."

The .22 to which he referred had been lent to Norman Parsley for the raid on the house of Mr and Mrs Howes, and although it has been suggested that Craig was unconscious during most of his time in hospital, he was sufficiently awake to implicate Parsley in the robbery; the .22 pistol was found in his room, wrapped in a sweater, and Parsley was later sentenced to four years' detention. A search of Craig's house would reveal 138 rounds of ammunition plus the sawn-off end of the revolver.

The inquest was held on 5 November, and evidence was given by the pathologist, Dr David Haler, that death had been caused to PC Miles by a bullet entering his forehead above the left eyebrow and exiting at the back of his head. Praising the police officers for their bravery, the coroner, Mr J. W. Bennett, released the body, and the following day at Croydon Parish Church, the Commissioner and the Home Secretary, Sir David Maxwell Fyfe, were just two of the many mourners who attended PC Miles' funeral service. He was cremated, and his ashes were scattered in Croydon cemetery.

On 17 November, Craig and Bentley were committed for trial to the Old Bailey, where their trial commenced on Thursday 9 December 1952, in No. 2 Court. Craig was represented by the barrister John Parris and Bentley by Frank Cassels; both youths pleaded not guilty to the murder of PC Miles. By now, Craig's former ebullience had evaporated, and when he piteously told the very hard-line trial judge, Lord Goddard, "I was in hospital and I woke up when someone hit me in the mouth and called me a murdering bastard, sir," he did not receive the sympathy which he undoubtedly thought was due to him. Evidence was given that Craig had said, "That night I was out to kill, because I had so much hate in me for what they'd done to my brother," although this was refuted. Craig also denied shooting Fairfax from a distance of six feet, saying that he was thirty-seven feet away from Fairfax when he fired into the ground, and claiming that the wound was caused by a ricochet. Evidence was also given by Lewis Nicholls MSc, the Yard's ballistics expert, that Craig's Eley revolver was "quite an inaccurate weapon", only reliable up to a distance of six feet, something which proved fortunate for several of the police officers on the roof, although less so for PC Miles. An attempt to modify the verdict to one of manslaughter in Craig's case, by alleging that he was only trying to frighten the officers, was seriously compromised by Craig's admission in court that he had fired nine shots, which meant that he had had to reload the revolver. Otherwise, the evidence was straightforward – at least as far as Craig was concerned; Bentley was quite another matter. He denied any complicity in any wrong-doing of any kind whatsoever and especially denied (and on this point Craig corroborated him) ever saying, "Let him have it, Chris" which rather ruined the chance for the jury to determine whether he meant "give him the gun," or "kill him".

In respect of this matter, Lord Goddard, referring to Fairfax, McDonald and Harrison, told the jury:

> Those three officers in particular showed the highest gallantry and resolution; they were conspicuously brave. Are you going to say they were conspicuous liars? Because if their evidence is untrue – that Bentley called out 'Let him have it, Chris' – those officers are doing their best to swear away the life of that boy. If it is true, it is, of course, the most deadly piece of evidence against him.

In any event, after a two-day trial, the jury deliberated for seventy-five minutes before finding both guilty of murder. Craig, who was aware all along that at the age of sixteen he could not be executed, was detained at Her Majesty's pleasure. Bentley – for whom the jury added a recommendation for mercy – was sentenced to death. At the conclusion of the trial, Fairfax, who had been commended at the committal proceedings at Croydon Borough Magistrates' Court, was called, together with PCs McDonald and Harrison, to stand before the trial judge, who said:

The conduct of the men from 'Z' Division on this night in arresting these two desperate young criminals is worthy of the highest commendation and of the thanks of the community to the police for their gallant conduct. It is no light thing to face a burglar or a housebreaker in the dark when he is firing a revolver in the way these two men did. No doubt all the police officers showed courage that night. They are all deserving of commendation, but I think it is these three officers in particular who were exposed to the worst, and had more opportunity to show their courage and resolution. The thanks of all law-abiding citizens ought to be given to you.

When Fairfax for his tremendous gallantry was promoted to detective sergeant within five weeks of the roof-top shootings – he had passed the examination five years previously – and then awarded the George Cross, a week before Bentley's appeal, it was accepted that this was a right and proper course of action. The same applied to PCs Harrison and McDonald, who were awarded George Medals; PC Jaggs was awarded the British Empire Medal for gallantry; and all of them received a £15 award from the Bow Street Reward Fund and commissioner's high commendations. A posthumous King's Police and Fire Service Medal for gallantry was presented to the widow of PC Miles.

Despite an appeal, petitions (one had 100,000 signatures on it) and protests – in the House of Commons, the Labour Member of Parliament for Northampton, Reginald Paget MP, QC, asked, "A three-quarter witted boy is to be hung for a murder he did not commit, which was committed fifteen minutes after he was arrested. Can we be made to keep silent when a thing as horrible and as shocking as this is to happen?"[2] – Bentley was hanged on the morning of 28 January 1953.

There had been an enormous upsurge in violence since the war, especially with the use of firearms, and, in fact, the year before PC Miles' murder, four other police officers had been shot dead. There was the growing menace of violent crime, perpetuated by youngsters of both sexes, and the police, with strong backing from the judiciary, felt that a firm line had to be taken against this growing tide of mayhem. This action was applauded by the general public, who had enjoyed the wartime

---

2. Paget, who fought passionately to correct what he saw as injustice, resurfaces again in the chapter *A Lapse of Memory* – and not to his credit.

'Dixon of Dock Green' style of policing – initially, at least. Members of the public yelled, "Let's kill the little bastard!" as Craig was taken into court. But on the night before Bentley's execution, a crowd of 300 assembled outside Parliament, chanting, "Bentley must not die!"

Fairfax's son Alan was eight years old at the time, and at the family home in Elmpark Gardens, Selsdon, he recollected seeing his father with his arm in a sling, and his mother telling him that he had been shot at work. "I remember going to school and a lot of my friends asking what had happened as they or their parents had heard the news on the radio," he recalled, almost sixty years after the event. "I also remember a lot of press people coming to the house," he added, and, "going to Buckingham Palace with Dad and Mum, in Dad's old 1936 Austin 10 when he received his medal. I remember quite well the details of the investiture and the interior of Buckingham Palace ... not the sort of thing you forget."

But the family of Derek Bentley did not forget either, and they commenced a series of actions to get their son's conviction overturned. Firstly his father, who died in 1974 and whose wife died two years later, and then Bentley's sister Iris took up the cudgels, and a curious campaign, supported by certain sections of the British public, commenced and gathered momentum. In 1958 it would happen again, when Ronald Henry Marwood murdered Police Constable Raymond Henry Summers and in the following year when Günter Fritz Erwin Podola shot dead Detective Sergeant Raymond Purdy. Both perpetrators were hanged, and resentment against the police reached boiling point. Bentley's case brought writers with a social conscience into the frame, as well as the inevitable lawyers, and the cause gathered support. Alan Fairfax recalled "some hostility from people," but was unable to remember the details. In the meantime, Fairfax – and the other officers who had acted so bravely – got on with their lives.

★   ★   ★

The detectives in charge of the investigation, John Smith and Stanley Shepherd (he was commended for his ability in a case of blackmail two weeks after the court case and, in the space of fifteen months, twice more) continued their distinguished careers and both retired with the rank of detective superintendent.

Norman Harrison was commended six years later for vigilance and devotion to duty, whilst actually off-duty, for his arrest of a man for larceny in a dwelling house; four years after that, he was promoted to sergeant. He was again commended, this time for ability in effecting the arrest of two persistent thieves, and ten years later he retired with an ill-health pension.

Three weeks after his award of the George Medal, PC McDonald was again commended, on this occasion for ability and determination in the arrest of three criminals. Just prior to being promoted to sergeant in 1955, McDonald was commended again, this time for alertness and initiative which resulted in the arrest of a man wanted for housebreaking. He retired with the rank of inspector, almost exactly thirty years after joining the police.

PC Jaggs remained on 'Z' Division and became a dog handler. He was commended a number of times: for alertness and determination leading to the arrest of five youths for larceny and highly commended by the Justices at Croydon Borough Magistrates' Court, as was his dog, 'Rajah III', for the arrest of eleven rowdy youths. His final commendation was for determination and initiative in effecting the arrest of two violent housebreakers. He resigned on an ill-health pension.

Following his promotion, Fairfax was posted to 'C' Division in London's West End, where he was commended twice, once for the arrest of a dangerous criminal and then for the arrest of two persons for robbery with violence. After eighteen months he was returned to 'Z' Division and nine months later was promoted to detective sergeant (first class). He remained at Croydon police station until his retirement, eight years later, having brought his total of commendations (which included arrests for housebreaking, indecent assault and blackmail) up to fourteen.

Christopher Craig was released from prison in May 1963, having served just over ten years. Half-hearted questions were raised in the House of Commons on 7 February that year regarding his intended release by Marcus Lipton, the Member of Parliament for Brixton, but he was simply going through the motions; it was expected to cause concern that a gun-toting police murderer was going to be released upon an unsuspecting public, so that was why the matter was raised. The Secretary of State for the Home Office uttered a few soothing phrases, mentioned that satisfactory arrangements had been made, providing of course that Craig's conduct in prison continued to be good, and honour was satisfied. Craig was released and disappeared into anonymity.

Meanwhile, with the murder of PC Miles largely forgotten by the general public (his widow, Mrs Catherine Elizabeth Miles, had been awarded the princely pension of £2 12s 4d per week), the Bentley campaign hotted up. Allegations which had been made during the trial were reiterated and new ones were formed. Because Bentley had denied uttering the words, "Let him have it, Chris" and Craig claimed he had never heard the words, it was strongly suggested that Fairfax and the other officers who had heard the words were lying. Then it was implied that there had been a *third* youth on the roof and that he might have shouted the damning words – this was hastily retracted when it was remembered that both Craig and Bentley had denied that those words had ever been uttered. Next, it was suggested that PC Miles' death had resulted from being hit by a bullet fired from a police marksman's gun. This was nonsense. Police firearms did not arrive at the scene until after Miles' death. But since the bullet which had killed PC Miles had not been recovered, the conspiracy theorists had a field day. Craig had used a number of different sized bullets in the revolver; mainly .41 and .45 calibre. A .32 calibre cartridge case was found on the roof and the so-called experts all but swooned with delight. They had convinced themselves that PC Miles had been killed with a bullet from a police-issued firearm and here was proof positive of their preposterous theories. They had conveniently forgotten that Fairfax had fired off two shots at Craig, using bullets of that calibre from his weapon, the cases of which had automatically been ejected, after Miles had been murdered.

It mattered little; it was far easier to allege the existence of some shadowy police marksman on some adjacent roof, armed with a rifle, whom no one saw ascend to the roof and who was so inept that instead of concentrating on the muzzle flashes from Craig's revolver, he turned his attention forty feet away from Craig and shot and killed a police colleague in full uniform. Having done so, he descended to the ground – witnessed by nobody – and returned to the station, where he cleaned the weapon and replaced it, somehow managing to avoid anyone seing him do so. How the spent round was accounted for and who authorized the booking-out of the weapon in the first place has never been satisfactorily resolved. It doesn't matter; this unmitigated nonsense is food and drink to the conspiracy theorists.

But with writers and lawyers poring over every deposition and every piece of evidence, taking months, sometimes years, to piece together their version of the events which took place during thirty highly dangerous minutes on a dark November night years before, it is hardly surprising that they discovered inconsistencies in the evidence. There had been discrepancies in the officers' testimony at the trial and these had been pointed out by Messrs Parris and Cassels at the time. It had not stopped Parris feeling relieved that following Fairfax's testimony the jury had been unable to hear Craig say, "I ought to have killed that fucker, as well!" And when Parris met Cassels, the latter's view of the whole matter was: "I think both the little fuckers [or according to various sources, 'buggers' or 'beggars'] ought to swing."

It prompted a freelance writer (and former scrap metal dealer) to apply for summonses at Croydon Magistrates' Court in 1986 against the officers, alleging unlawful arrest and claiming that evidence was withheld and that PC Miles had, of course, been killed by a police marksman's bullet. He was no more successful at the High Court than he was at the Magistrates' Court.

Four years later, it was the turn of a writer, M. J. Trow, who claimed that a dog handler, Police Constable 241 'Z' Claude Raymond Pain, had told him that he had climbed to the roof of the warehouse on the night of the shootings and that Bentley had not made his incriminating remark; and what was more, he had never been called to give evidence. This prompted Trow to demand access to the National Archives file, which was refused. The writer was convinced that this was a Scotland Yard cover-up, speculating that once the file was opened it would reveal that Pain's original deposition had mysteriously disappeared, and believing that Pain should have received a medal for his actions on the roof top that night.

He shouldn't, he didn't and it wasn't. The file was eventually opened but it revealed that far from inexplicably vanishing in a classic 'smoke and mirrors' piece of police duplicity, Pain's deposition was still with the papers; it placed him at ground level, with his dog, to intercept either of the intruders should they try to escape. Together with a number of other witnesses, Pain had not been called simply because his testimony could not add anything to the proceedings. Pain had not been in a position to hear anything. He was not in a position to say anything either, because he died, aged eighty-four, at the time of these revelations.

Books were written about the incident, plays appeared on television, a film was produced and even songs were performed. Iris Bentley had died and her niece, Maria Dingwall-Bentley, went to see Fairfax, now near the end of his life at his home; he – probably quite wearily, by now – stated once more that he had told the truth in court. The enquiry trundled on, with one Home Secretary after another re-affirming Bentley's guilt, until July 1993 when a royal pardon was granted in respect of the death sentence which had been passed on Bentley. It was not enough; Bentley's conviction for murder had not been quashed, and the lawyers got to work with a will. On 30 July 1998 the Court of Appeal decided that although there was substantial evidence of Bentley's guilt it was not overwhelming; they ruled that his conviction was unsafe and that the trial judge, Lord Goddard, had failed to put Bentley's defence fairly before the jury. In consequence, the conviction was set aside. This opened the floodgates. The police officers were now branded 'liars'. 'Experts' were called to say that Bentley was incapable of making the statements attributed to him by the police. It is only when one reads the whole of Bentley's statement, dictated by him and written down by Sergeant Shepherd, that it is possible to see how jumbled it is. It is in stark contrast to the flowing prose contained in the letters to his parents dictated by Bentley to the prison staff; and none of the 'experts' have commented on the content of these letters.

Following the court's decision, sixty-two-year-old Christopher Craig praised the result and stated in addition that he was "truly sorry that my actions ... caused so much pain and misery for the family of PC Miles, who died that night doing his duty." It is difficult to reconcile those unctuous comments with the swaggering, loud-mouthed, murderous young thug on top of a Croydon warehouse.

After Fairfax's death, aged eighty, in February 1998, his widow Muriel fiercely defended her late husband in a newspaper interview. She put matters very succinctly when she stated: "My husband was never a liar, he did his duty and he's been hounded for more than forty years."

There was never any question that Bentley had a history of violence, or that he was in possession of a gun or offered violence to the police officers. In fact, after he was under arrest and Fairfax momentarily left him to assist McDonald on to the roof, he could have used this opportunity to try to escape, but he did not. However, there was evidence to suggest that he knew that Craig had a gun and was prepared to use it, and that he uttered those fateful words. It was sufficient for him to be found guilty and to suffer the ultimate penalty; forty-five years later, the Court of Appeal thought otherwise.

But neither is there any dispute that a police officer was cold-bloodedly murdered by an out-of-control teenager with a hatred of police, who wounded another officer and shot at many more and who, after ten years' incarceration, walked free from prison. His brother Niven (whose photograph in the *Daily Herald* was captioned 'Young, dangerous Baby-Face') might have been there to greet his younger brother upon his release had he behaved himself, but he had not. Early in the morning of Sunday 30 October 1960, Niven Craig was one of four men concerned in an officebreaking with the use of explosives. He had been on weekend leave from Wormwood Scrubs Prison, now that he was coming to the end of his sentence. Instead of walking free, he was sentenced to another five years' imprisonment, with Reggie Seaton, the Chairman of the Inner London Sessions, warning him, "You will find yourself qualifying for preventative detention." The haul from the robbery at Waltham Abbey, for which Craig had received his original twelve-year sentence, had netted the five-man gang just £4 to share between them; his latest escapade had resulted in the gang accruing the princely sum of £26 16s 11d. Crime was beginning to pay, at last; the four-way split would have amounted to almost £7 per desperado. This was the brother whom Christopher Craig hero-worshipped; a persistent criminal he might have been, but a singularly inept one.

★   ★   ★

Police Constable Miles' widow later re-married. Her husband, Reginald Grasty, presented Miles' medals to the Metropolitan Police Historical Museum in 1977 and when he died in 1983 left the sum of £15,000 to the Widows' and Orphans' Fund. In 1994, the officers at Croydon placed a granite plaque in the police station's lawn to commemorate the bravery of Police Constable Miles. He had served his country well: a member of the Royal Army Medical Corps from 1926 to 1929 and a police officer who after joining the Metropolitan Police in 1930 had been commended at Croydon Petty Sessions and by the commissioner for making an arrest whilst off-duty for larceny and receiving.

The plaque serves as a reminder that we should not forget that on the night of 2 November 1952 a forty-two-year-old police officer gave his life in the line of duty and a number of ordinary police officers acted with extraordinary bravery, displaying gallantry that the pompous, sneering, self-serving writers, 'experts' and lawyers could never have even dreamt of showing themselves.

CHAPTER 3

A Screwed-up Piece of Paper

During the years following the end of the Second World War, a new breed of youth was seen in the tougher suburbs of London. Initially, they were known as 'cosh boys' because the cosh, usually made from the hanging strap with a ball-shaped end used on London Underground, was their favoured weapon. Later the cosh boys' arsenal extended to open razors, bicycle chains and knives – or in fact any implement which had maiming properties. Their appearance was distinctive; they wore long and often brightly coloured draped jackets, narrow boot-lace ties and 'drainpipe' trousers; their suede shoes with enormously thick crepe soles were colloquially known as 'brothel-creepers'. They greased their overlong hair, which was swept back into a huge quiff, and had the back cut into a 'V' which was known as a 'DA' or 'duck's arse'. As they swaggered around the streets, usually in packs of a dozen, their thinness accentuating their meanness (no cosh boy was permitted to be fat), they committed acts of vandalism, fought against rival gangs and beat up anyone whom they considered to be their social inferiors. These included newly arrived immigrants from the West Indies, who were considered a prime target; in Stepney in 1958, nine youths were jailed for participating in what they referred to as 'a nigger-hunting expedition'. Decent working- and middle-class citizens fearfully referred to them as 'delinquents'. As always, the press came to the rescue and provided them with a name which they considered socially acceptable and which lasted until their numbers started to peter out in the 1970s. Because their dress was reminiscent of the Edwardian era, they were re-christened 'teddy boys' or 'teds'.

These assorted tearaways thought themselves tough, and as long as they remained in large numbers, they were; they ensured that they were in sufficient numbers when they murdered a youth on Clapham Common in 1954. The following year, a soldier on leave died after his throat was cut by a gang, and two months after that, a boy was stabbed to death by a 'ted' wielding a flick-knife. It took very little to ignite irrational violence. On Thursday, 11 December 1958 it required just a screwed-up piece of paper, flicked at one gang member by another, to start a series of events which would end in murder.

★ ★ ★

It was a man named Flanagan who was the paper-flicker at Barry's Dancing Academy that evening; the paper may or may not have actually hit John Budd, aged nineteen and unemployed, from Stoke Newington, Church Street, N16 – but it appeared that Budd thought it was deliberately intended for him and believed the act carried more than a hint of disrespect. Budd, together with Brian Robert Murray, a twenty-one-year-old wholesale newspaper distributor of Phoenix Road, NW1, and George William Fletcher, a twenty-one-year-old glazier of Swinton Street, WC1, went out to collect some supporters and later returned. There was a minor brawl, and Peter Sydney Dean, aged nineteen, a junior warehouseman from Essex Road, N1, entered the fracas on the side of Flanagan. It appears that Dean got the worst of it and threatened Budd; and there the matter was left for the time being.

But tempers were on the boil, and on the following Saturday and Sunday there was talk about finding Dean to have a reckoning; whether it was to avenge Budd for having been the flickee or to remonstrate with Dean because he had sided with the flicker, mattered little. It was an example of *lèse-majesté* which had to be addressed.

★ ★ ★

Opinions vary as to why Ronald Henry Marwood failed to celebrate his first wedding anniversary with his wife Rosalie on Sunday, 14 December 1958; one version is that she was feeling unwell and told him to 'have a night out with the boys', another was that she preferred to stay at home and watch the television, and yet a third (and possibly the likeliest) was that Marwood insisted on going out without her. But whatever the circumstances, at 7.30 that evening, Marwood, a twenty-five-year-old scaffolder, left his parents' home where he lived with his wife in Huntingdon Street, just off Caledonian Road. At the Spanish Patriot pub at 14 White Conduit Street, Clerkenwell, 'by chance' he met a friend, Michael David Bloom, also a scaffolder, aged twenty-four, from Mackonnel House, Deeley Road, SW8. His companion was known as 'Big Mick' – both men were about six feet three tall – and they started their drinking spree. There were also a number of 'young fellows' in attendance. How long they stayed at 'The Pats' (as it was referred to by locals) is not clear, but at some stage, Marwood, Bloom and three other men moved to the east, to Bow Road, where a derelict shop had been transformed into a drinking club. It was known as 'The Double R Club', and the proprietor was a local Bethnal Green tough named Reggie Kray.

★ ★ ★

When his twin brother Ronnie was incarcerated in 1956 – he had received a three-year sentence for wounding and possessing a revolver – Reggie, without opposition from his psychotic sibling, had seized his opportunity. He realized his dream of meeting people and playing host and opened the club. It was a venue which attracted celebrities – Barbara Windsor and Jackie Collins – as well as a miscellany of riff-raff, but although violence sometimes erupted, Reggie was more than capable of dealing with it. There was no trouble on the evening of 14 December, but by Marwood's own reckoning, by the time he left the club at about ten o'clock, he had consumed ten pints of brown ale, in half-pint measures. At about 10.30 he and Bloom and some companions arrived in two or three cars at Gray's Dancing Academy, Seven Sisters Road, Holloway.

John Budd – the victim of the paper-flicking incident – and Bloom tried to get in to the dance hall but were refused admission. Dean was already inside, heard that there was a gang of people in the street and decided go outside "to meet trouble half-way." He and Budd met in the dance hall forecourt. In a later statement to the police, Dean said, "I went out and saw Johnny Budd and his mates. I said, 'What's it going to be, Johnny – you and me round the corner?' I pulled out a knife and he pulled out a chopper, but I was pulled back into the dance hall."

Peter John Healey of Andover Road, Holloway, was the man who led Dean back into the dance hall, saying, "I'm not having you getting into any kind of trouble." The remark was overheard by George Watkins of Marquis Road, Islington, a film artiste (although also said to be 'a bouncer' at the dance academy), who also heard Dean's alleged reply: "I'm not going to swallow it."

In the version he gave the police, Budd stated that he and his mates went to the dance hall tooled up with choppers, a shotgun and a cosh. "Dean came out with his friends standing behind him and said, 'Just me and you.' He pulled out a knife, like a butcher's knife. Fred Jackman put a chopper in my hand but I said, 'I want a straightener. I don't want it like that.' Then someone shouted 'police' and we ran off."

Matters were developing very quickly. Almost simultaneously, George Loizou, aged sixteen, of Playford Road, Finsbury Park, had run out of the dance hall, crossed the road and encountered some of Budd's gang. He was asked, "Which side would you like your hair parted?" and Loizou saw the questioner reach inside his coat. Believing – quite correctly – that he was reaching for a weapon, he kicked the man, whereupon two or three of the group set upon him. The remark to Loizou was overheard by James Henry Tuttle, a decorator's labourer of Harvist Road, Holloway. "The man put his hands in his inside pocket and I saw something that looked like a chopper," he said. "A couple of other chaps set about Loizou." Francis Patrick McLaughlin of Orleans Road, Upper Holloway, was walking home and later told the court, "I saw two fellows fighting one youth; the two chaps were fighting with heads and feet but one of them had a chopper. The one with the chopper was beating the youth above the head and shoulders with it." Stitches were later inserted into the wounds on Loizou's back. Frederick John Jackman, aged twenty-three, a newspaper worker of Brunswick Court, Percival Street, EC1 – already referred to above – was the alleged axe-wielder, although he stated that he was struck first. Someone shouted, "The law's coming!" and the majority of the crowd scattered.

At 10.45 that evening, the remainder of the crowd fell silent because the law had indeed arrived. At one quarter of an inch under six feet three, twenty-three-year-old Police Constable Raymond Henry Summers stepped in and took control of the situation.

Summers had been brought up in Broadstairs, Kent, had served in the RAF from January 1954 until April 1957 and within three weeks of his discharge had joined the Metropolitan Police. He was posted to 'N' Division's Holloway police station and four months previously he had successfully passed his intermediate probationer's examination with high marks and was now all set to be confirmed as a police officer. A single man, he lived at the Police Section House at Highbury Vale, was engaged to be married and was saving as much of his weekly wage of £9 15s 6d as he could. "A fine young uniformed officer who always had a ready laugh and was a very popular young man" was how the late Detective Sergeant Doug Archer recalled him.

Brian King had known Summers during their time in the RAF, when both expressed a desire to join the police at the conclusion of their National Service. Both did, but King never saw his RAF colleague again. Speaking over fifty years later, he told me, "The next I knew of him was his murder ... he was not a man who would flinch from enforcing the law even on his own, during those difficult times." As events would sadly prove, King's character assessment of Summers turned out to be utterly correct.

He was also remembered by Brian Cane who, prior to joining the Surrey Constabulary, had worked at North London Drapers in Seven Sisters Road. "What a credit he was to your Force," he recalled, since Summers was frequently seen on the beat in that area. "Everyone seemed to know and respect him."

But not everybody. Summers, who had seen the confrontation between the two gangs, moved forward, identified Bloom as a troublemaker, seized him by the arm and, as several more of the gang members decamped, led Bloom away towards Holloway police station. There were no personal radios in those days and assistance could only be summoned by the police officer blowing his whistle, telephoning from a police box or dialling 999 from a public telephone. But although Summers would have been fully justified in calling for assistance on this occasion, he did not.

"Ray Summers was very keen," former Police Constable Dick Elsey told me, "but practically every time he made an arrest he would dial 999 for a car to bring the prisoner in, and this was not always strictly necessary. The skippers [sergeants] got a bit fed up with this and asked me to have a word with him. So I said, 'Look, Ray, if you phone up every time you make an arrest, the wireless car might be taken off an urgent job, so if there's no need for it, just bring the prisoner in under your own steam.'" Speaking to me fifty-three years later, Elsey, who died shortly afterwards, said, "Ever since then, I've been haunted by those words."

It seems that Summers took the homily to heart, and this was commented upon by Ted Harrington, who saw him stride right past a telephone box. "Why doesn't he phone the nick?" he asked his friend Kieren Matthews. "Although I was only fifteen years old, I was streetwise and could not understand PC Summers taking on so many Teddy boys fighting," Ted Harrington – later a police officer with both the Metropolitan Police and the Surrey Constabulary – told me in 2011. "He walked into the road and went straight into the group. He started pulling people off one another and forced his way into the centre of the group. Within seconds, we saw his helmet come off and then he disappeared from view. We knew he was on the ground and then suddenly the Teddy boys started running in all directions and we saw PC Summers ... on his back being comforted by two girls in mini skirts."

One or two members of the gang had tried half-heartedly to pull Bloom from Summers' grasp but he brushed them away. Possibly their lack of enthusiasm stemmed from the fact that Holloway police station was close by, at 256 Hornsey Road, round the corner from Seven Sisters Road. Built in 1875, it had sustained enormous bomb damage in 1941 and was described as 'an awful place to work'.

But before Summers had gone very far, Marwood ran up behind the officer and stabbed him in the back with a thin, diver's knife with a serrated edge. The ten-inch weapon pierced five layers of clothing, penetrated Summers' body to a depth of four inches and severed his aorta. The young constable was dying by the time he hit the pavement.

With the exception of three young girls, aged sixteen, fourteen and twelve, who tried to help Summers, the rest of the group fled, including Marwood, who flung the knife over a garden wall in Isledon Road. A passing motorist stopped and telephoned for an ambulance and the police, but before the ambulance arrived another motorist had conveyed Summers to the Royal Northern Hospital, less than a quarter of a mile away, where he was declared dead on arrival.

It was initially thought that Summers had died from a heart attack, and the true cause of death was not discovered until twelve hours later. How anybody could have come to the conclusion that a strong, fit, twenty-three-year-old could have died from a heart attack simply beggars belief. Yet this was the initial diagnosis; a police spokesman said there were no wounds on the body. Summers' Central Record of Service (obviously hurriedly filled in first thing the following morning) reveals that he 'died whilst serving, on duty' instead of 'was murdered', and a generous senior officer, realizing that Summers had expired forty-five minutes after commencing night-duty at ten o'clock, graciously permitted him time to die before writing in Holloway's Occurrence Book, 'Pay until twelve midnight.' There was no reference to his conduct and no pension was payable; a gratuity of £45 18s 5d would later be paid to his 'legal personal representative'. A promising career had been cut brutally short; at the time of his death, Summers had served in the Metropolitan Police for one year, seven months and twenty-two days.

Nevertheless, the police had instantly responded to the call from Information Room directing them to a 'disturbance' – this was police phraseology to describe anything from a neighbours dispute to (as in this case) a murder – in Seven Sisters Road, and twenty minutes after the murder a police van stopped Marwood and 'a man named Bailey' half a mile from the scene. One of the officers was Police Constable 463 'N' Bill Burt, who was a local, acclaimed thief-taker. Blood was found on Marwood's hand and three of his fingers had been cut; Marwood claimed that the cuts had been caused during a fight at a hotel in Finsbury Park. Both men stated categorically that neither had been anywhere near the Seven Sisters Road that evening, but nevertheless they were detained.

★ ★ ★

The officer in charge of the investigation was Detective Superintendent Robert George Fenwick, who had joined the police in 1934 and was now forty-five years of age. It is clear that he was a careful, meticulous detective who favoured fraud investigations, which obviously suited his methodical way of working. After six years' service in the East End's 'K' Division, Fenwick would spend the following fourteen years with the Yard's C1 Department in the ranks of detective constable and detective sergeant, both second and first class. Most of his ten commissioner's commendations were for successfully investigating cases of false pretences, confidence tricks, company fraud and conspiracy to defraud, and this included a commendation for his contribution to what became known as 'The Lynskey Tribunal', a complex and lengthy investigation which threatened to bring down the Government.

What is also quite clear is that Fenwick was destined for high office. He spent two years as an instructor at the Detective Training School and was then posted to Chelsea as a detective chief inspector for a brief five months. He was seconded to the Foreign Office for another five months; whilst he was on secondment, he was posted to the Flying Squad but he saw just two weeks' service there before he was posted to the Fraud Squad for six weeks. His next posting to 'J' Division was even shorter – three weeks – before a posting to 'X' Division. There he lasted a full six months until 1 December 1958, when promotion brought a posting to 'N' Division.

Harry William Joyce had joined the police four months after Fenwick and like him had served at C1 Department, the Detective Training School and 'S' and 'B' Divisions, although not at the same time. Like Fenwick, he specialised in fraud investigations, although one of his sixteen commissioner's commendations, in 1944, was for the 'difficult arrest of a much-wanted criminal' and the next, three months later, was for 'arresting a violent criminal who was armed', for which he was additionally awarded £10 from the Bow Street Reward Fund. Promoted to detective chief inspector, he was posted to Holloway police station on the same day as Fenwick.

Two weeks later, the two of them commenced the investigation into Summers' murder.

★   ★   ★

At five o'clock on the morning following Summers' murder, Marwood told Fenwick that during the alleged fight at the hotel someone had swung an axe at him, he had raised his arm to fend off the blow and consequently his fingers had been cut. Marwood made a statement in which he described the fight at the hotel and once again denied being anywhere near Seven Sisters Road. Both Marwood and Bailey were released on police bail. That evening, Marwood vanished from the family home.

More than 100 people who had been in the vicinity of Gray's Dancing Academy were interviewed, but although many of them knew Marwood, none would place him at the scene. But simply because the man who would turn out to be the prime suspect had been released, it did not mean that the police were doing nothing. Marwood's and Bailey's alibi of being in the hotel was scrupulously investigated and was found to be untrue. The murder weapon – without fingerprints – was discovered in a manure heap in a front garden. Footprints found there were photographed. In response to a public appeal, two of the young girls who had tried to help Summers at the scene came forward and provided material assistance to Fenwick; and they were not alone.

That weekend, the older brothers of Ted Harrington and Kieren Matthews were home on leave from National Service, and upon being apprised of what their younger siblings had seen, insisted on taking them to Holloway police station. This caused some apprehension in the streetwise young Harrington, who had heard that the CID at Holloway were "as bent as nine bob notes", but both boys duly attended and made six-page statements. A senior officer told them that these differed completely from the 200 statements which had already been taken, but this may have been meant light-heartedly because he winked at them, laughed and thanked them for coming to the station. However, neither boy was called upon to give evidence at the trial.

Other enquires were made. On 15 December Detective Sergeant Jack Huntley found a chopper behind a wall at Thane

Villas, Holloway. Two days later, Detective Constable Stanley Crichton saw Brian Murray at his home address, and after he told him he was making enquiries about the incident, Murray replied, "I saw it. I did not take part in it." However, on the same day Sergeant Huntley found a weighted wooden stick under some newspapers at Central Mansions, near Hendon Underground Station, and when asked if it was his, Murray replied, "Yes." Also on 17 December, Sergeant Huntley found a chopper in a workshop at Engelfield Road, Islington, and Ronald Bergonzi, a nineteen-year-old labourer of Theberton Street, Islington, was seen by DCI Joyce and volunteered to make a statement. In a wardrobe on the top floor of Bergonzi's house Joyce had found a new chopper with a chip out of the blade.

Several other youths were arrested that day, and former Police Constable 178 'N' Paul Phillips recalled that the gang members were assembled in the room allotted to the Special Constabulary, with a police constable assigned to each. "I recall not a word was spoken, you could have cut the atmosphere with a knife," he remembered. And then one of the investigating team, Detective Sergeant Doug Archer, walked in and spoke to the youths. "I've just been up to the mortuary of the hospital where I've taken the fingerprints of my dead colleague; not a pleasant task," he told them.

"I can't remember the remainder of his address to these thugs," said Phillips. "I was too busy containing my own emotions. A chill ran down my spine as the hairs on the back of my neck stood on end."

The following day, Detective Sergeant Huntley was still hard at work, and at 58 Brunswick Court, EC1, he found two more choppers and a plasterer's hammer. He later gave evidence that Ronald James Jackman, a twenty-one-year-old window cleaner of that address, had referred to the choppers in his written statement as being in his possession at the material time of the offence; and that the hammer had also been in the possession of Jackman's brother Fred at the material time.

The Jackman brothers were among four more youths arrested on 18 December; six were released. One who was not was Frederick Robert Newbolt aged twenty, a porter of Holford Square, WC1, who when he was cautioned by Detective Sergeant Paxton replied, "I'll help you all I can about the killing. I do not think it would have happened if that Dixon had not come running out in the street with a knife," although it is not clear as to exactly who 'Dixon' was. Altogether, twelve had been questioned regarding their involvement.

Police Constable (later Detective Chief Superintendent) John Simmonds, who was attached to Stoke Newington police station, remembered Ray Summers from divisional instruction classes and attending Arsenal for football duties, and he was involved in escorting the suspects to and from Holloway police station from the surrounding stations, because there were insufficient cells at Holloway. Unsurprisingly, feelings were running high, but many of the constables providing the escorts were veterans of World War Two and knew the meaning of discipline. Therefore, it was remarkably tactless of Fenwick to call out to the escorting officers, just as the suspects were about to be returned to their respective police stations one evening, "If any of those men are injured, you will all be charged with assault!" As he left, one of the accompanying officers, John Simmonds, told me, "It was fortunate that he didn't hear the remarks made by some of the older PCs!" He described Fenwick as "a dapper man and bit of a 'gent' but not considered by many as the right man for the job."

It appears that this notion was endorsed by the area Detective Chief Superintendent Stephen Arthur Glander. This very tough, fifty-three-year-old ex-soldier was a veteran of the Flying Squad and, having been commended by the commissioner on forty-seven occasions, was known as 'The Ambush King' – as Fenwick certainly discovered to his cost. After Fenwick had addressed a meeting of all the officers, Glander turned to them and said, "Gentlemen, I have to tell you that your senior officer is a complete and utter cunt and what's more, as soon as he finishes this enquiry, he'll be off the division!" – and with that, he strode out of the room. Police Constable Dick Elsey was one of those officers present and was stunned at what he had heard; so was John Simmonds. "There was an absolute hush," recalled Simmonds, over fifty years later. "Fenwick went red and left the room. I was just a probationer PC and was agog to hear such an exchange by one of the Met's top five detectives, yet there was an undercurrent of comment and rumour as to Fenwick's ability and it was generally felt that Glander had hit the nail on the head."

Fenwick and Glander were not alone in making inappropriate comments. Sir Joseph Simpson KBE was a popular commissioner, being the first holder of the position to have risen from the rank of constable. However, he arrived at Holloway shortly after the murder, just as the late-turn officers were booking off duty and the night-duty were parading, and he addressed the men. Unfortunately he was totally unprepared, and amazingly he said to the officers, "I know you would all like to be in PC Summers' position, rather than him." The expression 'gob-smacked' was not then in popular use, but it would have adequately described the assembled officers' reaction. "A statement we considered to be a very bad choice of words," Police Constable Campbell Robertson told me, whilst PC Paul Phillips' reaction probably summed up the feelings of the officers: "What a pillock!"

But on Friday, 19 December eleven of the youths were charged with causing an affray, and they appeared in the dock – ringed by police officers – at North London Magistrates' Court the following morning, when they were all remanded in custody for one week.

On 27 December the youths appeared again. On the solicitors' table were set out weapons which had been recovered: six axes, a bread knife and a leather-covered cosh. In addition to the charge of making an affray, the youths were further charged with possessing offensive weapons, some of which were now in court, while others were identified by the defendant's own admissions. Murray was charged with possessing a weighted stick, Dean a knife, Fred Jackman a plasterer's hammer. Budd, Bergonzi, Newbolt, Fletcher, Ronald James Jackman and David Henry Bailey, an eighteen-year-old window cleaner of Margery Street, WC1, were charged with possessing axes. Brian John Thwaites, a twenty-one-year-old window cleaner of Malvern Road, Hackney, was charged with possessing an air pistol, although in respect of Bloom no additional charges were brought.

The matter was considered so serious that the case was heard before Frank Milton, later to become the Chief Metropolitan Magistrate. On this and subsequent remand hearings, the case was set out and the magistrate told Superintendent Fenwick that he assumed that further enquiries were being carried out in respect of the murder of PC Summers, since no charge had yet been made. "Not at this stage," replied Fenwick, adding, "exhaustive enquiries are being made to ascertain other persons who were present and we then may be able to clarify the position."

Bail was objected to by Fenwick. Referring to Summers' murder, he told the magistrate, "It is impossible to divorce the other matter from these charges in front of the court. There is a great deal of fear in the neighbourhood. There is considerable difficulty in making enquiries. There is a possibility there may be a resumption of the activities of these people." Mr Milton asked, "These are enquiries which you hope may result in the arrest of a person in connection with the death of a policeman?" and Fenwick replied that they were.

Nevertheless, bail was applied for, with David (later Sir David) Napley stating that his client Murray came from a respectable home and had no previous convictions. Mr Body, appearing on behalf of Budd, appeared to distance himself from the assertion that it was Budd who had allegedly started the trouble in the first place, and actually distanced Budd from the affray by saying he was in the dance hall at the time of the murder. Additionally, Body asked Fenwick if it was true that in his statement Budd had said that he knew, respected and admired PC Summers. Fenwick replied that that was so, but wisely added the corollary that he was not in a position to say if that was true or not.

It is possible that Mr P. Weitzman, appearing for Bergonzi, muddied the waters for everybody by asking if it was right that persons accused of one offence should be refused bail because of a different matter in which 'enquiries were being made', and then went on to allege that his client had been forcibly dragged from his home and at the police station threatened and struck in order to obtain a statement. At committal proceedings, Weitzman delivered an attack upon the character of Detective Chief Superintendent Glander, who denied that in dealing with the murder of a police officer the officers concerned were 'more zealous' than usual; when it was suggested that he had told Bergonzi that he would 'put a rope around his neck if he did not start talking', Glander smoothly replied, "He was ready to talk from the moment he came into the police station."

With a police officer dead and no one held to account for his murder, gang warfare with a miscellany of weapons on the streets of London and representatives of 'The Angel Mob' and 'The Finsbury Park Lot' in the dock, Weitzman's was not the most compelling argument to use to secure bail. It failed to work for the accused, who were committed in custody to stand their trial at the Old Bailey, with the exception of Newbolt who, the magistrate said, did not go there armed – he was granted bail in his own recognizance of £50, with two sureties each of £200.

It was now thought that the wound to Marwood's fingers had been caused outside the dance hall by a member of his own gang who was brandishing an axe. But no one – including Bloom – would say that it was Marwood who had killed PC Summers. What was known, however, was that after his release Marwood had telephoned Bloom, telling him he was frightened and that he was going to stay out of the way.

Fenwick released Marwood's photograph to the press, and the hunt was stepped up. Meanwhile, Reggie Kray, himself an habitué of Gray's Dancing Academy, gave him shelter in a flat at

49 Lake View Estate, Edgware. Opinions vary as to whether or not Marwood fled there with his wife; if she did accompany him, she either did not tarry long or else was incredibly broadminded, because in his often unintentionally hilarious memoirs, *Born Fighter*, Reggie Kray describes how Marwood was kept supplied with beer and ex-club hostesses.

Kray claimed that 'a police chief inspector' came in to the Double R Club and let him know that he was aware of the address of Marwood's hideout. It may be true, it may not be. Criminals usually tend to allege that it is officers of substantial rank who mark their cards, for no other reason than to display their hold over supposedly venal, high-ranking police officers. One corrupt officer, who was referred to by Ronnie Kray as 'a police inspector', was in fact a detective sergeant. Reggie Kray also asserted that the local police told him they knew he was harbouring Marwood and they would be keeping a close eye on his future activities. That, too, may or may not be true.

But what Kray also stated is that during a visit to Marwood (who had apparently dyed his hair ginger and grown a moustache) he saw that the latter had got hold of a revolver, which he showed to Kray, saying, "I will shoot the bastards if I'm cornered." When it was later suggested that he regretted hiding Marwood, Kray haughtily repudiated this slur on his integrity, claiming that it was "a diabolical lie". But was it? If pressure was being put on Kray by the police, it is quite possible that he was beginning to regret his quixotic action in shielding Marwood, who was becoming an embarrassment, as well as fearing his (Kray's) possible culpability as an accessory before or after the fact, in the event that Marwood did shoot police officers.

Reggie Kray should have learnt his lesson; that February, after Ronnie had been certified insane and transferred to Long Grove Hospital, Surrey, Reggie had helped him escape, and six months later hoped that the time lapse would prove that his brother was not insane at all. Unfortunately, by now Ronnie was raving and his behaviour had become so outrageous that, just prior to Marwood being shielded, the Kray family had handed Ronnie back to the authorities. He would be released in 1959.

So with the recent memories of his lunatic brother, and now Marwood threatening to shoot the police, it is highly likely, notwithstanding the fact that Reggie Kray was five inches shorter than his lodger, that he brusquely gave him notice. However, it was clear that Kray failed to profit from the experience of hiding wanted men. Almost exactly eight years to the day after shielding Marwood, he arranged the escape from prison of Frank 'the Mad

Axeman' Mitchell, who behaved in the same way, getting a gun and threatening to shoot anyone coming to arrest him. On that occasion, Mitchell was unlucky; he ended up being fatally shot. Marwood merely postponed his execution; at eight o'clock on the evening of 27 January 1959, six weeks after the murder, he went with his father to Caledonian Road police station and gave himself up.

★   ★   ★

After Marwood admitted being in the Seven Sisters Road on the night of the murder, Fenwick asked him if he wished him to make a written record of the incident. "Yes, you can later," replied Marwood. "I want to think."

Three hours later, he was seen again. "You can write it all down," Marwood told Fenwick and Detective Inspector Thomas O'Shea. "I did stab the copper that night. I'll never know why I did it. I've been puzzling over in my mind during the last few weeks why I did it, but there seems no answer."

In his written statement under caution, Marwood explained how on the night he had gone out for a drink and met up with Bloom "and some younger kids". Bloom had told him that there had been trouble between three youths, and eventually they went to Gray's Dancing Academy. "I saw Mick and one of the younger blokes go up to the door of the dance place to see somebody about some argument," Marwood told Fenwick, "the next thing I know is that a lot of people come running out of Gray's. A few scuffles started on the pavement. Someone swung a chopper at my head." Marwood said he felt "dizzy and sick" after being hit by the axe and then saw Bloom being pushed along by PC Summers. As he walked up behind Summers, the officer half turned and said, "Go away" or "Clear off" and punched him on the shoulder. "I remember I had my hands in my overcoat pockets," Marwood said, "I pulled out my hand, intending to push him away from me. I must have had my hand on the knife."

In common with most criminals who endeavour to minimize their misdeeds, Marwood stated that he aimed a blow at the officer's arm and that the knife had been given to him earlier that evening by a youth who had told him, "Here you are; you might need this." "At the time, I thought it was a bit silly," said Marwood, "and I put it in my overcoat pocket. I had forgotten all about it and I never realized I had it until I struck the policeman with it."

Like many officers who specialize in the investigation of fraud, Fenwick did not try to browbeat suspects; he let them say whatever they liked in a voluntary statement, and then 'looked for the lie'. In fact, there were a number of lies in Marwood's statement, including his acquisition of the knife; Fenwick was able to prove it had been in his possession for several months, and the following day Marwood was charged with murder.

★   ★   ★

But whilst Marwood was being remanded from North London Magistrates' Court, the youths who had been involved in the incident at Seven Sisters Road had problems of their own. On 6 February they appeared at the Old Bailey before the Common Serjeant, Sir Anthony Hawke. All pleaded not guilty to causing an affray, and this was accepted by the prosecution after they had all – with the exception of Dean – pleaded guilty to unlawful assembly with intent to disturb the peace. All of the defendants – with the exception of Bloom – pleaded guilty to possessing offensive weapons. Passing sentence, the Common Serjeant told them:

> You are a shocking example to other young people. You are really nothing but intolerable nuisances and you become a little more dangerous when you carry weapons.

Budd was sentenced to fifteen months' imprisonment, Fletcher to twelve months and Ronald Jackman and Thwaites to nine months each. Frederick Jackman, Newbolt and Bloom each received six months' imprisonment and Bergonzi, four months. Sentence was postponed on the other defendants until later, Sir Anthony Hawke telling them, "I don't propose any of you to get away with it." He sentenced Bailey to five months in a detention centre, Dean to three months in a detention centre and fined Murray £20, or three months' imprisonment in default. As the prison van drove off to deposit them at various places of incarceration, one of the gang was heard to shout to the others, "Blow this for a lark; next time it'll be balloons on sticks at twenty-five yards!"

★   ★   ★

After Marwood was remanded at North London Magistrates' Court, DCI Joyce later told the court, he had taken Marwood's wife and father to his cell. His father immediately asked his son, "Did you do it?" Marwood replied, "Yes, dad. I have told them the truth." Mr Mordecai Levene, on behalf of Marwood, later suggested that Marwood's father was referring to the statement which his son had made, although DCI Joyce thought he might well have been referring to the fatal stabbing. The Magistrate, Mr Milton, commented that this was a matter of interpretation, although more credence may have been given to DCI Joyce's understanding of Marwood's remarks, since Fenwick had given evidence that when Marwood was formally charged and cautioned he had replied, "I have already told you the truth, how it happened in my statement."

One week into his six-month sentence, Bloom appeared as a witness for the prosecution at Bow Street Magistrates' Court and stated that Marwood had telephoned him on the night after the murder, telling him that the police had arrested him but had let him go. He had told Bloom that he was frightened and wanted to keep out of the way. Asked by Mr Peter M. J. Palmes for the Director of Public Prosecutions if Marwood had said why he was frightened, Bloom replied, "It was something to do with a policeman getting killed."

Bloom told the court that a police officer had come up behind him outside the dance hall and had said, "What's all this about?" The officer had "nudged him along" and then said, "Clear off out of it," to someone who had come up from behind him. "The policeman took hold of my arm," said Bloom, "and said, 'Just a minute, I want to talk to you.' I hear a blow at the back of the policeman and he let go my arm and I ran away across the road and down Thane Villas."

Marwood's trial commenced at the Old Bailey on 18 March 1959, before Mr Justice Gorman. The prosecution was led by Christmas Humphreys QC and the defence was represented by Neil Lawson QC and Mr Levene. Marwood pleaded not guilty to the capital murder of PC Summers.

Asked by the defence if he had anything in his hand when he struck PC Summers, Marwood replied he had not. The basis of the prosecution's case was Marwood's voluntary statement – and Marwood now claimed it was a fabrication. He told the jury that the police had written it down and after being in the police station for ten hours he had signed it without reading it. This, not unnaturally, was denied by Superintendent Fenwick.

Summing up, the defence suggested to the jury that if they did not dismiss the statement out of hand, and came to the conclusion that Marwood had indeed stabbed the constable, they should return a verdict of manslaughter, due to the accused's befuddled state after drinking ten pints of brown ale. It was a defence of double standards; either Marwood had stabbed Summers or he had not.

In his summing up to the jury, Mr Justice Gorman mentioned the statement in which Marwood alleged that the police had written the exact opposite of what he had told them. He told them:

> How do you describe in mild terms the putting of this devilish concoction in the document? If you come to the conclusion that this statement substantially represents the truth, and you are sure that there was a knife in the hands of the defendant that night, then it may help you to arrive at a view as to whether the prisoner did, or did not, strike the fatal blow.

After the jury had deliberated for over two and a half hours, Marwood was found guilty, and was subsequently sentenced to death.

An appeal, heard on 20 April before Lord Chief Justice Hubert Parker (who had just been appointed Baron Parker of Waddington), sitting with Mr Justice Donovan and Mr Justice Salmon, was dismissed, and the date for the execution at Pentonville prison was set for Friday, 8 May 1959.

It was high time for Marwood to be transformed into a martyr.

⋆   ⋆   ⋆

Albert Evans, the Labour Member of Parliament for Islington (South-West), drew up a petition for a reprieve, which was signed by 150 of his fellow MPs. Feelings were running high on both sides of the fence. John Grey, then a probationary police constable, recalled an idiotic police constable in the canteen at King's Cross singing, "Lay down your head Ron Marwood, tomorrow you're gonna die!" – a parody of the ballad 'Tom Dooley', made popular by the skiffle artiste Lonnie Donegan in 1958. When the local priest set up a table in Chapel Market to collect signatures for a petition against the death sentence, some of the more predictable police officers, known as 'canteen cowboys', were all for having the priest arrested for highway obstruction – as long as they were not called upon to do it themselves, of course. Fortunately, this offensive nonsense was stopped because wiser heads – notably Jim Jardine, who would later become chairman of the Police Federation – prevailed.

The day before his execution, Marwood's family attempted to get the Attorney General to permit the case to be referred to the

House of Lords, but this appeal was ruled to be out of time, as indeed it was. That evening, there was a noisy demonstration by some of the Pentonville inmates; prisoners screamed, smashed crockery and set fire to material which was pushed out of cell windows and fluttered down to the yard below. A crowd of some 500 people gathered in the street outside the prison, some with placards, reading 'Hanging no Deterrent' and 'Don't Murder Marwood'. By the morning of the execution, the crowd had swollen to 1,000 and was becoming more unruly. Ted Harrington was stopped by a mounted police officer but explained he was going to work at a nearby paint-spraying company and was let through. *Pathé News* was on hand to film the disturbances, and the *Manchester Guardian* told its readers:

> Not since the execution of Derek Bentley six years ago has there been such a display of emotions and physical violence. During the last fifteen minutes of Marwood's life, a mob went wild – punching, kicking, screaming and cursing. Once again, as at the hangings of Bentley and Ruth Ellis, dozens of men and women had arrived in a state of macabre anticipation. If one has ever wondered about the mentality of the festive crowds that used to line the route to Tyburn, a visit to the gates of Pentonville yesterday showed that there are still many of the same sort of people in our midst today. It is not a pleasant thought.

The *Daily Mail* reported that tulips and lilies in the prison chapel had been sent by Marwood's twenty-year-old wife, 'who became a widow as she prayed', and the *Observer* thought that 'a revival of the campaign to abolish capital punishment is overdue.'

Marwood was hanged at nine o'clock that morning, Friday, 8 May 1959, by executioner Harry Allen, assisted by Harry Robinson.

The nuns who had been kneeling in the roadway, praying, stood up, crossed themselves and glided away. The assembled police officers returned to their respective stations for a belated breakfast. The mounted branch returned their steeds to the stables – "They were not needed," remarked former Chief Superintendent Mick Patten, although Assistant Commissioner 'A' Department Douglas Webb thought otherwise – and the crowd dispersed. There were jobs to go to, wages to be picked up at the end of the day, and the weekend beckoned.

Two days later, Canon Collins told the congregation in St Paul's Cathedral, "Surely the offence against Christian principle committed on Friday morning must make us do more than wring our hands in despair," and in the House of Commons on 12 May Samuel Sydney Silverman, the Labour Member of Parliament for Nelson & Colne and a vocal opponent of capital punishment, introduced a motion to abolish the death penalty. His campaign had started in 1948; it would not be successful until 1965.

Not to be outdone, Mr E. L. Mallalieu QC, MP, drew up a motion to disallow confessions made to police unless they were written in the presence of a magistrate. And one month later, Sir Frank Mendicott, Member of Parliament for Norfolk Central, mentioned that Marwood had had twenty drinks served to him on the night of Summers' murder and demanded that the Secretary of State for the Home Department give an assurance that in future the authorities should exercise their powers under various sections of the Licensing Act. The Secretary of State mildly replied that at his trial Marwood denied he had been drunk and that the evidence of the police who stopped him after the murder suggested that he did not appear to be anything other than sober.

★   ★   ★

It would appear that the police did indeed 'keep an eye' on Reggie Kray's activities; later that year he was arrested for demanding money with menaces and was sentenced to eighteen months' imprisonment.

Two months after Marwood's execution, Superintendent Fenwick was seconded to the Home Office; he was appointed Deputy Chief Constable of Gloucestershire and in 1969, as a member of Her Majesty's Inspectorate of Constabularies, he was awarded the Queen's Police Medal for distinguished service. Whether or not he had been 'the best man for the job', every person involved in the case which he dealt with had been properly convicted.

Harry Joyce was promoted to the rank of detective superintendent and took Fenwick's place, but not for long. Within a few months, he went to spend his last remaining four years of service as head of the Detective Training School, where he had previously served as a detective inspector. He retired after exactly thirty years' service and enjoyed forty years of retirement, dying at the age of ninety-one. Joyce was remembered with great fondness by Bob Roach. "He had been an instructor at the Detective Training School when I was there, and his English pronunciation was wonderful," Bob recalled. "One could never doubt anything he said because he was such a clear speaker. One of his favourite openings when giving instruction was, 'The facts at issue are ...'" It was also a phrase he used when giving evidence against Marwood.

Roach sat through the trial of Marwood and was present when the judge donned the black cap prior to delivering the death sentence. Also present was former Detective Superintendent Geoff Parratt. He was then a young constable who was a witness in an arson case, and the jury in his case had been sworn in the court where Marwood's trial took place. Suddenly, the proceedings in Parratt's trial were temporarily halted as the jury in Marwood's case returned to deliver their verdict. As they did so, Parratt's detective inspector said quietly, "Stay where you are; I don't suppose you'll ever see anything like this, again." Speaking to me over fifty years later, Parratt – who had joined the police just a couple of months before Summers – said, "And he was right; I never did."

★   ★   ★

Some thirty years after the event, a memorial plaque was erected to the memory of PC Summers at Holloway police station. The old police station had been demolished, and the present station was built in 1965, further along at 284 Hornsey Road. In 1980, Raymond Gosman, who had been a police constable at Caledonian Road police station and knew Summers slightly, retired from the Metropolitan Police and went to live in Broadstairs, Kent. One day, and quite by chance, he saw Ray Summers' grave in St Peter's churchyard, in a village close to Broadstairs. From time to time flowers were placed on the grave, but although he made local enquiries, Gosman was unable to trace any relatives or friends who might have lived nearby. As the years went by, the flowers stopped being placed there, and so Gosman made it his responsibility to clean up the headstone. As he said on the thirty-seventh anniversary of his comrade's death, "I feel, in some way, responsible for it now."

The grave overlooks the Thanet countryside where Ray Summers grew up. His parents, Henry Percival and Ruby Summers, are buried in the same grave, as is Summers' fiancée, Sheila McKenzie. She died on 26 September 1959, aged twenty-one, ten months after Summers' murder. Official records reveal that she died of an asthma attack. However, the romantics prefer to believe that she died of a broken heart; I know I do.

CHAPTER 4

A Lapse of Memory

I t is important for a writer of history to be, if not utterly certain of his facts, then as positive as he possibly can be. Therefore, permit me to acquaint the reader with certain facts and fallacies concerning the murder of Detective Sergeant Ray Purdy in 1959. The first fact is that he was murdered by Günther Fritz Erwin Podola, and the next is that Podola was executed for his crime. Now the fallacies. There was a popular misconception that at the time of his arrest and following his detention at Chelsea police station, Podola was subjected to savage and sustained beatings. Despite questions being raised in the House by a near-hysterical Member of Parliament and the public outcry which followed – thanks to some completely irresponsible press coverage – this was not true. Another fact is that Purdy, who was murdered in the line of duty, received less and less attention, while the belief that Podola was a victim gained more and more prominence. Podola was not a victim. He was a convicted housebreaker in Canada who continued his burglarious enterprises in England. And as well as being a gun-toting, cold-blooded murderer, he was a cunning and duplicitous blackmailer, who unsuccessfully played the legal system for all he was worth but became the last murderer of a police officer to be hanged in England. That's just to set the record straight. But although Purdy was a victim (and Podola quite conspicuously was not) there was another victim who, following Purdy's murder, carried his self-imposed guilt around with him for over fifty years. This is the story of all three.

★   ★   ★

Podola was born on 8 February 1929 in Berlin and during the war became a fanatical member of the Hitler Youth movement. In 1952 he escaped from East Berlin to the Western sector of the city, conveniently leaving behind Ruth Quandt with whom he had had a child, Micky, and emigrated to Canada. During the following four years, Podola had a number of jobs, as a labourer, mechanic and welder, nearly all of short duration. On 1 March 1957 he was convicted of burglary in Montreal and sentenced to ten days' imprisonment. Following his release, on 26 March he was convicted of another eleven counts of theft and burglary and this time was sentenced to two years' imprisonment. He was released on 25 July 1958 and deported to West Germany, arriving there on 4 August 1958. He worked in Gerlingen and Stuttgart as a labourer before flying from Düsseldorf to England, but already he had formed his plans. "I was determined to make myself a big-shot in crime," he wrote from prison, whilst awaiting execution. "I bought an automatic pistol for £5 and touted myself as a gunman for hire." The automatic which he purchased was a 9mm FB Radom V15, a pistol of Polish origin; the manufacturers originally produced 40,000 of them before the war and then, after the Germans' invasion and with their encouragement, another 300,000.

Following his arrival at Heathrow on 21 March 1959, Podola was directed to a hotel near the West London Air Terminal, where he registered as 'G. Jodola' from Montreal. After ten days he left for a guest house in the Cromwell Road, from where he was ejected on 23 June for failing to pay his rent. On 25 June he booked into the Claremont House Hotel, 95 Queen's Gate, Kensington. The management of the thirty-five-shillings-per-week hotel knew him as Paul Camay of Montreal, and in adopting this alias it is clear that he was now commencing his English career of criminality.

Swaggering around Soho and calling himself Mike Colato, but attracting little attention as a gangster, Podola carried out a series of housebreakings to provide himself with funds. In order to dispose of some of the stolen property, Podola required an outlet. He found one and jotted down his contact's telephone number in a notebook. It would prove to be his undoing.

On 3 July 1959 Podola broke into a flat in Roland Gardens, South Kensington, just south of the fashionable Old Brompton Road, whilst the occupier, a thirty-year-old British-born American model, Mrs Verne Schiffman, who was on holiday in London, was absent. Among the property stolen were a mink stole and jewellery, valued at £1,785, plus passports belonging to Mrs Schiffman, her daughter and a friend. The loss was promptly reported to Chelsea police station.

On 7 July Mrs Schiffman received a letter from a person purporting to be R.M. Levine – it was, of course, Podola – who claimed to be an American private detective and informed her that he had been hired to check on her private life; as a result, he was in possession of a number of compromising tapes and photographs which would be handed over to her upon receipt of

$500. In that eventuality, stated 'Mr Levine', he would send a favourable report to the person who had commissioned the investigation. Mrs Schiffman knew that this was a bluff pure and simple and, knowing she had nothing to be worried about, handed the letter to the police. On Sunday, 12 July she received a telephone call at home from a man claiming to be a Mr Fisher – Podola, again – asking if she would be willing to pay. Acting on police advice, Mrs Schiffman replied that she would. Podola told her he would phone back, giving details of how the payment should be made. She then contacted the police, who quickly arranged for an intercept to be put on her telephone.

The next call came the following morning, when Podola instructed her to withdraw $500 from her bank and await further instructions. That afternoon, Mrs Schiffman received a further call; she got a neighbour to contact Chelsea police station and kept 'Mr Fisher' talking. In the meantime, the Post Office engineers traced the call to a public call box, KNIghtsbridge 2355, situated by South Kensington Underground station in Thurloe Street, just a quarter of a mile from Mrs Schiffman's address, and a telephone call was made to Chelsea police station; it was the breakthrough for which John Sandford had been waiting.

⋆　⋆　⋆

Detective Sergeant (Second Class) John Leslie Sandford was born in Portsmouth in 1926 and joined the Metropolitan Police in 1946, immediately after demobilization from his wartime service with the RAF. He was married with one child, and had spent all of his service in 'B' Division, first as Police Constable 70 'B', then as an aid to CID, a detective constable and, since June 1958, as a detective sergeant. He knew the area inside out and was an active thief-catcher; at this stage of his career he had been commended on nine occasions, of which the first was for the arrest of violent criminals.

The Schiffman case was allocated to him and now, on the afternoon of Monday, 13 July, having asked a colleague, Ray Purdy, to come with him, he ran from the office to a police car.

Raymond William Purdy was born in Fulham in 1916 and following a higher elementary education was employed as a fitter's mate. He joined the Metropolitan Police on 28 August 1939, aged twenty-three and, a married man, he was initially posted to 'Y' Division, on the border of the Metropolitan Police Area adjoining Hertfordshire Constabulary. Within a year he was transferred right to the other end of the Metropolitan Police Area, to Kingston police station on 'V' Division, and in 1941 the first of his three children was born. In 1943 he volunteered for the army and for the next two and a half years saw active service, before demobilization returned him to the Metropolitan Police and 'V' Division. There he applied to be an aid to CID, and two commendations from the commissioner – one for zeal and ability in a case of larceny dwelling, the other for initiative, in another case of larceny, where he was also commended by the justices at Richmond Magistrates' Court – helped him on his way to being appointed detective constable in 1947. His second son had been born a year previously, and one year after his appointment his daughter was born.

Purdy was a bright officer; he passed his examinations at the first attempt for second- and first-class sergeant, and upon promotion to detective sergeant (second class) in 1955 he was posted to Hammersmith police station on 'F' Division, close to the place of his birth. Less than three years later came promotion to detective sergeant (first class) and he was posted to Chelsea police station, next door to Fulham, on neighbouring 'B' Division.

He was admired at the station; former Police Constable Ken Walker remembers him on what he believes was Purdy's last appearance at the Old Bailey, when he oversaw a case in which a general practitioner had been charged with bribing, attempting to bribe and assaulting Walker. As Walker laconically remarked, "We won." Walker told me, "He was a dedicated officer, a very quiet and thoughtful individual, very meticulous in his work." In addition, Purdy had been commended by the commissioner for alertness and initiative in effecting the arrest of two men for armed robbery.

Purdy did not normally work with Sandford and in any event he had just been about to book off duty when Mrs Schiffman telephoned; but Sandford's regular partner was unavailable, and therefore Purdy deputized for him.

Mrs Schiffman had done well to keep Podola talking on the telephone for fifteen minutes and she had obviously lulled him into a sense of false security, because at 3.50 that afternoon she suddenly heard the man who had introduced himself as 'Mr Fisher' exclaim, "Hey! What do you want?"

There were sounds of a scuffle before she heard another, more authoritative voice say, "Okay lad, we're police officers." A moment later, the same man picked up the receiver and said, "Mrs Schiffman? This is Detective Sergeant Purdy – remember my name."

Podola was pulled from the telephone kiosk, and a small black leather notebook which he had been holding was taken from him and placed in Purdy's pocket. As the two officers led Podola up the steps to the street he suddenly broke away, and as Purdy stumbled, Podola dashed off into Onslow Square. Sandford flagged down a passing taxi, both officers got in and were in time to see Podola run into a block of flats situated at No. 105. Following him into the hall, they found Podola hiding behind a pillar and again seized him.

"Behave yourself!" Purdy admonished him, and told Podola to sit on a window sill while his colleague went to ring for the hall porter. It was Sandford's intention to get the porter to telephone the police station for assistance and when it arrived to retrace his steps to recover the abandoned police car. But he could get no response and he called out to Purdy, "The porter must be out." At the sound of Sandford's voice Purdy was momentarily distracted and glanced in his direction; Sandford then saw Podola slide off the window sill and slip his hand inside his jacket; with mounting horror, he saw Podola withdraw a pistol, and shouted, "Look out – he's got a gun!"

It was too late; Podola immediately fired at point-blank range, hitting Purdy in the chest and mortally wounding him. Sandford started after the fleeing Podola but, realizing he would be unable to catch him, turned to his companion to see what assistance he could render. Alas, there was nothing that he or the two passers-by who had heard the shots could do. Sandford telephoned Chelsea police station, and when the two senior officers, Detective Superintendent David Hislop and Detective Chief Inspector Bob Acott, DFC, arrived, they were just in time to see Purdy die.

The very shaken John Sandford gave what was, in the circumstances, an extremely creditable description of the wanted man: aged about thirty, five feet nine or ten, clean shaven, thin build, quietly spoken with traces of an American or German accent, with brown, crew-cut hair, wearing dark glasses, a light sports coat and trousers and light brown suede shoes. But of the suspect there was no sign.

With a shocked reaction registering throughout the Metropolitan Police District – Deputy Commander Reggie Spooner (late of the wartime MI5 and former head of the Flying Squad) entered the office of Assistant Commissioner (Crime) Richard (later Sir Richard) Jackson CBE, and told him, "You'll be sorry to hear, sir, that one of our sergeants has been shot. He's dead" – the investigation moved into top gear. House-to-house enquiries were carried out, underworld informants were pressed to reveal what they knew and Detective Sergeant Hughie Coulston was present when the autopsy was carried out on his friend Ray Purdy. It was so harrowing that the matter was never referred to again, by anybody. Fingerprints were found on the marble window sill in Onslow Square, but could not be identified; Podola had no criminal record in England.

Gillian Purdy was then eleven years of age. She had returned from school, changed and had gone out to play with friends, when two smartly dressed men, with buttonholes and wearing bowler hats, approached – they were obviously senior police officers – and asked the whereabouts of Mrs Purdy's house. She told them that Mrs Purdy lived at No. 15, the two men went to the house, and Gillian followed five minutes later. "There the two men sat with my mother, looking very serious," Gillian told me, almost exactly fifty-two years after the tragedy. "My mother told me, 'Daddy went to work and he's not coming back.' We waited for my eighteen-year-old brother to return from work, praying that he wouldn't pick up a copy of the *Evening Standard* before we saw him. Later, I looked out of the upstairs window and along the pathway I could see a line of pressmen and photographers." Gillian and her younger brother – who was profoundly affected by his father's murder – were shielded from the news. "There was a news 'black-out' in our house," Gillian recalled. The house which originally had been full of laughter was now silent.

★   ★   ★

And then something curious happened. Purdy's personal effects had been returned to his heartbroken widow, Mrs Irene Eileen Purdy, but she contacted the station to inform the investigating officers that a small address book which had been returned to her had not belonged to her husband.

Detective Sergeants Fred Lambert and Peter Darke (both of whom had served on the Flying Squad and would both later achieve the rank of detective chief superintendent) were attached to Gerald Road police station, also part of 'B' Division, and were seconded as part of the investigating team at Chelsea. Now, Lambert perused the address book – the one which Purdy had taken from Podola – and recognized one of the many telephone numbers which Podola had jotted down. It belonged to a character named 'Little Jack', who owned a shop which bought anything of value, in Lisle Street, a narrow thoroughfare just off the Charing Cross Road, by Leicester Square Underground station. He was a very useful contact to the police, as was his son, who owned a similar establishment in Little Newport Street, a short walk away.

★ ★ ★

When 'Little Jack' was offered an item which was identifiable, if he had doubts regarding the honesty of the customer, he would refuse the offer but direct the seller to the shop of his son, who, he would assure the customer, "would buy anything". Once the customer had left with the property, he would flash his 'anything bought' sign in the window on and off, in the hope that it would attract the attention of a couple of aids to CID. If none were in the vicinity, Jack would telephone the local police station, which was West End Central, in which case the customer could be intercepted in the street before he reached the Little Newport Street premises.

A few days prior to the murder, Podola had gone to 'Little Jack's' in possession of a tape recorder. Jack had flashed the shop's sign, and a couple of aids to CID, Police Constables Geoff Anderson and Charlie Body, who were in nearby Momma's Café, noticed this and entered the shop on the pretext of examining Jack's books. They got into conversation with Podola regarding his ownership of the tape recorder and invited him into Momma's Café. Leaving Body to "see what he was made of", Anderson went to the nearest telephone box and checked with the Yard, both at Criminal Records Office on Podola and at Property Index on the serial number of the tape recorder. Although the tape recorder was indeed part-proceeds of a housebreaking committed by Podola, the details of the property had not yet been sent to the Yard and therefore it dutifully reported, "No trace on either." Recording Podola's details in his police pocket book, Anderson asked him to sign his name in it, which he did. The signature appeared to be 'Jodolar', which was slightly at variance with the signature in his passport, so Anderson asked him to sign his name again on the back of his pocket book, and once more Podola obliged. There was a further short conversation, and then Podola, together with the tape recorder, was allowed to go on his way, which he did – to Little Newport Street, where he sold his merchandise.

Anderson and Body had behaved perfectly correctly, except for one matter. Aids to CID carried out so many stops in the street in those days that although every person they interviewed should have had their details correctly recorded in the Book 66 (colloquially known as the 'Stop Book') at the local station, unless a stop was resented or resulted in an arrest (in which case, the stop was triumphantly recorded in red ink), this piece of documentation was often neglected. Of course, it was a disciplinary offence to omit to enter a person's details in the Book 66, but with this pleasant man who had an accent which varied from American to German and had been no trouble at all, it seemed scarcely worthwhile. Therefore, Podola's details remained in Anderson's pocket book.

★   ★   ★

When he saw the address book which had been in Purdy's possession, Lambert immediately realized that the killer must have had dealings with 'Little Jack', so he and Darke drove over to Jack's home address in Kennington Lane. Jack remembered the man, and his description fitted the suspect. He said that he had tipped off a couple of aids to CID, but that when they informed Jack that the tape recorder had not been reported as being stolen, it had been purchased by his son. The tape recorder was still in the son's shop, and upon checking the serial number it was discovered that by now it had indeed been reported as stolen; furthermore, Lambert was told that the aids to CID had taken details of the suspect from documents which were in his possession. The next stop was West End Central police station for examination of the 'Stop Book' – only to find there was no relevant entry at the time. Lambert correctly guessed what had occurred; after all, he had been an aid himself. He reported his findings to Superintendent Hislop back at Chelsea police station. By now, it was midnight; Hislop contacted the duty officer at West End Central and directed him to ensure that all the aids to CID were to parade at four o'clock the next morning. Since the aids were mostly single men who lived in the nearby police section house, this did not represent a great problem.

Hislop addressed the aids and told them that if the officers who had stopped the suspect at 'Little Jack's' in possession of the tape recorder came forward, the fact that they had neglected to enter the necessary details in the Book 66 would be overlooked.

Anderson and Body immediately stepped forward. "Of course, Charlie and I were mortified to learn of the shooting of Ray Purdy," Anderson said. "Superintendent Hislop could see how upset I was. When I produced my pocket book, Mr Hislop seemed to forgive my errors, and Charlie and I worked at Chelsea until Podola's arrest."

Now the investigating officers had a name. Podola's movements since his arrival in England were traced through the Aliens' Registration Office and enquiries were made about him to the Royal Canadian Mounted Police at Ottawa and the *Bundeskriminalamt* (German Federal Police) at Wiesbaden. Fingerprints sent from both countries matched the prints taken from the marble window sill in Onslow Square, also from the black address book which had erroneously been returned to Purdy's widow. With the fingerprints came a photograph; and Podola's photograph was inserted in a frame with eleven others of similar appearance and shown to Sandford to determine if he could identify the man who had shot Purdy. Without hesitation, Sandford identified Podola, and now his photograph was released to the press.

Everyone, it seemed, wanted to help. And then, three days after the murder almost to the exact minute, at 3.45 on Thursday, 16 July 1959, the police paid a call to the Claremont House Hotel, 95 Queen's Gate, Kensington.

Since the day of the murder, the man who called himself 'Paul Camay' had not left his room. His behaviour was so strange that the manager called the police, and upon being shown a photograph confirmed that Podola and Camay were one and the same and that the gunman was presently ensconced in Room 15 on the third floor.

Hislop had chosen the arrest party well; all of them were veterans of the Flying Squad. His second in command was Detective Chief Inspector Basil Montague – always known as 'Bob' – Acott who, following an interruption in his police career during which he had distinguished himself in the wartime RAF, had been showered with commendations during his time on the Flying Squad as a detective sergeant, particularly with regard to his contribution to the 1948 'Battle of Heathrow'[3] and his work with the ultra-secret post-war Ghost Squad.[4]

At half an inch over six feet and weighing sixteen stone, Detective Sergeant Albert Eric John Chambers had already been brought to prominence on the Flying Squad when he was awarded the George Medal. Four years previously, he had tackled John Cohen, one of an armed gang of three who had carried out

---

3. For full details, see *The Sweeney – The First Sixty Years of Scotland Yard's Crimebusting Flying Squad* (Wharncliffe Books, 2011).
4. For full details, see *Scotland Yard's Ghost Squad* (Wharncliffe Books, 2011).

a robbery at a jeweller's. Despite being shot, Chambers had disarmed and arrested Cohen, who failed to attract the sympathy he undoubtedly thought due to him when he explained to Lord Goddard at the Old Bailey, "I panicked and did my nut." Goddard then sentenced Cohen to twenty years' imprisonment. "A big guy, very quietly spoken, with a wealth of CID experience," was how Bob Roach remembers Chambers, and Ken Walker recalls him as being, "Of the old school of detectives, a fine officer."

The hardest man in the group was undoubtedly Detective Inspector Jasper Peter Vibart. An ex-soldier, Vibart had served for twelve years on the Flying Squad, where he and the legendary Tommy Butler were known as 'the Terrible Twins'. Both had been commended for their part in the Brighton Police corruption scandal and both had been seconded to the British Police Unit in Cyprus in the hunt for Colonel Grivas. Vibart made a speciality of arresting dangerous armed criminals and he had been commended time and again for doing so. Twelve months previously, he had arrested Ronnie Easterbrook for shooting a police officer in the face and had been awarded the Queen's Commendation for Brave Conduct.[5] Despite being slashed in the face with a razor wielded by the gangster William 'Billy-Boy' Blythe, Vibart's success with violent criminals stemmed from the fact that he was absolutely fearless in his dealings with them.

These were a selection of the officers whom Hislop had chosen to accompany him to the Claremont House Hotel. But just as this powerful posse started to leave Chelsea police station, so a large number of pressmen, journalists and photographers started to move off with them. The car carrying Hislop stopped, he got out of the car and addressed the representatives of the Press. "If any of you fucking lot cock this up, I shall personally come looking for you," he said. Then in a more conciliatory tone he added, "Now, wait for a while and let me do what I have to do."

The Press had already responded very helpfully in this investigation, so Hislop's words were not the most tactful that he might have used to further Police/Press relationships, as he was soon to find out.

These officers – and others, including a police dog-handler with his charge, 'Flame' – stood outside the door of Room 15 of the Claremont House Hotel. They had established from the manager that Podola was still in the room. Vibart charged the

---

5. For full details, see *The Brave Blue Line* (Wharncliffe Books, 2011).

door but without success, so he shouted, "Police – open the door!"

There was silence; then from the other side of the door there came an ominous 'click', very much like a gun being cocked. At that, Chambers launched his bulky frame at the door and this time it gave in. Podola was crouching behind the door, perhaps looking through the keyhole or about to unlock the door, but as the door flew open it struck him in the face, knocking him backwards. "I caught a glimpse of Podola as the door hit him in the face," Chambers later told a packed courtroom at the Old Bailey, "and the force of it hitting him made him stagger back across the room. He went over the arm of a chair and he finished up lying on the floor face uppermost, with his head in the fireplace. I let myself go forward and fell down full length on top of him." Podola struggled furiously, and Chambers held his arm to stop him reaching his gun. Other officers crowded in and held him down, then Vibart and Acott put him on the bed, where he was searched and handcuffed. Whatever else the officers had heard from the other side of the door, it was not the cocking of a gun; the murder weapon was later found in the hotel's attic, wrapped in a copy of *The Times* from the day of the murder.

Podola suffered a small cut above his eye as the result of the impact with the door, and there was a great deal of blood on the bed's pillowcases, the coverlet and Podola's trousers, undoubtedly the result of a nose-bleed sustained during the struggle. In addition, his left eye was rapidly swelling. The officers washed the wound and stopped the bleeding. Within half an hour of their entry into the room, Podola was taken to Chelsea police station. Reg Davis, then a detective sergeant, who was one of the officers later to be highly commended by the commissioner for his part in the arrest, told me, "Some members of the Press were outside the house at the time of the arrest, saw his injuries and assumed that he had been assaulted by us, which was completely untrue. He was not badly injured but he used his injuries as an excuse for not being able to remember anything of the murder or his arrest." Half an hour after Podola's arrival at the station, Dr John Shanahan, the Divisional Surgeon, arrived to examine the prisoner as to his fitness to be detained. He carefully examined Podola, noted his injuries and cleaned and dressed the cut above his eye. The doctor felt that whilst Podola was fit to be detained he was not fit to be interviewed. The prisoner was uncommunicative, and the doctor found him to be "dazed, frightened and exhausted". Podola shivered constantly, which Dr Shanahan diagnosed as "withdrawal reaction to his arrest".

However, the personnel at Chelsea police station had a more prosaic explanation: "He was shitting himself because he knew he was going to hang for the murder of a police officer."

After half an hour Dr Shanahan left, and Podola, under continuous observation in the cells, slept, smoked and drank tea. The doctor was recalled at 11.30 that evening; he examined the prisoner, decided that he was not making the progress which he would have expected and recommended his admission to hospital. Podola was taken to St Stephen's Hospital shortly afterwards on a stretcher, where he was guarded by two police officers and was handcuffed by one wrist to the frame of the bed (this would later lead to accusations in the House of Commons that Podola had been 'chained' to his bed). He was examined by Dr Philip Harvey, the consultant physician, but although Podola appeared shocked and professed to remember nothing prior to his arrest on 16 July, tests revealed no fractures or internal bleeding. He was kept under observation until the morning of 20 July, when Dr Harvey permitted him access to both the police and a solicitor. That afternoon, he was returned to Chelsea police station, where in the presence of his solicitor he was charged with the murder of Ray Purdy, taken before the justices at West London Magistrates' Court and remanded in custody at Brixton Prison. Now he would be examined by a number of doctors in order to determine if he really had lost his memory. Meanwhile, the general public were in danger of losing their memory about the cold-blooded murder of a police officer, thanks to irresponsible members of the press and an even more reckless Member of Parliament.

★   ★   ★

When Podola was taken from the Claremont House Hotel there was a blanket covering his head, since identification might well prove to be an issue during his trial. Some disgruntled members of the Press suggested that the blanket had been used to cover Podola's injuries and that the police had severely beaten him up. One of the press photographs later taken of Podola, complete with black eye, being conveyed by Detective Sergeants Lambert and Darke to Brixton Prison, added fuel to the fire of suspicion that Podola had been beaten up by the police upon his arrest and had then been subjected to another savaging at Chelsea police station. Added to this were allegations that police dog 'Flame' had been slipped from its leash and had bitten Podola either on the cheek or the arm – or both. In fact, the dog had not been released. It had entered the room with its handler and had guarded the window in case Podola tried to escape. But the accusations caught the public's imagination about what might have happened during the period of arrest and before the appearance at court. The police had said Podola had killed a police officer. Podola now had a black eye. Ergo, the police had beaten him up. A group of businessmen clubbed together to provide Podola with a solicitor and claimed, incorrectly, that the police had prevented the solicitor from seeing his client. In fact, it was the consultant physician who had prevented Podola from seeing either the police or his solicitor. When a group of rowdy students were arrested for obstruction outside a coffee bar in the King's Road, Chelsea, Marlborough Street Magistrates' Court was informed on 23 July that they shouted, "Do we get the Podola treatment?"

But most contemptible of all were the bellowings of the Labour Member of Parliament for Northampton, Mr Reginald Thomas Paget QC (later Lord Paget of Northampton), who in the Commons on 20 July – the day upon which Podola was charged – demanded to know from the Home Secretary, Mr R. A. (Rab) Butler, what had happened to Podola during the six hours at Chelsea police station which necessitated his removal to hospital on a stretcher, and why his lawyer was denied admittance.

Butler replied that the hospital authorities had agreed Podola should be permitted to leave hospital, that he had been charged with murder and was being taken before a magistrate, and that being the case, it would not be proper to say any more.

"I am not concerned about the charge against Günther Podola," roared Paget. "I am concerned about the people who beat him unconscious! Have charges been preferred against them? If charges have not been preferred against them, the subject matter of this question is not *sub judice*."

"The honourable and learned gentleman has no right to say that this man was beaten unconscious, and he has no proof that it is so," riposted Butler hotly.

The Speaker of the House ruled that any further questions might have an effect upon the trial, but not before Paget made a further attack, saying, "The idea that either vengeance or beatings up occur in British police stations is utterly unacceptable. Because the person who was the victim of that beating up is also the subject of a charge, that ought not to prevent us from investigating the beating-up, which is eminently our business."

The then Prime Minister, Harold Macmillan, later stated, "I always enjoy Paget's interventions but never know whether they are epigrams or paradoxes." Macmillan didn't know the half of it.

⋆   ⋆   ⋆

The trial commenced at the Old Bailey on 10 September 1959 before Mr Justice Edmond Davies, who five years later would preside over the trial of the Great Train Robbers. Maxwell Turner led for the Crown and Frederick Lawton QC appeared for the defence. It was a most extraordinary case, the like of which had never been heard in an English courtroom before. Lawton told the jury: "I stand here today, my learned friend by my side, Podola's solicitor in front of me, and the three of us have no idea what his defence is at all." The Judge ruled it was up to the defence to prove that Podola's loss of memory was genuine and that if they succeeded, they would have to submit that he should not be tried for murder.

The nine-day trial got underway, with Lawton telling the jury, "In all fairness, I should state specifically that there is no evidence of any kind that any violence was done to Podola at Chelsea police station. Indeed, such evidence as exists points the other way." This tended to discount one very popular theory, that every member of Chelsea police station had been invited to line up and hit Podola once.

Five doctors called by the defence concluded that Podola's amnesia was genuine; two called by the prosecution believed he was malingering and faking his symptoms. When Podola gave evidence, he recalled that whilst he was in hospital he had heard Superintendent Hislop whisper to him, "I am your friend – say it went off accidentally." Asked by the prosecution if he believed this to be true, Dr Michael Ashby, who had been called by the defence, stated blandly that he did and that it was the police's job to trap criminals – which unsurprisingly drew fierce criticism from the judge. Dr Edward Larkin – also for the defence – thought that Hislop's alleged whispering was no more than a morbid hallucination. This was a view shared by Dr Denis Leigh, called by the prosecution, who had examined Podola on ten occasions and had reached the conclusions that Hislop's whisper was either a hallucination or a lie and that Podola's amnesia was definitely faked.

A man named Ronald Alan Starkey, who had met Podola three times and stated that he had stayed with him on one occasion, had sent Podola a postcard while he was on remand, asking him if he would like some cigarettes and food. Podola claimed to have no knowledge of the man, but the waters of the defence were muddied when it was revealed that Podola had responded by writing a letter containing the words:

> Dear Ron. Thank you for your card. I was very pleasantly surprised to hear from you. How are you keeping these days, old boy? I reckon you have heard all about the mess I'm in … I think it is very nice of you to write and now you want to come all the way to London to see me …

The defence were not helped by the fact that Starkey had opened his postcard to Podola with the words, 'My dear Mike', a reference to Podola's alias 'Mike Colato', which he had been using just prior to the murder, a time which he now claimed he could not remember.

Summing up to the jury, Mr Justice Edmund Davies told them:

> The case for the Crown is that no man in his senses, using his intelligence, could regard that reply sent by the accused as a reply written to a man who was to him unknown and a complete stranger. If ever there was a point fitted for a jury's determination, it is this. If I had the privilege of exercising the function you are called upon to discharge, I think I would begin my deliberations by coming to a conclusion on which side the truth lies in regard to that letter.

After retiring for three and a half hours, the jury concluded that Podola was not suffering from a genuine loss of memory and was fit to stand trial. The following day, 24 September, a fresh jury was sworn in, in front of the same judge and counsel, to try the case against Podola for murder.

The main witness for the prosecution was of course John Sandford, who testified that he had seen Podola shoot his colleague at point-blank range. The defence suggested that Podola had tried to hand the gun to Purdy and that the gun had gone off accidentally. This was refuted by Sandford as it was by Mr Nickolls, a ballistics expert who also confirmed that the bullet which had killed Purdy had been fired from the pistol found in the attic of the Claremont House Hotel.

Podola, giving evidence from the dock (which meant he could not be cross-examined by the prosecution), told the jury, "I understand the various accusations that have been made and now the time has come for me to defend myself against these accusations. I cannot put forward any defence ... I cannot remember the crime. I do not remember the circumstances leading up to the events or to this shooting. I do not know if I did it or whether it was an accident or an act of self-defence. For these reasons, I am unable to admit or deny the charge against me. Thank you, my lord."

It took the jury of ten men and two women just thirty-seven minutes on 26 September after a two-day trial to return a verdict of guilty to a charge of capital murder. Mr Justice Edmund Davies had the black cap placed on his head – for the last time for the murder of a police officer – and told Podola:

> You have been convicted on evidence of the most compelling character and certainty of the capital murder of a police officer by shooting him down in the prime of his manhood. For that foul and terrible deed but one sentence is prescribed and that, I now pronounce.

Podola was sentenced to death, but although he did not appeal against his conviction, the Home Secretary referred the case to the Court of Appeal (Criminal Division) under Section 19(a) Criminal Appeal Act, 1907, to determine whether the onus of proof of unfitness to plead rested on the prosecution or – as Mr Justice Edmund Davies had ruled – the defence. On 15 October the appeal judges dismissed the appeal, reserving their judgement for a later date, and Podola's request for the Attorney-General's fiat (allowing a proceeding for which the consent of the Crown was necessary – in this case, an appeal to take the case to the House of Lords) was rejected.

The Home Secretary then established a medical committee to examine Podola's mental condition, and the three doctors, Snell, Mather and Pearce, unanimously agreed that Podola's amnesia had been faked and that they had no medical recommendation to make. On 20 October the Court of Appeal announced their judgement, stating that the trial had been fair and just. So Podola was set to hang – and then a miracle occurred.

★ ★ ★

With every legal avenue of appeal exhausted, Podola's memory astonishingly returned. He now claimed that at the time of the murder he had broken into a flat in Sloane Avenue. In fact, the address of this flat was found in Podola's address book, and it was revealed that the flat had indeed been burgled on the day in question and that the culprit had not been apprehended. It all pointed to Podola being the perpetrator, and it is highly likely that he was, but since the burglary had occurred between 8.30 in the morning and 2.30 in the afternoon – over an hour before Podola had telephoned Mrs Schiffman – it was no alibi at all.

This was a setback but not an irrevocable one, because Podola now also remembered that he had a double – a man named Bob Levine and they were as alike as two peas in a pod. They had known each other in Canada and West Germany and they had agreed to meet on the day of the murder at 105 Onslow Square. In fact, he said, they had already met at that location previously, because they intended to stage a break-in there. And oddly enough, whilst they were there, Podola had actually sat on that window sill and <u>that</u> was how his finger and palm prints had been found there. And because he had failed to keep the later appointment, it must have been Bob Levine who turned up and murdered Ray Purdy, and Sandford had mistakenly identified him as being Bob Levine.

Well, it was providential that this whole ghastly mistake had been sorted out just in the nick of time. Except that it hadn't. A search at the Ottawa and Wiesbaden bureaux revealed that 'Bob Levine' only existed in the imagination of Günther Podola. On 2 November the Home Secretary decided that the law should take its course, and on 5 November 1959, amidst a fresh burst of public controversy, the hangman, Harry Allen, slipped the noose around Podola's neck and consigned him to oblivion. He was buried in Grave 59 at Wandsworth Prison.

It sounds almost incredible, but as well as the usual, predictable crowd of abolitionists who appeared outside the prison, a small group found out where the Purdy family were living and arrived outside their house. Mrs Purdy thought they were morbid and curious people who got a kick out of others' bad news, closed the curtains and requested the attendance of one of Purdy's close friends, a fellow police officer whom Gillian now recalls simply as 'Uncle Ernie'. He duly arrived and dispersed the crowd with the minimum of fuss and, no doubt, a complete lack of political correctness.

★   ★   ★

Purdy had been buried at Surbiton Cemetery, Surrey, on 21 July. Gillian and her younger brother did not attend, Mrs Purdy once more seeking to protect them from the tragedy which had enveloped the family. The funeral procession was a mile long and the last half-mile contained 1,000 police officers who wished to pay their respects. He was well liked. Mrs B. Osborne, the wife of a former police officer and the mother of six children, all of whom joined the Metropolitan Police, had a "vivid memory" of the funeral service, which was held at St Mathew's Church, Tolworth. Leonard 'Nipper' Read QPM, the man who smashed the Kray empire, was Purdy's replacement as a first-class sergeant at Chelsea and, he said, "found it a difficult task trying to live up to the reputation of a man who had become a police hero."

A police hero Purdy undoubtedly was, but far less consideration was given to his widow and children, living in police married quarters at Berrylands Road, Surbiton. With insensitivity bordering on utter crassness, a faceless clerk at Scotland Yard had almost immediately authorized a telegram to be sent to her, demanding that she vacate the married quarters within three months. "It was," as Purdy's daughter Gillian recalls with masterly understatement, "a bit brutal." Four days after Purdy's funeral the matter was raised in Parliament, and the Home Secretary scarcely dealt with it any better, declaring, "The widow of a police officer living in a police house has no security of tenure in law, and all police houses are needed for serving officers."

Purdy's widow received a police pension of £7 4s 6d per week; with other allowances for the children, it brought her income up to £10 10s 8d per week. At the date of her husband's death, times were very hard, since there was no life insurance, the police married quarters had to be vacated and the Criminal Injuries Compensation Board had not yet been set up. The Mayors of Kensington and Chelsea organized an appeal fund but the sum raised was not as great as it might have been, thanks to Paget's repugnant behaviour and the anti-police feeling generated by the Press, which had convinced many of the public that Podola had indeed been beaten up. However, there was sufficient money raised to purchase a small house in Surbiton which Gillian described as 'a life-saver'. There was much support from Purdy's colleagues, and the family received letters from victims of crime, with whom Purdy had dealt with compassionately; paradoxically, there were also letters of support from criminals whom Purdy had 'put away'. One special supporter was the world-famous conductor Sir Malcolm Sargent, whose immaculate appearance earned him the nickname of 'Flash Harry'; before his death in 1967, he would send Purdy's children postcards and gifts from all over the world.

Due to Mrs Purdy's emotional state, there were several house moves; every time a police officer was murdered, the press would telephone, and one by one the family emigrated to New Zealand.

A commemorative plaque to Purdy was unveiled inside Chelsea police station in February 1999.

★　★　★

And what of the bellicose Reginald Paget, the Member of Parliament who had made those damaging and unfounded allegations of police misconduct, safe from defamation proceedings as a result of Parliamentary privilege? The magazine *Police Review* (which acted on behalf of all federated ranks of the police) was furious and demanded a retraction. Incredibly, Paget in turn criticized *Police Review* for their alleged inability to judge the difference between a question and an assertion, stating that he had merely asked the Home Secretary a question. His letter ended with the words:

> I would like to say now that I am entirely satisfied that Podola was not assaulted at Chelsea police station and I have no criticism at all to direct against the police conduct. I have, however, no apology to make either for asking the question or pressing for an answer.

Police Review published Paget's reply but added that Paget's words, 'the people who beat Podola unconscious', contained an assertion, not a question. Paget declined to reply.

Regarding the other officers in the case, Bob Acott went on to rise through the ranks to become a CID commander. He investigated what became known as 'the A6 Murder' which, after James Hanratty was convicted and hanged, became even more controversial than the Podola case. Acott died before it was proved beyond a shadow of a doubt in the Court of Appeal that Hanratty was indeed guilty.

Bert Chambers was one of those officers highly commended by the commissioner for the arrest of Podola. He retired three years later and died aged seventy-four in 1990. Of the other commended officers, Peter Vibart rose to the rank of detective superintendent and was awarded the Queen's Police Medal for distinguished service. He had been commended on sixty-five occasions and died aged sixty-two in 1974. Reg Davis rose to the rank of Deputy Assistant Commissioner (Crime) and retired in 1977. He achieved a BA (Hons) degree in law and became a solicitor. John Vaughan, a detective constable at the time, was promoted to detective sergeant, posted to the Flying Squad and later achieved fame as

'Sid Green, the Chopper Man' when he went undercover to unmask Dr Christopher Swan for conspiracy to murder. He retired in 1973, having collected twenty-six commendations ("good ones," he told me) and he died aged eighty-five in November 2010.

Of the two aids to CID who had originally stopped Podola, Charlie Body (now deceased) married a German girl and later retired. Geoff Anderson married Winnie, a Danish girl, and in 1962, en route to a day out at Southend, their 1938 Ford 8 was suddenly passed by a gleaming Armstrong Siddeley Sapphire. It contained 'Little Jack', his wife, son and grandchildren. They all met up on Southend's sea front later and had a pleasant chat, accompanied by the traditional ice-creams. Unfortunately, Winnie's comprehension of the English language was rather limited at that time, and she was somewhat baffled by the conversation. It took another forty years until at their retirement home in Denmark she was fully acquainted with the part her husband had played in the investigation into a police murderer.

★   ★   ★

So was Podola beaten up by the police? The simple answer is 'no'. Make no mistake, when Vibart & Co smashed their way into Room 15 at the Claremont House Hotel, they sought to arrest a man strongly suspected of murdering a police officer and who was still in possession of a firearm. These were tough men, who had all seen the hard side of police work and all been commended previously for disarming gunmen. And when there was that ominous 'click' from behind the hotel room door, as one of the officers later readily admitted, "I thought it was the cocking of a gun and I expected the door to open and the man to start shooting." No, there can be little doubt that the furiously struggling Podola was strongly subdued. But once he was arrested and handcuffed, that was the end of the matter. And the thought that he was systematically beaten up at Chelsea police station is risible; Superintendent Hislop wanted evidence to convict and hang him, and the very idea that he would have permitted every officer in the station to attack his prisoner – the prisoner who had been examined by a doctor (and his findings recorded) almost as soon as he had entered the station – is laughable. Of course, anyone is at liberty to believe anything they wish, but I hope perhaps that after the foregoing words a clearer picture of what did – or rather, what didn't – occur during the Podola case will emerge.

Which leaves us with the last victim.

★   ★   ★

John Sandford had passed his examination for detective sergeant (first class) early in 1959. One month after Podola was hanged, Sandford was promoted to first-class sergeant and transferred to C1 Department at the Yard. Although in the next twelve months he was commended twice, both times for his work in fraud cases, he was a broken man.

Like many people in similar situations, he blamed himself for what had happened to Purdy, feeling that he could – or *should* – have done so much more to remedy the situation. Sometimes this might be true; but not in Sandford's case. There was absolutely nothing he could have done to save his colleague, but of course counselling or indeed any type of therapy was unknown in the police at that time. And as the years went by, so Sandford's guilt grew.

Peter Elston, who in retirement lives in Canada, remembered Sandford at the Yard, investigating fraud cases. "He was a very quiet, unassuming man," Elston recalls. "He seemed to be embarrassed that he was involved in the shooting. He may have laboured under the belief that he had let Purdy down by not searching the prisoner or leaving him with Podola alone, to get transport. But in those days, we did not have cell phones and never suspected that prisoners carried guns."

Bob Roach met 'Sandy' (as Sandford was known to everybody) after Sandford had been promoted to detective inspector in 1966 and now headed the Interpol office. "I always remember him as a rotund young man who, at times, showed his nervousness if the subject was brought up. He was usually serious as he had become quite famous at the time, although not the way he would have liked." And Fred Cutts, who then worked at Interpol, recalled that with regard to the thousands of enquiries which passed through the radio section and correspondence department every year, Sandford "knew every detail that was logged in either docket or message, in and out." Tony Roots remembered Sandford as "a very quiet, introverted individual. Every Friday his wife came to the office at about 5pm, was shown to his office with nary a word [spoken] until he would say it was time to go, sometimes at gone 6pm." Roots naturally knew of Sandford's background, but what brought matters home to him was that his uncle and aunt had travelled to England on a ship from New Zealand and had got into a conversation with a woman who turned out to be Purdy's widow. But when Roots mentioned this, Sandford looked blankly at him, remarked, "Oh, yes?" and carried on working on the Interpol dockets. Referring to the shooting, Roots was of the opinion that, "there was more than one victim".

"He was a gentleman but terribly reserved and withdrawn," said Dave Patrick, and former Detective Inspector Mick Masson remembered at the age of sixteen joining the Metropolitan Police's civilian support staff and being posted to Pensions Branch, situated (then) at Tintagel House. The officer in charge was Sandford, and Masson remembered him as somewhat of a disciplinarian and with "the sort of presence which prevented anyone from stepping out of line."

In 1974 Sandford was promoted to chief inspector and worked at C11, the criminal intelligence department, until his retirement in May 1977. He was fifty years of age and had served almost thirty-one years. Derek Godfrey recalls that, precise to the last on his final day in office, Sandford waited until a couple of minutes to midnight before booking off duty, walking down to the foyer of Scotland Yard and on the stroke of midnight handing in his warrant card to the Back-Hall Inspector. Pedantic? Obsessive? Or believing that if anyone should wish to criticize his actions in the shooting of his colleague, they would never have the justification to do so, again? Difficult to say.

That was the way in which the Metropolitan Police dealt with those situations then. It was expected that one should 'just snap out of it', but if this proved impossible and the criteria for an ill-health pension did not apply (or it was not wanted by the officer concerned), then matters were usually brushed under the carpet, and the unfortunate officer would be posted to a series of non-stressful jobs, where his subordinates, according to their temperaments, either regarded him with compassion or as 'barmy'.

John Sandford died on 24 November 2009. He was eighty-three and he had carried his burden of guilt for over half a century. Nowadays, there is little doubt that he would have been diagnosed with Post Traumatic Stress Disorder and received the appropriate treatment, but as Mick Masson opined, "I think then, he was simply left to cope with his own demons."

★   ★   ★

Mrs Irene Purdy, who had been confined to a care home, died from a heart attack in November 2011, aged ninety-three. Although the two Purdy sons still live in New Zealand, Mrs Purdy and her daughter had returned separately to the United Kingdom in the late 1970s. Mrs Purdy had been forced to sell her house in New Zealand, on which there was still a mortgage outstanding, and any money she had saved had dwindled away;

she still received her pitiful pension. "My mother used to say, 'The police always look after their own' but it wasn't true," her daughter told me. "It was my father's colleagues who looked after us – not the Force." It was only after the Police Dependants' Trust came into existence that Mrs Purdy received, as her daughter puts it, "cash injections, every year", when gathering household bills were dealt with by a very welcome cheque.

Fortunately, the rest of the Purdy family now have families of their own and lead happy and productive lives. But despite this, the loss and horror of those tragic events over fifty years ago never leaves them, and every 13 July is a time for a day of quiet reflection.

Irene Purdy was cremated, since she had left no instructions that she should be buried with her husband. Perhaps it was just as well. Gillian was told that her father's grave would be maintained for seventy-five years. It has not been. The headstone, together with several others, has been snapped off and the grave is in disarray. She has tried to contact the cemetery by telephone, without success. She intends to go there and do something about it. As a result of what has been written about her father in this book, she might have some help.

CHAPTER 5

"I'm Calling from WANstead 4199"

Following serious crime – and few crimes in the criminal calendar can be more serious to police than the murder of two of their colleagues – the question is raised: could anything have been done to prevent it happening? In respect of the cold-blooded murders of Inspector Pawsey and Sergeant Hutchins in 1961 an unequivocal answer cannot be provided; perhaps just an ambiguous 'maybe'.

Just a few years prior to the dreadful murders, Detective Constable Tommy Thorburn was serving at Chadwell Heath police station, then part of the Metropolitan Police's 'K' Division, a huge area stretching from Plaistow in the west to Dagenham in the east, with the River Thames as its southern boundary. One morning, he received a telephone call from a concerned neighbour in Donald Drive; the occupier of a house who was on business in Germany had asked the neighbour to keep an eye on his premises during his absence, and now it appeared there had been a break-in. Thorburn visited the premises and discovered there was indeed a broken window at the rear of the house but that this might have been caused by a 'stone thrown up by a passing lorry' – the usual excuse put forward by investigating officers when there was no obvious criminal intent. Nevertheless, Thorburn checked for fingerprints and other clues, but without success. However, he decided to search the premises, in company with the neighbour, to see if there was any other evidence of a burglary having taken place. Upon entering a small bedroom, Thorburn was shocked to discover at least fifty handguns hanging on the walls, including Mausers and Lugers, all of which appeared to be in good working order. He gathered all of them up, took them to the police station and carried out checks on the occupant of the house. He discovered that the owner was John Hall, who was in his late twenties. A flamboyant character, he was married, a car salesman and held a pilot's licence. He was also a member of a rifle club and owned 'several guns'. Thorburn also discovered that he had a minor criminal record and as a youngster had been sent to an Approved School. Hall was six feet one, a well built man, and he had an explosive temper; he had attacked a motorist who failed to show him due consideration, had been discharged from the Royal Air Force because of mental instability and had also received treatment at a psychiatric hospital – although not, as events would show, treatment of sufficient intensity or for long enough.

Thorburn set out a comprehensive report to S1 (Firearms) Department at Scotland Yard, describing the circumstances of his discovery and suggesting that the weapons should be permanently confiscated and Hall's firearms licence (if indeed he possessed one) revoked. Within days Hall returned home, and upon being apprised of the situation with regard to his firearms stormed into Chadwell Heath police station and berated Thorburn for having the impudence to enter his home and seize his collection. A few days later, Thorburn received a reply from S1 Department – it was run by a civilian staff – instructing him to return the firearms to Hall. Thorburn did so, but would later state, "I was extremely unhappy with the situation."

★   ★   ★

Several years passed. Hall and his wife Joyce divorced, and on 1 April 1961, after a whirlwind nine-week courtship, he married Sylvia Roberts. He was now working as one of three salesmen for a company supplying motor spares in the Romford Road, E7. Unfortunately, by all accounts the owner of the company was one of the most obnoxious beings whom God had seen fit to blow breath into; he verbally abused his long-suffering wife in front of the shop's customers and was to all intents and purposes cordially loathed by all who met him. In consequence, it was not long before Hall ran out of patience with his employer, and one Friday afternoon he returned to the shop, placed his takings on the counter, inelegantly told the proprietor precisely what he could do with his job and walked out. His employer immediately checked Hall's takings against the stock left in his van and discovered a discrepancy of £5; it was sufficient for him to rush into Forest Gate police station at three o'clock and demand in strident tones that Hall be found and the missing £5 be returned to him. The CID officer to whom he addressed his bellicose demands was Detective Constable Terry Corbett, who despised the shop owner as much as anybody else but nevertheless told him that, 'he would look into it.' Not, however, that day, because (a) he was on the early – nine to five – shift, (b) he had arranged to take his wife out for the evening, but most importantly of all, (c) because he was on an ARD.

The ARD – or Additional Rest Day – no longer exists in the

Metropolitan Police, but then, because police officers were only allotted three days off per fortnight, they were granted an ARD for which they were paid at time-and-a-half. CID officers were expected to work all the hours possible, for which (until 1975) they were paid no overtime at all. However, the thought of any senior officer authorizing overtime on an ARD was anathema, especially Jack Williams, the divisional detective superintendent. So Corbett telephoned West Ham police station and spoke to Detective Sergeant Russ Lewis, who checked Hall's particulars and noted that he had only a few minor convictions. Therefore at five o'clock Corbett booked off duty.

However, within two months of Hall's new marriage he and his wife Sylvia had begun living apart, and on the evening that Corbett had booked off at the appropriate time, there was a marital dispute at Hall's in-laws' house in Tavistock Road, E15, which escalated into serious assaults. Hall had requested a loan of £5 with which to repay his former employer, and when this had been refused, he had picked up a chair and hit his wife with it; the wound in her head required twenty-two stitches. Next attacking Mrs Roberts, his mother-in-law, Hall broke her wrist; she required the insertion of ten stitches in her head and twelve in her arm. In addition, he injured his young sister-in-law Eileen, albeit less seriously. The assaults were reported to West Ham police station, a short distance away at 64-66 West Ham Lane, E15, and the area car, 'Kilo One', attended. Police Constable Alfie Wells told me that he took details of the assaults and noted the injuries, and Hall's wife told him that her husband would be staying with relatives 'across the water'. Of course, Wells' brief did not extend to leaving his division, let alone 3 Area, to travel to 4 Area across the River Thames, and he dutifully recorded the matter at West Ham police station. But Sylvia Hall's assumption was only partly correct; although when her errant husband left the house in Tavistock Road, he had initially gone to his parents' home in Empress Avenue, Woodford Green, he had later crossed the river and now, unknown to the police, he was ensconced in a flat in Erith, Kent. And what was more, the police were also unaware that he was in possession of a small arsenal of weapons.

At ten o'clock that evening, Detective Constable (later Detective Chief Superintendent) Peter Thompson booked on duty to commence night-duty CID with two aids to CID, to cover the entire division and to deal with matters of crime as they were reported until six o'clock the following morning. At West Ham police station he saw a friend, Inspector Philip Pawsey, who was just finishing his late-turn shift. Pawsey mentioned the assaults committed by Hall – his version of the occurrence was slightly muddled because he erroneously believed the matter had arisen as a result of money going missing in Hall's in-laws' household – and asked Thompson, if he should see Hall during his tour of duty, to bring him in so that he might be interviewed by the day-duty CID. Pawsey also mentioned that the following day, instead of resuming late-turn, he had arranged to swap duties with another inspector so that he (Pawsey) would be working the early-turn shift. He had arranged to do something which involved his wife, possibly shopping. "A very sad move, as it turned out," Thompson told me, half a century later.

So Thompson commenced the night-duty CID patrol. On a quiet night, the CID officer would keep his eyes peeled for arrests of his own, but not on this Friday night, which was an exceptionally busy one. Therefore, Thompson had no opportunity to look for any suspects, including Hall – which, given the turn that events would take, was probably quite fortunate for him.

The following day, Saturday, 3 June 1961, Terry Corbett booked on duty at nine o'clock at Forest Gate and shortly afterwards received a telephone call from Russ Lewis, who informed him of what had occurred in Tavistock Road the previous evening. He told Corbett that he was dealing with the allegation of assault, that he intended to bring Hall in to the police station and, at the same time, he would deal with the matter of the missing fiver. "Thanks," replied Corbett and turned his attention to other work.

However, it was Hall himself who made the first move in the matter of the assault allegation. Here the waters become a little muddied, because it is the popular belief of those officers to whom I spoke that it was Detective Sergeant Russ Lewis who dealt with the matter from beginning to end; however, Detective Inspector George Jones told the inquest that it was he who did so. It probably makes little difference; in any event, according to Jones he received a telephone call from John Hall at midday. "I understand you want to see me about the affair last night," said Hall. "Can I come and see you? Can I speak to the officer who is dealing with it?"

Hall agreed to come to the station and he arrived in a red Austin Healey Sprite an hour later, at 1.05. Jones met Hall at the door and told him, "It's in your favour that you've come here of your own accord. But, as you know, your mother-in-law, wife and her younger sister were badly hurt at Tavistock Road, last night."

"I know," replied Hall, "and I'm sorry. I went down on my knees to them and asked forgiveness. But they started pushing me about. I lost my temper and hit them with a chair. Are they badly hurt?"

In the CID office Jones told Hall he would be detained while further enquiries were carried out and asked him to empty his pockets. From his left-hand trouser pocket Hall produced six bullets and placed them on the desk. Jones stared at the bullets, as did Detective Sergeant Russ Lewis and Detective Constable Walton, but before anybody could react, Hall suddenly pulled out a Walther 9mm automatic pistol, pointed it at the officers, said, "You're not keeping me here!" and backed away towards the door. "Don't be silly," retorted Jones, but Hall dashed out of the office and down the stairs.

Police Constables Charles Edward Cox and Leslie Charles England were chatting at the foot of the stairs when they heard a voice – it was DI Jones – shout, "Stop that man!" and Hall, brushing aside Police Constable Eddie Turner who was ascending the stairs, rushed past the two officers into the charge room, thence to the station entrance, where he stopped and pointed the pistol at them before dashing into West Ham Lane. Crossing the busy road, Hall ran into the recreation ground opposite the police station. In hot pursuit was PC Cox. Having served four years with the wartime Royal Armoured Corps, the former Trooper had joined the police in 1947 and since 1950 had been stationed at West Ham. Married, with two daughters aged twelve and ten, thirty-eight-year-old Cox was now rapidly closing the gap between him and the gunman.

Hall stopped and pointed the pistol at his pursuer, but Cox, undaunted, ran on. When Hall reached the north-west boundary of the recreation ground, he climbed the fence and disappeared into one of the back gardens of the houses in Whalebone Lane. Cox ran along parallel to the fence, having no idea which direction Hall had taken after scaling the fence but hoping to head him off. But he took the wrong route, and by the time he had clambered over the fence, there was no sign of Hall.

Meanwhile, PC England got on to his 'Noddy' bike – a lightweight Velocette motorcycle with a quiet water-cooled engine which made them particularly useful on night-duty patrols – and tore off into the recreation ground. England had served with the Irish Guards in 1944 and after his demobilization in 1948 he had been employed as a bank messenger. He had married and had two children (who by now were aged ten and eight) and in 1953 he joined the police; his eight years' service had been spent at West Ham. Now, as he drew up, there were a number of police officers in the recreation ground, and although matters were

somewhat confused, England discovered that Hall had last been
seen in Whalebone Lane, so turned his bike around and rode into
that thoroughfare, where he met up with PC Cox.

Hall, however, had crossed the lane and dashed through the
back door of 54 Farringdon Road, along the passage, out of
the front door, across the road and straight into No. 35, where the
son of the household, Leonard Hilliard, was busily painting
the exterior of his parents' house. As he rushed into the kitchen
where Mr Hilliard's mother was reading to his nine-year-old
daughter, Hall shouted, "I'm wanted by the police!" but he was
grabbed by Hilliard's seventy-year-old father, who turned him
round and in true East End style shouted, "Git 'art of 'ere!" –
which is precisely what Hall did.

Now, Hall turned left into Tennyson Road, which led to the
busy thoroughfare of Romford Road, close to Stratford
Broadway. After his meeting with Cox, England had ridden into
Farringdon Road, but Hall was seen by Cox and by Police
Sergeant Frederick George Hutchins who was in plain clothes
and had joined in the chase. Hutchins had been called to the
police station to be admonished by a senior officer for a minor
breach of discipline – hence being in 'civvies' – and he was the
oldest of the officers in the chase; born in 1912, he had joined the
Metropolitan Police in 1933. In 1941 he had been commended
by the commissioner and awarded a bronze medal from the
Society for the Protection of Life from Fire after rescuing a man
from a burning house and six years later he received another
commendation for keenness and determination in a case of
receiving. Promoted sergeant in 1954, he had been posted to West
Ham the following year. He was married with two children, aged
twenty-five and fourteen.

Hutchins rushed forwards and leapt onto Hall's back, grabbing
him in a bear-hug and trying to seize the pistol. But the
powerfully built Hall flung him from his back and ran off.
Hutchins picked himself up and ran at Hall again, but when he
was a foot away Hall turned and fired at point-blank range,
hitting him in the stomach. Despite this, Cox did not hesitate; he
dashed towards Hall, who fired again, hitting him on the left-
hand side of his upper abdomen. As he fell to the pavement,
Hutchins, who had been staggering from the bullet's impact,
collapsed across Cox's legs.

This was witnessed by Les England, who had turned into
Tennyson Road, and it had also been seen by a number of people
who had emerged from their houses. England rode up to the two
wounded men, and as he did so Hutchins lifted his head and

recognised him. "Get him, Les," he groaned. "Get him – he's got us!"

"Call for an ambulance!" shouted England to the astonished bystanders and roared off along the pavement in pursuit of Hall. Mrs Doris Bethell, the wife of the proprietor of the greengrocer's shop in Tennyson Avenue, did just that; she and her husband also got blankets and pillows for the wounded officers. Now, England rode straight at the gunman. When he was a yard away, Hall fired and England braked, swerved and ducked. This was witnessed by Mrs Winifred Norcott of 71 Tennyson Road, who had just called her son Roy, aged thirteen, to come in for his lunch. Roy was sitting on a wall with his friend Keith Pearman when he saw Hall racing towards them, gun in hand. "He turned around and shot a man in plain clothes coming after him," Roy said. "This man fell to the ground. He fired at a policeman who was also chasing him and hit him, too. When he saw us he turned back, but a policeman on a motorbike was coming after him, so he came towards us again. I was scared." The two boys and Mrs Norcott ran into the house and out into the back garden. Roy then heard another shot. It was the sound of the second fatality.

★   ★   ★

Hall was panting up to the junction with the Romford Road when a police car driven by Inspector Philip Pawsey turned into the junction. Aged forty, Pawsey had served during the war years with the Essex Regiment and had married a year after joining the police in 1946. Commencing his career in London's West End, Pawsey's later postings were all in the East End, 'G', 'H' and now 'K' Division, where promotion to inspector had brought him in 1956. He was well liked and industrious, and ten years previously he had been commended by the commissioner for good work in connection with proceedings taken under the Betting Acts. In fact, on this particular day, due to a shortage of senior officers, Pawsey was aid to Ilford police station; this suited him, because he lived in Oaks Lane, Ilford. The Duty Officer's car from Ilford which he was driving – an unmarked Hillman, registration number VGU 15 – was the only one on the entire division which possessed an RT set. Had he been driving any other Duty Officer's car, he would have been completely unaware of the drama which was unfolding in and around Romford Road; but quite evidently he had heard the RT call, which sent him racing to Tennyson Road.

Seeing Hall, Pawsey drove to the same side of the road as him, stopped the car, opened the door and started to get out. But Hall pointed the pistol at him, so Pawsey shut the door but then opened it again as Hall made to get past the police car, leaving the watching England in no doubt that he was about to tackle Hall. Again at point-blank range, Hall shot the inspector in the chest and he collapsed on to the steering wheel, causing the horn to sound. As England drove up, Pawsey gasped, "Get after him!" and England's last sight of Pawsey alive was as he tried to grab the microphone of the car's radio to alert Scotland Yard to the gunman's route. As Pawsey's life ebbed away, two passers-by, a woman then a man, used the police radio to call for an ambulance as well as reinforcements. It was too late. Detective Inspector George Jones arrived and held Pawsey's hand, but he died there in the street.

Police Constable Harry Tester was the plain-clothes observer on the area car 'Kilo One', with Olympic wrestler Police Constable Dennis McNamara as driver and Police Constable Freddy Craddock as RT Operator. They were patrolling High Street North, East Ham, when they received the first of two calls from the Yard's Information Room: "Man escaped from 'Kilo Whisky' [West Ham Police Station]", followed shortly afterwards by a second, "Police officers shot in Tennyson Road." Blue light flashing, siren wailing, the area car turned sharply into Plashet Grove, flashed across the junction with Katherine Road and, barely pausing at the busy junction with Green Street, drove into Plashet Road, straight through the junction with Upton Lane, into Portway. As they turned into Tennyson Road, they were confronted with the full horror of the situation; Cox and Hutchins lay on the pavement, both grievously wounded – the ambulance had not yet arrived – with householders emerging from their homes and Pawsey already dead. "He was lying on the front passenger seat," Tester told me, "as though he was trying to call for help on the radio."

Hutchins and Cox were taken to Queen Mary's Hospital, West Ham Lane. Cox was seriously wounded but expected to survive. Hutchins was in a parlous state, and the staff at the hospital required a resuscitator which was held at East Ham Memorial Hospital, Plashet Grove. The station officer dispatched 'Kilo One' to fetch it, and although McNamara paid scant lip-service to the niceties of the Road Traffic Act as his car thundered east towards East Ham, he arrived minutes too late to save the brave Sergeant Hutchins.

By now, Hall had crossed the Romford Road diagonally and had run into Deanery Road. As England followed, with great difficulty due to the heavy traffic in the Romford Road, Hall hid behind a parked-up furniture van; every time England approached him Hall pointed his pistol, and England was in no doubt that he intended to shoot. As Hall crossed over a bomb-site, so he re-loaded the pistol. "Is that a real gun, mister?" asked thirteen-year-old John Wright, and the re-loading of the pistol was also witnessed by Janet Bilverstone, also thirteen. Additionally, she saw Hall enter a house through the rear door on the north side of Romford Road. This was also seen by England, so he drove round to the Romford Road where another officer told him he had just seen a man getting into a yellow lorry. Another officer said Hall had been picked up in a red saloon car. Both vehicles were seen heading towards the area of Ilford, but although road-blocks were set up and the lorry was stopped, neither the driver nor his passenger was Hall, who had disappeared.

★   ★   ★

In the 132-year-old history of the Metropolitan Police, it was the worst murder count of officers: two men dead, another seriously wounded and the perpetrator still at large.

It was a hot day, and Tommy Thorburn, by now serving at Dagenham police station, was sitting in his back garden sipping a cold drink with an aid to CID, the late Wally Boreham (later Chief Constable of the MOD Police). They were on a split-duty shift when Thorburn received a telephone call telling him that there had been a shooting at West Ham and to get there as soon as possible.

Terry Corbett returned to Forest Gate police station from having consumed his lunch in the nearby Princess Alice public house to find the area car in the yard, engine running, awaiting his return. The car set off to West Ham, Corbett was quickly made aware of the tragic events, and en route Corbett, who was aware that Hall had been in possession of a red Austin Healy Sprite, sent out a radio call for all units in the vicinity to be on the look-out for such a distinctive vehicle. As the Yard's Information Room received Corbett's call, so it was sent out 'All Stations' by means of a teleprinter message. Two police constables at Ilford police station saw the message, then left the station to go out on patrol. As they reached Ilford Broadway, there, stationary in the traffic, was a car exactly fitting the description of the suspect vehicle, with a man at the wheel. When questioned, the driver was extremely evasive in his replies, so much so that he and the car parted company, and at Ilford police station he was rigorously questioned. However, it was quickly established that Hall's red Austin Healy Sprite was where it had been left, in West Ham Lane, following his flight from the police station, and therefore a further teleprinter message was sent, informing the surrounding stations of this and cancelling the previous communication. The suspect at Ilford was so relieved that he was not going to hang that he confessed that the sports car he was driving was stolen, on false plates and he had been about to deliver it to a client. After charging him, the officers tendered apologies which were accepted by the driver; he also declined the offer of medical aid.

Maurice Marshall, then a detective constable at Dagenham (and later, detective chief superintendent) heard that "two of our own had been shot" and immediately made his way to West Ham police station, as did practically every other CID officer on 'K' Division – and the surrounding divisions, as well. As he told me, fifty years after the event, "I was not really privy to the course of the investigation other than knowing the name and description of the suspect and that every uniform officer on foot, bicycle and car was out looking for him."

The mood of the officers was one of cold fury that two of their fellow officers had been murdered, and this was demonstrated in an extraordinary scene which would certainly never be replicated in these days of health and safety.

As the officers sat in the canteen, so a uniform superintendent entered the room with a bulging cell blanket like a sack slung over his shoulder which with a heave – rather like Father Christmas who had arrived six months early – he laid out on the floor. The blanket contained a large number of Webley & Scott .38 revolvers, gathered from all over the division, together with a mass of ammunition; the senior officer invited the assembled officers to 'help themselves', and there was a mad scramble as the men did just that. It must be remembered that this was before the days of a dedicated firearms unit, and although some of the assembled police officers had received small-arms training in the armed services, many had not, and consequently the standards of expertise and experience in the handling, loading and firing of firearms varied considerably. This was demonstrated when one officer from Ilford loaded his revolver, put it on full cock and simply did not know what to do thereafter. As the majority of the investigating team hit the floor, an enterprising detective sergeant from Dagenham stuffed a pencil between the hammer and chamber and relieved his counterpart of the gun.

When Tommy Thorburn arrived at West Ham, the weapons had all been issued; he would later say that everyone seemed to be "running all over the place, handling hand guns." It was a fraught situation; Thorburn recalled one police officer in the canteen holding a police issue revolver and asking where the safety catch was.

Having discovered the name of the suspect, Thorburn saw the detective superintendent of the division, Jack Williams, and told him of his previous report regarding Hall's firearms and his encounter with him; there was no doubt in his mind that one of those weapons which he had seized and had, on instructions from Scotland Yard, returned to Hall, had been used in the murder of his colleagues.

The search for Hall had now moved into top gear. Road blocks were set up, and his name and description were circulated to all areas of the Metropolitan Police plus the adjoining constabularies. His known haunts were kept under observation, including the Herts & Essex Aero Club, Stapleford, Essex, where he had once been a member. Hall's rented rooms at Balfour Road, Ilford, were searched, as was his in-laws' house in Tavistock Road and the premises belonging to his parents in Empress Avenue, Wanstead, E12, a turning just off Aldersbrook Road and opposite to Wanstead Flats. The message to his relatives, friends and associates from the police was unequivocal: 'If you see him, call us!' But nobody did.

⋆   ⋆   ⋆

Apart from being a psychotic, self-pitying, cold-blooded murderer with a lunatic temper, John Hall possessed one other character defect: he suffered from claustrophobia. When he walked into a strange house he would open all the doors and windows; when he drove a car it would invariably be a convertible with the hood down or, if it was a saloon, all the windows open. Therefore, it can have done Hall's psychological state no good at all when he squeezed his bulky, six-foot-one-inch frame into the confines of a telephone kiosk measuring just twenty-four by thirty inches, situated at the junction of Lake House Road and Aldersbrook Road, Wanstead. The door hissed shut behind him, and as the shadows lengthened across the Wanstead Flats at 8.30 on that summer's evening, Hall picked up the telephone and dialled the number of the *Sunday Express*.

Telling crime reporter Nelson Sullivan that he was speaking from a call-box, WANstead 4199, Hall informed the incredulous journalist that he was the police killer. Whilst a colleague listened on an extension, making copious notes of the conversation, another reporter contacted the police, giving them the number of the kiosk so that its location could be pinpointed. It is a tribute to Sullivan that he was able to keep the conversation going for fourteen minutes; Hall had stated he still had the pistol, plus twenty rounds of ammunition. The murderous aggression he exhibited seven hours previously had now resurfaced, coupled with his claustrophobia and sobbing hysteria. "If any policeman comes near, I'll shoot him!" he told Sullivan.

Meanwhile, Information Room at the Yard had sent out a message to all cars 'J' and 'K' Divisions, giving Hall's location. The first to arrive were the unarmed crew of 'Kilo Three', the wireless car from East Ham police station. "There are police all around," Hall told Sullivan. "But I'll shoot the first person who comes forward – I expect they'll try to rush the door."

Colin Harding, a resident of Lake House Road, saw one police officer standing at the back of the kiosk and two more approaching the door. "I heard a shot," he said, "and a man fell out of the kiosk just before the police got right up to the door."

"I saw the man suddenly collapse," said Mr E. F. Lloyd, "The door opened with his weight and he slid half-out to the ground. As the man fell out of the box, he groaned. One police officer in a flat cap seized the gun." The police officer in question was Police Constable Ron Askew, the RT operator from 'Kilo Three', who saw a bullet wound in Hall's side where he had shot himself. He picked up the telephone, told Sullivan that the suspect had been arrested and thanked him for his help. Found in the kiosk was a copy of the *Evening Standard*, upon which Hall had written in large capital letters, 'I AM SO SORRY'.

Hall was conveyed to Whipps Cross Hospital, where the following day he was taken off the emergency list and moved to a private room, guarded on a twenty-four-hour basis by two detectives. One of the CID officers was Terry Corbett, and from time to time Hall would mumble, "I'm sorry, I'm sorry, tell them I'm sorry." These sentiments were duly recorded in Corbett's pocket book, which he still possesses.

Meanwhile, south of the Thames at Erith police station, information had been received that Hall had spent the previous night in a flat at Pier Road, Erith. This had certainly been the case; the CID searched the flat and discovered pistols and ammunition. Believing that Hall could return to the flat in order to re-arm, armed officers were posted in and around the flat and there they remained until word came through that Hall had shot himself and was now in custody. It was then discovered that one of the murdered officers was Phil Pawsey; this caused great distress to one of the armed officers at Erith, Police Sergeant 82 'R' 'Dixie' Dean, who had struck up a friendship with Pawsey after they had attended the same pre-promotion course to sergeant in 1952.

Philip Pawsey's widow Muriel was inconsolable. They had no children and just the previous year they had moved into a police house in Oaks Lane, Ilford. Now she would have to move out. She was awarded a widow's police pension of £10 1s 1d per week. Mrs Betty Caroline Hutchins – her husband had been due to retire in three years' time – received a weekly pension of £8 7s 2d plus a special child's allowance of £1 2s 4d for her teenage daughter Sharon. Letters of condolence were sent to both widows by Mrs Irene Purdy, the widow of Detective Sergeant Raymond Purdy, also murdered by a gunman two years previously.

The dead officers were highly respected – Thorburn described Hutchins as being "a diamond, and fearless," and Pawsey as "an excellent officer, fair and much loved by the men." "'Hutch' was a great guy," recalled Police Constable John Merry, "and he was well-liked by the troops ... he was an efficient officer, without being officious ... it was a pleasure to work with him." Merry also remembered Pawsey; it was he who encouraged Merry to join the police after he left the army in 1950, and he described Pawsey as "a popular man with both his colleagues and the supervising officers." Police Constable Dennis Walland remembered Pawsey as being "a most pleasant gentleman" and had one other chilling memory of the incident; when the Duty Officer's car was returned to Ilford, he noticed the bullet hole in the driver's seat, where it had passed right through Pawsey.

On the Monday morning following the shooting, John Hall (no relation to the murderer but also a salesman and working in the same area) arrived for work to be confronted by his manager, who detested him and who quite obviously had heard the news of the events over that weekend at Wanstead Flats. "Christ!" exclaimed his supervisor, bitterly. "I thought you'd been fucking shot!" Describing those events to me fifty years later, almost to the day, Mr Hall recalled, "It wasn't too long before that firm and I parted company!"

A subscription from residents of the area flooded in to West Ham police station, eventually amounting to more than £5,000. The joint funeral was held the following Friday, 9 June at the City of London Cemetery, Aldersbrook Road. In excess of 200 wreaths and floral tributes were sent, and over 2,500 police officers from all over the country lined the three-mile route taken by the nine-car cortège. A detour was made so that Charlie Cox,

Police Constable Nathanael Edgar

The arrest of Donald George Thomas
– PC Edgar's murderer

Police Constable Sidney George Miles

Fred Fairfax GC and his wife, Muriel

Derek Bentley – hanged for the murder of PC Miles

Christopher Craig – guilty of PC Miles' murder

Ronald Henry Marwood – hanged for the murder of PC Summers

Police Constable Raymond Henry Summers

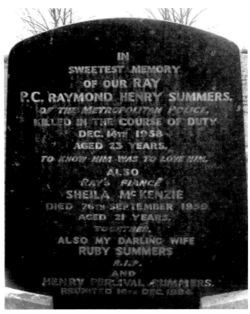

Raymond Summers' gravestone

Detective Sergeant Raymond
William Purdy

Purdy's gravestone

The arrest of Günther Fritz Erwin Podola

John Hall – the murderer of Inspector
Pawsey & Sergeant Hutchins

Police Sergeant Frederick
George Hutchins

Inspector Philip Pawsey

The scene at Wanstead flats after Hall had shot himself: the officers in plain clothes, left to right: Commander John Bliss, Detective Constable Maurice Marshall, Detective Sergeant Robert Bowley, Detective Inspector Jack Weisner

Police officers at the scene where Hall shot himself

Detective Sergeant Christopher Tippett Head

Temporary Detective Constable David Stanley Bertram Wombwell

Police Constable Geoffrey Roger Fox

Murderers of the crew of 'Foxtrot One-one'

Harry Maurice Roberts

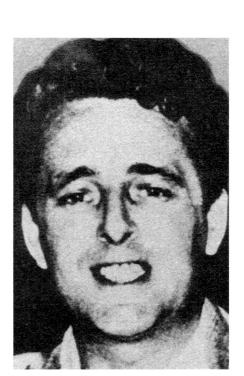

John Duddy

John Edward Witney

The funeral cortege for the crew of 'Foxtrot One-one'

Staff at Shepherd's Bush police station taking details of donations for the families of the murdered crew of 'Foxtrot One-one'

Police Constable Stephen Andrew Tibble

Artist's impression of the murderer of PC Tibble – William Joseph Quinn

The funeral cortege for PC Tibble

Inspector Stephen John Dodd

Woman Police Constable Jane Philippa Arbuthnot

The scene following the explosion outside Harrods – the windscreen of the Rolls Royce has been sucked out by the blast of the bomb

The memorial to the three police officers, murdered outside Harrods

The scene of devastation outside Harrods in Hans Crescent

Bomb damaged Harrods

Woman Police Constable Yvonne Joyce
Fletcher

The memorial to WPC Fletcher in St
James Square

Colleagues attending the injured WPC Fletcher

Police Constable Patrick Dunne

Kwame Danso

Gary Lloyd Nelson – who with two others, murdered PC Dunne and Danso

The memorial to PC Dunne in Cato Road, Clapham

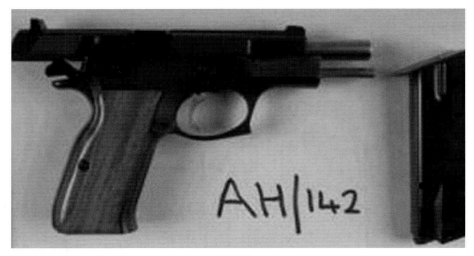

The Tanfoglio pistol, used to murder PC Dunne

The funeral cortege for PC Dunne, passing Clapham Fire Station

still seriously ill and in a wheelchair, could see the procession from a window in Queen Mary's Hospital. The Reverend Lawrence Pickles told the congregation:

> People don't join the police force with any sense of heroics, but just go in to do their duty. If it involves them in danger, as it often does, then they still carry out their duty to the best of their ability.

In a strange coincidence, the bed next to Cox's was occupied by a railway worker who had been injured in an accident. He was visited by Ted Jolly, then a young apprentice at the Stratford works, who later joined the police and as an aid to CID at Forest Gate was a crew member of the 'K' Division 'Q' car, 'Kilo One One', which was driven by Police Constable Peter Chapman, Charlie Cox's brother-in-law.

The day after the funeral, Hall's condition suddenly deteriorated, and he died. Although he might be regarded as a pitiful figure by most, these were not the sentiments expressed by one Reggie Kray. In 1957, Reggie had been acquitted at the Old Bailey following an attack on Terry Martin, a young docker, who had been repeatedly stabbed with a bayonet. Martin and his brothers had given evidence, with the result that Ronnie Kray, who had been stopped in possession of a revolver ("Careful with it," he told the police. "Can't you see it's loaded?") was sentenced to three years' imprisonment, and two associates were similarly imprisoned. Later, Reggie was approached in the Double-R Club by John Hall, who apparently told him, "If you like, Reg, I'll shoot them slags the Martins for nicking your brother and the other two." Reggie was genuinely touched by this beneficent offer but graciously declined. However, Reggie Kray's sources of information were somewhat awry when he related that Hall later shot dead a desk sergeant with a revolver and, having gone to a telephone kiosk where he paused to make a call, 'resounding shots were heard' and Hall lay dead with a bullet in his brain. It was darkly rumoured, said Reggie ominously, that the police were responsible for Hall's death.

The Kray brothers' reputation for accuracy was best summed up by their trial judge, Mr Justice Melford Stevenson, who sentenced them both to life imprisonment for murder. Later, he would say that during their trial they only spoke the truth twice: when one of them called the prosecuting barrister 'a fat slob' and when the other remarked that the judge was biased.

At the inquest at West Ham Coroner's Court just under two weeks after the officers' funeral, the jury found that Hall had murdered the two officers before killing himself. The Coroner, Mr J. Milner Helm, told the court:

> The country has come to expect a high standard from the police and in this case the police knew they were dealing with an armed man. They were all taking their lives in their hands in the course of duty and each of them did that duty without hesitation. I think the whole handling of the case on the evidence we have had shows great courage and devotion to duty on the part of the police. They all knew they were likely to be shot and we owe them a debt of gratitude.

Charlie Cox was in hospital for four weeks, and his wound troubled him for years afterwards. Six weeks later, he and England were highly commended by the commissioner, and six weeks after that, both officers were awarded £20 from the Bow Street Reward Fund. That November, it was announced in the *London Gazette* that Cox would be awarded the George Medal and England the British Empire Medal for Gallantry. The investiture at the Palace took place on the same day that the widows of Pawsey and Hutchins accepted the Queen's Police Medal for Gallantry, which had been posthumously awarded to their husbands.

The old West Ham police station was soon considered to be unsuitable for further use, and in 1969 it closed. A new one was opened the same year further along the road at 18 West Ham Lane, and on the tenth anniversary of the murders a local police constable met an elderly lady in the front office. She placed a £10 note in the Widows and Orphans Box on the front counter, saying, "Did you know, it's ten years since the shootings?" Apparently, the woman had been making similar generous donations every year since the murders.

Charlie Cox retired in 1977, aged fifty-four, on an ill-health pension; the gunshot wound, which had affected the nerves in his leg, made it impossible for him to continue his police duties any longer. In 1981 a plaque was unveiled in the station foyer to commemorate the bravery of the four officers by the Commissioner, Sir David McNee QPM.

Les England served in Anguilla in 1968 for a year before later moving across the division to Hornchurch, where I first met him in 1970 when I was an aspiring CID officer. I admired him very much – to me, he represented everything a police officer should be: calm, professional, brave, unflustered and hard-working. He was a Home Beat officer, but this did not mean that Les had put himself out to graze. He made a number of impressive arrests and in 1972 he was commended by both the trial judge at the Old Bailey and the commissioner for courage and determination leading to the arrest of three men for possession of a firearm. He had divorced, and re-married eighteen months prior to his retirement in 1979.

So I knew Les England, and a few years later, as a detective constable at Forest Gate, I met Charlie Cox, who at the time of my writing this book in 2010 had sadly suffered a minor stroke which had practically robbed him of his power of speech. But what men they were! Their courage, and the gallantry displayed by Pawsey and Hutchins, rubbed off on their fellow officers; it was a pleasure for a young detective to work with them.

Tommy Thorburn was later posted to the Flying Squad and achieved considerable success working on a small, select team, under the direction of Jack Slipper, and carrying out arrests of the Great Train Robbers. He died in 2000, and in connection with his discovery of John Hall's firearms would say, sadly, "I wish I had been able to change things and often think to myself, 'if only'."

Tommy did his best, which was more than can be said for some nameless civilian, smugly sitting in his or her ivory tower in S1 (Firearms) Department at the Yard. Nevertheless, the Department were spurred into action. By a curious coincidence, in the same edition of *Police Orders*, dated 4 August 1961, which contained details of the commissioner's high commendation for Cox and England, an amnesty was announced in respect of illegally held firearms and ammunition. There would be immunity from prosecution for persons surrendering these items to police, whether or not a firearms certificate had been issued, as long as the submission had been carried out by 31 October. However, the notice robustly added, 'Applications for firearms certificates by persons in unauthorized possession of firearms will not be entertained.'

Well, that was a big relief then. As long as – to use that repulsive phrase, so beloved of civil servants, senior police officers and other politicians – 'lessons had been learnt'.

CHAPTER 6

Operation Shepherd

I have to explain to the uninitiated reader exactly what a 'Q' car is – or rather was, because like many other crime-fighting initiatives in the Metropolitan Police they do not exist anymore. Their name came from the 'Q' Ships of the First World War, which appeared to be ordinary merchantmen or fishing smacks. Originally referred to as 'Special Service Ships', then as 'decoys', they possessed a phenomenal turn of speed, were heavily armed and were used to hunt down the marauding German U-boats. The names of these ships were continually altered, many of the officers came from the Mercantile Marine and they exhibited great courage and took enormous risks. Of necessity, their work was kept secret; awards, including the Victoria Cross, were shrouded in mystery – these ships were working in disguise.

The 'Q' cars were first introduced to the police in 1934 and they were used in the divisions of the Metropolitan Police in the same way that their Flying Squad counterparts were deployed across London. They were fast, nondescript cars, fitted with two-way radio, with which they could communicate with the Yard, and a gong for warning vehicles to stop. The driver was a uniform police constable in plain clothes who had been classified at Hendon Driving School as Class I or II, and the rest of the crew consisted of a detective sergeant or constable, plus an aid to CID. They patrolled their division on the lookout for suspicious vehicles and persons, following up snippets of information, tracking down wanted criminals and, of course, being used when it was advisable for an anonymous vehicle to attend the area of criminal activity rather than advertise a uniform presence. They were not to be used for long, protracted investigations; they used 'hit-and-run' tactics to achieve a quick turnover of arrests. The Press, with their love of hyperbole, referred to the crews of the 'Q' cars as 'the Commandos of the CID', and the comparison was not ridiculous. Their call-sign was the phonetic letter of the division to which they belonged, followed by the numbers 'one-one', and the most famous of them all in police history was the ill-fated 'Foxtrot One One'.

★　★　★

The Metropolitan Police's 'F' Division took in some very busy areas, including Shepherd's Bush, Fulham and Hammersmith, and on the morning of Friday, 12 August 1966, the crew of 'Foxtrot One One' was the early-turn shift; all 'Q' cars worked fairly elastic hours, usually ten to six during the day and six to two at night, thereby giving the division a sixteen-hour coverage, although when enquiries were progressing, the hours were far longer.

That morning, the driver was Police Constable Geoffrey Roger Fox, who was aged forty-one. He had served in the Royal Navy for almost four years, seeing war service, and after demobilization he married Marjorie in 1947. Their first daughter, Ann Margaret, was born a year later, and in 1950 Fox joined the police and was posted to Shepherd's Bush, which suited him because he lived in Northolt, just to the north-west of the police station. Two more children were born, a boy, Paul Geoffrey, in 1950 and another girl, Mandy Ann, in 1963.

Fox's education had proved that he was academically very bright; he sailed through his courses at training school and his probationary examinations and, had he felt the need to pursue promotion, could have done so without sitting the Civil Servant's Examination, because his standard of education was such that he was exempt from it. But promotion did not interest Fox; his love was driving, and he had passed the advanced course at Hendon Driving School as a Class I driver in November 1963. He was therefore much in demand as an area car – and a 'Q' car – driver. "He was very much a 'copper's copper'," recalled Police Constable Dick 'Taff' Bowen. "He was a top thief-catcher and knew mostly all the villains on the patch. He was, even by advanced police driving standards, an exceptionally skilful driver."

The CID officer in charge of the car was Detective Sergeant Christopher Tippett Head, who was single and aged thirty. Born in Dartmouth, he had joined the Devon Constabulary's Cadets for eighteen months before almost immediately carrying out his National Service as a Leading Aircraftsman in the RAF. In 1958 he joined the Metropolitan Police and spent almost five years on 'B' Division as a police constable and an aid to CID, before being posted to 'F' Division in 1963 as a detective constable. Several postings followed – to 'C' and 'E' Divisions, as well as C10 (the Stolen Vehicle Squad) and C1 Department at the Yard – before promotion to detective sergeant (second class) brought him back to 'F' Division in February 1966. Head was well remembered by former Police Constable 405'C' Harry Greig, who after one week at Tottenham Court Road police station carried out his first arrest for grievous bodily harm. "Chris Head was so helpful to me and was such a methodical worker," Greig told me in 2011. "I was shocked to hear of his death; I always felt that although he was then just a DC, he had the ability to go a long way in the job."

Head had been part of the 'Jack the Stripper' murder enquiry – the assailant had murdered six prostitutes, scattering their naked bodies around the area. But by August the chief suspect had committed suicide and the enquiry was wound down; instead of resuming normal CID duties, Head was asked to run the next 'Q' car tour.

The youngest member of the crew was Temporary Detective Constable (TDC) David Stanley Bertram Wombwell, who was aged twenty-five and was married to Gillian. They had two children, Daen Andrew who had been born in 1963 and Melanie Ann, born one year later. Formerly a trainee car salesman, Wombwell had joined the police in 1963 and been posted to 'F' Division. A keen youngster, he had applied to become a TDC (the new title for what had previously been aids to CID) and had been accepted eight months earlier. A posting on a 'Q' car – working with an experienced CID officer and making a lot of arrests – was considered an excellent way for a TDC to gain experience and to ensure acceptance into the Criminal Investigation Department.

★   ★   ★

'Foxtrot One One' was a blue Triumph 2000 with an automatic Borg-Warner gearbox. It could accelerate from 0–60mph in 14.9 seconds, had a top speed of 96mph and was considered ideal for this type of work; commonplace, but fast and highly manoeuvrable. Sitting in the front passenger seat was Head; as officer in charge of the car, it was to him that a constable or witness would naturally speak first upon the car's arrival at the scene of an incident, and he was also responsible for receiving, acknowledging and transmitting messages on the RT set concealed in the glove compartment.

That morning, Police Constable Dick Bowen was driving 'Foxtrot Two' area car, which covered the Hammersmith and West Kensington areas, when he received a call from Information Room stating that 'Foxtrot One One' required urgent assistance outside a scrap metal dealer's in Scrubs Lane, NW10. Bowen powered the area car into top gear, but whatever had prompted the 'urgent assistance' call had abated, because upon his arrival,

Geoff Fox emerged from the yard, waved and shouted, "It's OK now, Taff – cheers, mate," and 'Foxtrot Two' resumed its patrol. "And that was the last I ever saw of Geoff, or his oppos, Detective Sergeant Chris Head and TDC Dave Wombwell," Bowen sadly told me.

Lunch at the Beaumont Arms pub in Shepherd's Bush followed, and later the patrol resumed, with Chris Head following a suspected bicycle thief on foot in the vicinity of Western Avenue, Acton, before 'Foxtrot One One' received a call from Detective Inspector Kenneth Coote. The 'Q' car had been used to convey him to Marylebone Magistrates' Court that morning, because he had a number of bulky exhibits to present to the magistrates in a prison escape case. Now the court appearance had concluded, Coote had asked the Yard to send out an RT call to the car to come and pick him up. Head returned to the car – he had stopped and questioned the suspect, who was completely guiltless – and after he had found a telephone box, he called Coote at the Magistrates' Court and told him that he would pick him up in twenty minutes. The time was 3.10; it was the last RT transmission that 'Foxtrot One One' would make.

On that sunny afternoon, the 'Q' car headed east towards the Marylebone Road, gliding past groups of children playing as the end of their summer holidays approached. There was no intimation that the car was on a course set for disaster, which would culminate in the greatest number of Metropolitan Police officers being simultaneously murdered since the formation of the Force in 1829.

★　★　★

Elsewhere in London, three men had been consolidating their plans to rob a rent collector. John – often referred to as 'Jack' – Edward Witney was aged thirty-six and the possessor of ten previous convictions; the longest sentence he had served was one of eighteen months' imprisonment. He had been a soldier and a lorry driver and had failed at both. Witney lived with his wife Lilian in a basement flat at 10 Fernhead Road, Paddington. Telling his wife he was going to work – he was in fact unemployed – Witney drove over to Treventon Towers, North Kensington, the home of John Duddy, a thirty-seven-year-old Scot. The son of a former police officer, Duddy, like Witney, had been a lorry driver and had previous convictions. He had served a term of Borstal training and two sentences of imprisonment, each of three months, the last of which had been recorded fifteen years previously. Married, with two teenage daughters, Duddy was similarly unemployed and had started to drink heavily. His wife had left the marital home weeks previously because of her husband's friendship with the third member of the gang, whom she detested.

Waiting with Duddy was the third and most dangerous member of the group. Harry Maurice Roberts was a thirty-year-old former bricklayer, who had been convicted as a juvenile for receiving stolen goods. He had a rebellious and violent streak; he had attacked his mother and he would later assault his wife. Roberts was sentenced to Borstal training for a robbery in which he attacked a shopkeeper with an iron bar, and following his release he was called up for National Service. He joined the Rifle Brigade and saw active service against the communist terrorists in Malaya. He was taught guerrilla skills, and by his own admission had killed a number of the enemy. Following demobilization, it appeared that the conflict had affected Roberts, who often spoke about killing, conflict and danger. Married in 1958, less than a year later he was convicted of storebreaking and larceny at Chelmsford Assizes and was sentenced to a total of twenty-one months' imprisonment. However, it was soon revealed that Roberts had also attacked a seventy-eight-year-old man in his home and in order to steal a ring from him had cut off the old man's finger. The judge, Mr Justice Maude, told him, "You are a brutal thug. You came very near the rope this time. It is to be hoped you do not appear before us, again." Roberts was sentenced to seven years' imprisonment for robbery with violence and was more fortunate than he knew; the elderly man died one year and three days later. Had he expired two days earlier, Roberts could have been tried for his murder, for which the death penalty was still in place. Divorced, and released after serving four years and eight months of his sentence in 1963, Roberts went to live at Wymering Mansions in Maida Vale with Lilian Perry, who was divorced from her police officer husband, and he then fell in with Witney. The men had stolen lead and scrap metal, before meeting up with Duddy. Apparently, the three then started a series of robberies and burglaries, targeting betting shops and rent collectors, and both Duddy and Roberts would later say that Witney was 'the boss'. However, their successes and remuneration must have been extremely limited; Witney was the owner of a clapped-out, second-hand, blue Standard Vanguard estate, registration number PGT 726; it had failed its MOT, the exhaust was tied on with string, the vehicle was untaxed and the insurance had run out at noon on that day, 12 August.

The plan to rob the rent collector was to be put into action the following week. In the meantime, a getaway car was required, and that afternoon the men planned to steal a car, a Ford Cortina, from one of the area's station car parks. In the back of the car were a set of false number plates – JJJ 285D – which had been acquired that day. These matched a blue Cortina which they had seen previously in the Shepherd's Bush area, and Roberts had also brought a bag, which at first glance appeared to be full of overalls. But the weight of the bag betrayed its contents. A closer examination would have revealed that amongst the clothing in the bag lodged between the two front seats were three loaded handguns.

⋆ ⋆ ⋆

Braybrook Street is more like a crescent than a street. It commences at the junction with Wulfstan Street and its northern boundaries skirt Old Oak Common and Wormwood Scrubs. Before the street dips southwards to return to the junction with Wulfstan Street, its eastern boundary abuts Wormwood Scrubs prison. Therefore, because of the possibility of an escape from the prison being arranged by outsiders, any vehicle containing three men loitering in the vicinity – especially one in the wretched state of Witney's Vanguard – would attract the attention of police officers. So it was ironic that Roberts & Co, who had no thought of assisting anybody to escape from anywhere, simply happened to be driving aimlessly through Braybrook Street at 3.15 that afternoon, at the same time as 'Foxtrot One One'.

A number of former police officers have told me that considering Fox's sixteen years' knowledge of local criminals he probably recognized Whitney at the wheel of the Standard; and although we will now of course never know for sure, this could well be true. It is easy to imagine Fox nodding in the direction of the estate car and muttering, "That lot's worth a pull!" But whatever the reason, the 'Q' car accelerated, overtook the estate and gonged it, and Witney reluctantly stopped. Head and Wombwell got out of the Triumph and strolled back to the suspect vehicle, leaving Fox at the wheel, the engine ticking over. There was general conversation between Head and Witney concerning the ownership of the Vanguard, and upon examination of the insurance certificate, Head mentioned that it was three hours out of date. "Can't you give me a break?" pleaded Witney, but by now Head had seen the holdall and pointing to it he said the six words which would seal his fate and that of his two companions: "Let's have a look in here."

Wombwell was holding the Book 85, the police document in which to record details of vehicles and their occupants, and he leant towards Witney to speak to him through the open window. Without a word, Roberts shot him in the left eye.

Head, aghast, turned and ran towards the 'Q' car as Roberts told Duddy to grab a gun. Both men tumbled out of the car and chased Head, with Roberts shouting, "Get the driver!" and also firing a shot which missed. "No!" shouted Head. "No, no!" Catching up with him at the front of the car, Roberts shot Head twice in the back, and he turned and fell on to his back, mortally wounded.

Duddy, meanwhile, holding a .38 Webley service revolver, fired a shot at Fox through the nearside passenger window which missed, as did his second shot, both bullets shattering the windscreen. His third shot hit Fox in the left temple, killing him instantly.

Witney had got out of the estate to see what was happening and was attempting to prise the documentation from Wombwell's lifeless hand, as Roberts and Duddy ran back and got into the Vanguard and Roberts shouted, "Drive!"

"You must be fucking potty!" gasped Witney, to which Roberts replied, "Drive, you cunt, unless you want some of the same!" Just four minutes had elapsed since the Vanguard had been stopped.

Witney reversed, narrowly missing Bryan Deacon who was driving towards him, then the estate roared into Erconwald Street, sparks flying from the exhaust pipe which was in contact with the road. Deacon, believing there had been an escape from prison, shouted to his wife to get the registration number. Then he saw the bodies. First, he saw Wombwell, lying on his back, apparently looking skywards, his fingers still clutching the pen in his right hand, his legs straight, his ankles crossed. Then he saw Head, who was underneath the car. Fox's foot was still on the accelerator, and with the automatic gearbox in 'drive' the front wheels had run over Head, the exhaust system had burned him and the rear wheels bumped against his lifeless body.

This was the sight which faced nineteen-year-old David Jenkinson as he and two friends cycled into Braybrook Street. Two days later Jenkinson was due to join the Royal Military Police (and six years later, the Metropolitan Police), but now he was horrified at this scene of carnage. "Me and my pals were just out, cruising around," Jenkinson told me. "I lived in Portobello Road at the time. We were confronted by the surreal scene of a car with its engine racing, the rear drive wheels were off the ground and seemed to be propped up on the body of a man. We were certainly amongst the first on the scene, if not the first, although the area was very quickly swamped and the police put screens up across the road."

A lorry driver ran over and switched off the Triumph's ignition. Now, the sound of crying from the frightened children who had witnessed the massacre could be heard. Householders spilled out of their homes. Mr Deacon, who had called the police from a butcher's shop in Erconwald Street, returned to the scene and handed the piece of butcher's wrapping paper upon which was written 'PGT 726' to Police Constable David Owen, who was in the first police car to arrive at 3.22. Mrs Ida Collis of Braybrook Street had heard the sound of three gunshots in quick succession but had not seen the men responsible, who had escaped. Ten-year-old Jimmy Newton and fourteen-year-old Tommy McCormack had witnessed the murders. They were unable to describe the men but they were able to state that the men who had shot the police officers had escaped in the blue Standard van, of which Mr Deacon had correctly recorded the registration number. A little girl described the driver of the van – Witney – as looking "just like the footballer, Bobby Charlton" – as indeed he did.

The Yard's Information Room immediately broadcast the message that "a very serious assault had taken place in Braybrook Street, W12 and that the occupants of a Standard Vanguard, probable registration PGT 726, were to be approached with the utmost caution if seen or stopped." What the operator did not know was that it was the occupants of 'Foxtrot One One' who were the victims, and therefore, ironically, the message was directed to that unit as well.

★   ★   ★

Everybody had memories of that day. Ken Law was employed as 'duties sergeant' at Shepherd's Bush and was probably one of the last officers to see the crew alive. The three men came to his office because Chris Head wanted Law to arrange Fox's duties so that he might remain with them for an extra month, as driver on the 'Q' car. "I was only one of many who could not believe the news we heard about an hour later," recalled Law. "I was stood beside Chief Inspector Fred Rooke in the front office when he telephoned the news through to the 'F' Division commander. I don't know what the person who received the call said, but I remember Fred's reply: 'Sir, do you really think I would joke about such a dreadful thing?'" Law added, "Anybody who remembers Fred Rooke will know that humour was not his strong suit."

Station Sergeant Gordon Hunter returned from a course to Shepherd's Bush on foot to discover a police constable posted on the steps of the police station. Rather flippantly, he asked, "Hello, Taff, expecting the Commissioner?"

"Could be, Sarge, haven't you heard?" replied the constable. "The crew of the 'Q' car have been shot."

"Christ, Taff!" exclaimed Hunter. He then asked, "Are they in hospital?" and received the chilling reply, "Worse than that, they're all dead."

"I remember the day as though it were yesterday," Bernie Davis told me. "I was the operator on the 'Q' car for 'B' Division – 'Bravo One One' – on the same shift as 'Foxtrot One One'. In fact, we used to communicate with them regularly, being on adjoining divisions. We had just pulled into the yard at Notting Hill when Jim Neville, the DI at the time, stuck his head out of the CID office window. 'Get down to Shepherd's Bush, now!' he shouted. 'Three of our guys have just been killed!' On arrival at Shepherd's Bush, you can imagine, there was mayhem. I don't think I'd seen so many police officers at a nick at any one time. Officers responded from all over the Met."

Geoffrey Anderson was working as the CID Clerk at No. 1 District Headquarters when the call came through; he was shocked, because he knew Chris Head well, and he contacted Detective Chief Superintendent John 'Bill' Bailey at West End Central police station, who went straight to the scene. Detective Sergeant (Second Class) Harry Clement BEM (later Detective Chief Superintendent) was attached to the Regional Crime Squad (RCS) and was in the vicinity of Wormwood Scrubs at the time of the shooting, but his radio was switched to the RCS channel and therefore he missed the initial call to the wireless cars. Upon his arrival at the RCS office at Tottenham Court Road police station, he was informed what had happened and was told to leave for the scene immediately. "The senior man at the scene was Detective Chief Superintendent John Bailey," Clement told me. "He asked me to get some of our team to collect the dead lads and put them on the grass at the side of the road." Forty-five years had passed since that day, but as Clement told me, "Friday, 12 August 1966 will long remain in my mind."

At the Yard, Detective Superintendent (later Deputy Assistant Commissioner) Dick Chitty of C1 Murder Squad had returned from Gloucester Assizes, where he had notched up his fourteenth conviction for murder. He was called into Commander Ernie Millen's office and was annoyed when Millen told him to get down to Shepherd's Bush to take over the investigation of three police officers who had been shot, because he was the third detective superintendent 'in the frame' to be called in the event of a serious investigation. "But I'm not on call," expostulated Chitty, before the full import of what he had been told had sunk in and he asked, "Are they injured?"

"They're dead," replied Millen with his usual bluntness. "All three. Get down to the Bush as quickly as you can. I'll see you there." Millen's choice of Chitty was a wise one, whether or not he was the third officer on call; he had worked on 'F' Division previously and he had an acute knowledge of the area. As Chitty left, so Millen telephoned Chiswick police station, spoke to Detective Chief Inspector John 'Ginger' Hensley and appointed him second in command.

★   ★   ★

In retrospect, nobody should have been surprised at this atrocity. In the previous two years crime in London – particularly violent crime – had gone through the roof. And with the abolition of the death penalty nine months previously, no deterrent to violent criminals existed.

However, everyone wanted to help. The five-line switchboard at the police station was jammed by the colossal number of calls coming in; GPO engineers quickly set up further lines. Police officers, not only from the Met but from all over the country, volunteered to help; thirty-six officers from Southampton used their annual leave, hired a coach and arrived at Shepherd's Bush, offering their services. So too did the AA, the RAC, local businesses and just ordinary people who turned up at the counter. The Territorial Army and even the Boy Scouts and Girl Guides offered to assist. The late-turn at Shepherd's Bush had no intention of booking off at ten o'clock, and the night-duty came on early. Everyone was desperate to do something, anything to help. Police Constable Peter Sheldrick had taken over driving the area car, 'Foxtrot Two', from Dick Bowen for the late-turn shift and when he arrived at Braybrook Street, he was, as he told me, "Profoundly shocked. Geoff Fox couldn't at first be seen, although he was behind the wheel. Head was underneath the car and Wombwell was lying in the road, ten or fifteen yards away."

Later that evening, Sheldrick acquired a large number of loaves of bread to help make sandwiches in the canteen for the enormous number of people now at Shepherd's Bush. As he pushed his way through the throng outside, a press photographer took a picture of him carrying the loaves, which were in plain white wrappers. The following morning, the photograph appeared in the national press, bearing the caption, "Officer carrying ammunition."

In the meantime, the eminent pathologist Donald Teare had gone straight to the scene, and the experts from the Yard's forensic department were making an initial inspection of the 'Q' car, prior to it being lifted on to a low-loader and transported to the Forensic Laboratory (then) at Theobalds Road. And at Shepherd's Bush, Scotland Yard's top crimebusters were arriving; first, Millen, purely in an advisory capacity, then 'the Grey Fox' and head of the Flying Squad, Detective Chief Superintendent Tommy Butler, fresh from his success with the Great Train Robbery investigation. Detective Inspector (later Detective Chief Superintendent) Jack Slipper was being driven through West London in a Flying Squad car when he heard the initial call from the Yard; it was followed by a second message almost immediately: "All C8 units are to telephone D99, immediately." Having contacted the Squad's control centre, Slipper, too, headed straight for Shepherd's Bush. The officers who would make up the sixty-five-strong team of detectives forming the nucleus of 'Operation Shepherd' were quickly being assembled.

The burning question for the enquiry team was why had the crew of the 'Q' car been murdered? If they had known they were going into a potentially dangerous situation they would certainly have called for back-up; in fact, they had already done so, several hours earlier when they had gone to the scrap yard. It was clear from the witnesses that the men in the Standard had been responsible for the shootings, but why? What were they up to? Was it to do with a planned prison break? Had they carried out a robbery? But there was no suggestion from Wormwood Scrubs that an escape attempt had been envisaged, and no robbery or any other offence involving firearms anywhere in the vicinity had been reported. One theory was that the 'Q' car crew might have been caught in the cross-fire in a confrontation between two rival gangs. But only one car had been seen leaving the scene, and nobody else had been seen running off on foot. No, the answer lay in the Standard Vanguard. It had not been reported stolen, so the van had to be found – quickly – and with it, the owner.

★   ★   ★

But although the registration number of Witney's van had been correctly recorded by Mr Deacon, no computerized records showing the details of the registered owner, retrievable in an instant, then existed. The paper records were kept in four London County Council offices situated around the capital which kept strict office hours and closed promptly at five o'clock. Therefore authority had to be granted to get one of the offices reopened and a search made; however, Witney had not registered the vehicle in his name, so the last recorded owner of the van had to be found – he lived in Finchley and had sold the vehicle to a dealer. He, in turn, had sold the Vanguard to a man in Kilburn. Eventually, a dealer was found who admitted he had sold the van for £55, with a Ford Anglia in part-exchange, almost a year previously, in October 1965. He was able to provide the name and address of the man to whom he had sold it.

It was not until nine o'clock that night that Detective Inspector (later Deputy Assistant Commissioner) Ron Steventon arrived at Fernhead Road and told Witney that he was making enquiries about the blue Vanguard. "Oh, no – not that!" gasped Witney and explained that he had seen the reports of the van and the murders on the television. Witney told the officer he had sold the van earlier that day to a stranger outside the Clay Pigeon public house at Eastcote for £15, but then Witney's wife chipped in, "You told me you'd been to work; you didn't tell me you sold the car. What's going on?" Witney, who was perspiring freely (as well he might), told her he had not been to work for some considerable time. Although a search of his flat failed to disclose anything incriminating, he was arrested and taken to Shepherd's Bush police station.

In the early hours of the following morning, Witney made a statement, which took two hours and twenty minutes to record. In it, he sedulously stuck to his story of selling the car to an unknown man, also stating that he had had a drink with a tobacco salesman in the pub and had later gone to a betting shop.

Jack Slipper had previously worked in that area and knew a lot of the inhabitants, including the manager of the betting shop. Slipper obtained a statement from him and his staff which completely contradicted Witney's assertion that he had been there. In addition, he traced the tobacco salesman, who confirmed he had had a drink with Witney but added that Witney was in company with two other men.

Roberts, meanwhile, had returned to the flat at Wymering Mansions, and when his girlfriend, Mrs Perry, mentioned that police officers had been shot, Roberts told her that he had been involved. He kept repeating, "If only that fool hadn't asked to look inside the car." Roberts had commenced his journey towards transforming himself into a victim. It was not his fault that three police officers had been murdered nor, indeed, that he had been in illegal possession of firearms. No, Head had been at fault for having the colossal impertinence to ask what was in the bag.

The following day, Duddy came to the flat. He was in possession of the guns, and Roberts hid them under a bed. Roberts knew where Witney had garaged the van, in a lock-up in Tinworth Street, Vauxhall, and he and Mrs Perry visited the garage and could see the Vanguard inside through the cracks in the door, but Roberts did not possess the keys to the garage or the vehicle. Nevertheless, rather than do anything himself, he wanted Duddy to do something, perhaps burn the vehicle to dispose of any clues. But Duddy refused.

That evening, due to the enormous amount of coverage given by the media, police received information that a blue Vanguard had been seen to be driven into the garage in Vauxhall the previous day. The motorist providing the information stated that he had particularly noticed the vehicle because it had been driven at speed and scratched its side along a wall. The vehicle was discovered in the lock-up, together with the false registration plates, sets of overalls, part of a woman's stocking for use as a mask and the three .38 cartridges from the gun fired by Duddy. Like the 'Q' car, the Vanguard was removed to the Forensic Science Laboratory. What was more, it was established that the garage had been rented by Witney; the garage owner later positively identified him as the lessee. He had initially denied that it was Witney who had rented the garage; after Jack Slipper had had a quiet word with him he changed his mind and acknowledged that it was Witney who was the leaseholder. The garage owner admitted taking possession of lead stolen by Witney & Co from a company at Acton and was afraid that identification of Witney would lead to his being charged with receiving the stolen property.

Meanwhile, on the Sunday morning, Roberts and Duddy went to Hampstead Heath where they buried the weapons, although Roberts later returned, dug up the cache and removed two of the guns. Duddy travelled to Scotland and Roberts spent the night in the Russell Hotel with Mrs Perry, registered under the names of Mr and Mrs Crosby. The following morning, Monday, 15 August, Roberts purchased some camping gear – a haversack, a primus stove and a sleeping bag – in King's Cross and travelled to Epping; he knew the area quite well through camping there as a boy. Mrs Perry returned to London. Roberts, who had previously used the aliases of Ronald Ernest Hall and John O'Brien, was armed, on his own and on the run.

By the Sunday evening over forty-eight hours had passed since the killings. John McCafferty, a ballistics expert, had confirmed that the three cartridges had been fired from the same gun. Witney was still denying any involvement in the murders, but Chitty was of the opinion that if he had sold the car to a complete stranger, it would have been somewhat unlikely that that stranger had parked the car in a garage rented by Witney; so he was charged with the three murders. However, Witney later called Hensley to his cell and made a further statement, in which he said:

> As God is my judge, I had absolutely nothing to do with the shooting of the three policemen. I just drove into Braybrook Street where a small car pulled up alongside. Two men got out and one asked if it was my car. I said, 'Yes'. Then he asked me for my Road Fund Licence, and I told him I hadn't got one. The elder of the two policemen walked round to the other side of the car and said, 'Let's have a look in here'. Without anything further Roberts leant across and shot the young officer in the face. The sound of the shot deafened and dazed me. The other officer ran to the front, and Roberts, followed by Duddy, gave chase, still shooting. I saw the second officer stumble and fall. Roberts fired again, I don't know how many times. Duddy raced alongside and shot through the window of the police car. They ran back to the car, jumped in, and said, 'Drive'.

Having named Roberts and Duddy as the gunmen, Witney said he knew where they lived but was unaware of their exact addresses. Therefore, from the back of a Flying Squad taxi, he pointed out to officers where the other two lived.

At five o'clock on the Monday morning, armed police raided the two addresses, but the birds had flown. Duddy's teenage daughters were on their own. They told the detectives that they had last seen their father on Saturday; their mother had walked out weeks before. The flat at Wymering Mansions had also been kept under observation, and when Mrs Perry returned, she was questioned and told the police everything she knew of Roberts' last movements.

Later that morning, an inquest was opened and adjourned on the three officers, and the West London Coroner, Cyril Baron, stated:

This was an appalling and dreadful crime which has resulted in the deaths of three courageous police officers, officers who have been killed in the execution of their duty. They were officers whom the police and the public could ill afford to lose.

On Tuesday, 17 August, Detective Chief Inspector Robert Brown from Glasgow's Flying Squad brought in the Duddy family, and after questioning, Duddy's brother Vincent agreed to take the officers to 261 Stevenson Street, Calton, where a family named Crummer lived. At 1.20 that afternoon Vincent Duddy knocked on the door of the premises which was opened by Mrs Crummer; the detectives rushed in and extracted a quivering John Duddy, who was lying in bed. Detective Chief Inspector Hensley and Detective Inspector Jack Slipper brought him back by plane to London. Duddy had initially denied involvement in the shootings but during the flight he made a statement to the officers which read, in part:

> I must tell you what happened ... It was Roberts who started the shooting. He shot the two who got out of the car and shouted at me to shoot. I just grabbed a gun and ran to the police car and shot the driver through the window. I must have been mad. I wish you could hang me now.

Later, at Shepherd's Bush, Duddy made a further statement which in part read, "I didn't mean to kill him. I wanted quick money the easy way. I'm a fool," and he, too was charged with the murders.

On Thursday, 500 police officers, some armed, some with dogs, searched the 6,000 acres of Epping Forest. A reward of £1,000 was offered for the arrest of Roberts, and 16,000 wanted posters were circulated. Chitty made an appeal on television for Roberts to give himself up; so did Roberts' mother Dorothy, although many members of the investigation team thought her plea less convincing than Chitty's. Roberts' divorced wife, Margaret Rose, now known as 'Mitzi Roberts', was working as a stripper in a Northern club – since the murders, the club manager complained that her fee for performing had rocketed – and she, too, made a public appeal for her erstwhile husband to surrender. Since Roberts believed – with some justification – that she had provided police with the information which had led to his seven-year sentence, if he heard her entreaty to capitulate, it was likely to fall on deaf ears.

On 31 August a funeral service was held for the three officers, with 600 police officers in attendance. Superintendent Gordon

Maggs, the head of Traffic Patrol, was in charge of the seven-man motorcycle unit who accompanied the cortège from Worcester Park to the parish church of St Stephen with St Thomas; all of the junctions were manned, so that the funeral procession would have an uninterrupted journey. "On that day, as we travelled, all oncoming traffic stopped, bus drivers got down from their cabs, conductors got off and stood by the buses, other drivers got out of their cars or lorries, the pavements were lined with people, men raised their hats, women were weeping and the normal hustle and bustle stopped and it was quite eerie," remembered Reg Humphries, one of the police motorcyclists. "All we could hear was the sound of our bikes as we rode along. I had been told to keep the speed down to 20mph for the whole journey, and during the many escorts I carried out during my service, this four-mile ride was the saddest and seemed the longest I was ever called to do."

And for the bereaved, it seemed there was no end to the suffering. Mrs Fox had been comforted by the wife of Police Constable Sid Seager, a traffic patrol officer from Barnes Garage. Geoff Fox had been the best man at their wedding, Seager had been one of the first to arrive at Braybrook Street and now Seager too, had been killed, at the Hogarth roundabout, when an articulated lorry carrying seventeen tons of axles toppled over, killing him instantly.

After the service, Christopher Head was buried at St Luke's Church, Torquay, Geoffrey Fox at Mortlake and the ashes of David Wombwell were interned at St Thomas' Church, Acton. A memorial tablet was erected in the foyer of Shepherd's Bush police station.

On 6 September there was a memorial service at Westminster Abbey, and 2,000 police officers attended, as well as the Commissioner, Sir Joseph Simpson KBE, Prime Minister Harold Wilson and the leader of the opposition, Edward Heath MP. The Queen had already sent her condolences from Balmoral. It was on these two occasions only during the whole of the investigation that the personnel of 'Operation Shepherd' left their enquiries to attend the services.

For the rest of the time, enquiries to trace Roberts were continuing at top speed. Within a fortnight of the murders, the team had received 3,714 telephone calls and 521 letters. Information – some wildly inaccurate, some malicious, some well intentioned and a small amount correct – continued to flood in; 6,000 sightings of Roberts were reported, all over the United Kingdom and beyond. He was allegedly seen on 160 occasions in

Liverpool, and 106 times in Bournemouth. There were not enough officers or hours in the day, but every sighting was followed up. Criminals thought to be sheltering Roberts learnt the hard way not to be obstructive; for the officers leading the raids, 'No' did not feature in their vocabulary.

Ken 'Pedlar' Palmer had been on the same advanced driving course as Geoff Fox and admired him greatly. He was on a lone patrol when he stopped a car, the driver of which was "the spitting image of Harry Roberts." The innocent motorist was able to prove his identity, but as eighty-two-year-old Palmer told me in 2011, "Perhaps this will give a lead as to how a team unite in their search for justice when one of us is involved."

A man thought to be Roberts was dragged out of his seat at London's Victoria Palace Theatre during a performance of *The Black and White Minstrel Show*, but turned out to be a steel worker from Cardiff. The officers apologized for having stuck a pistol in his mouth. A performance of Offenbach's opera *Barbe-Bleue* was halted at Sadler's Wells Theatre after it was thought that Roberts was in the audience. As the patrons spilled out into Roseberry Avenue they were meticulously checked, but it was discovered that the only murderer in evidence was Offenbach's hero, Bluebeard.

A Spanish boxer, Jose Luis Velasco, was seized at Victoria Station in the mistaken belief that he was Roberts. It was an unedifying start to his trip to England, which got worse on 23 August, when at the Civic Hall, Wolverhampton, he was beaten on points by the English heavyweight, Johnny Prescott. That very fine character actor Victor Maddern, who had been born a stone's throw away from Roberts' birthplace and who bore an uncanny resemblance to the 'wanted' photograph, wearied of the number of times he was pointed out to the police as being the killer.

But Roberts *was* seen; a man wearing a combat jacket regularly made purchases of food from a grocery shop near Thorley Wood, Bishop's Stortford, Hertfordshire, just three miles away from Epping Forest; the manageress thought it was Roberts but said nothing because she was afraid of being ridiculed. Then three boys who were hunting rabbits in Thorley Wood discovered a camouflaged tent; a radio was playing and they could hear someone inside. One of the boys, who thought the tent's occupant might be Roberts, told his mother; she laughed and described his notions as 'fanciful'.

On 10 November a gipsy named John Cunningham saw the tent, half buried in the ground and obviously containing an occupant. Cunningham could see a light inside the tent and heard the rattling of a tin can. He mentioned this to his father Thomas but said nothing about his discovery to the police. The following day, at 5.30 in the morning, there was a break-in at a factory in Bishops Stortford, and Roberts later admitted attempting to break open a safe there. A police dog picked up Roberts' scent but the trail petered out. It was not until the following day, 12 November, that Cunningham mentioned his sighting to a police officer who was making enquiries regarding thefts in the area and took him to the tent, which was expertly constructed. It was sited so that the occupant of the tent had an uninterrupted view of anyone approaching, but at the same time it was almost unrecognizable as a tent. There was a framework of twigs and branches covered with a tarpaulin, camouflaged in military style with brown and green paint. It was well stocked: two blankets, plenty of food, cooking utensils and a baited fishing rod. But Roberts had gone. Observation was kept, but when Roberts failed to return, fingerprints were taken from items in the hide – a whisky bottle and a pistol holster – by the local police which were positively identified as being those of Harry Roberts.

On 14 November the trial of Duddy and Witney commenced at the Old Bailey and Chitty was informed of the find in Hertfordshire. At dawn on Tuesday, 15 November, Thorley Wood, which had been ringed by over 100 police officers, was searched, and Roberts was found in nearby Nathan's Wood, just before noon. Police Sergeant Peter Smith and Police Constable Oswald Thorne entered a disused hanger at Blount's Farm and under some bales of straw they discovered a sleeping bag, which contained a dishevelled Harry Roberts. Inside the sleeping bag was the Luger which had been used to kill Wombwell and Head, as well as an Army .38 Colt, but although both were loaded Roberts made no attempt to use them – possibly because Sergeant Smith was holding a rifle. "Don't shoot," pleaded Roberts, who had spent 96 days on the run. "You won't get any trouble from me; I've had enough. I'm glad you caught me."

The trial at the Old Bailey was halted and Chitty travelled to Bishop's Stortford. Roberts admitted killing Wombwell and Head but denied killing Fox. A statement was taken down by the late Detective Sergeant Ted Fosbury which read, in part:

Since I have been living rough I have been living by thieving either food or money to buy food. What you have found in the tent I have stolen or bought with stolen money. I'll tell you the truth. I shot the policemen on that Friday afternoon and it was Duddy who shot the driver. I don't know what we were doing near the Scrubs. We were going to nick a car but not that particular day. We had the plate in Jack's van. We were going to rob the rent collector. When the police car pulled up I thought they were going to find the guns in the car and so I shot the officer who was talking to Jack and then shot the one who was talking to Jock Duddy. Jock got out of the car and went to the police car and shot the driver. We then got back into the car and Jack drove back to the arches at Vauxhall. We first decided to abandon the car and some of us decided to take it back to the arches. We were going to burn it later.

Roberts described where the guns had been hidden, and Hensley found the third gun – the one used to kill Fox – after Roberts told him where to look.

Richard Slater was a young detective constable who was one of many in the charge room at Shepherd's Bush when Roberts was charged. "I recall the charge room being lined 'several deep' with officers who just watched the charging, at the desk in the middle of the room, in absolute silence, and it remained absolutely static until Roberts had been led from the room," Slater told me. "That moment has remained in my memory to this day."

Roberts appeared at West London Magistrates' Court and was sent, on a Bill of Indictment, straight to the Old Bailey, where on 6 December 1966, before Mr Justice Glyn-Jones, Duddy, represented by Mr W. M. Hudson, and Witney, represented by Mr James Comyn QC, pleaded not guilty to the three murders and the charges of possessing firearms. Roberts, represented by Mr James Burge QC, pleaded guilty to the murders of Wombwell and Head, of being an accessory to the murder of Fox and of possessing firearms. The prosecution was led by the Solicitor-General, Sir Dingle Foot QC.

After a six-day trial, the jury at the Old Bailey took barely thirty minutes to find the men guilty of the senseless murders, and Mr Justice Glyn-Jones passed sentence on all three, saying:

I pass on you the sentence prescribed by law for the crime of murder, on each count of which you have been convicted, that is, of imprisonment for life. You have been justly convicted of what is perhaps the most heinous crime to have been committed in this country for a generation, or more. I think it likely that no Home Secretary regarding the enormity of your crime will ever think fit to show mercy by releasing you on licence. This is one of those crimes in which the sentence of life imprisonment may well be treated as meaning exactly what it says. Lest any Home Secretary in the future should be minded to consider your release on licence, I have to make a recommendation. My recommendation is that you should not be released on licence, any of the three of you, for a period of thirty years, to begin from today's date.

There was one other piece of unfinished business: the man who had supplied the guns to Roberts for the sum of £90. It took a lot of time, but an informant in the Greek community of North London eventually steered Jack Slipper towards Costas Christos, a bellicose Greek-Cypriot newsagent. Although Roberts was produced from prison, he refused to identify Christos as the armourer; but there was separate, compelling evidence, and Christos was sentenced to six years' imprisonment. Slipper later commented, "I haven't often seen a man more shaken in court."

★　★　★

As soon as the news broke regarding the murders of the three officers, money for their families came pouring in. It was much needed. The officers did not have private insurance, and the Criminal Injuries Compensation Board, set up in 1964, did not at that time cater for the dependants of victims who had been murdered. The Irish labourers who frequented the pubs in Shepherd's Bush and who were paid in cash made massive donations (so much so that it was thought that many of them must have handed over their entire wage packets), retired people turned up with their state pensions, and children with their money boxes. The morning following the shootings, the postal donations started arriving, first a full postman's bag, then two, then three and then a van-full. The volunteers at Shepherd's Bush simply could not cope with the sheer volume, and the operation of dealing with the donations was transferred to Scotland Yard. Within just one month the donations had amounted to £100,000. These included an anonymous donation of £10,000, although the culprit was later revealed to be Sir Billy Butlin, and eventually, £210,000 was raised for the families of the dead police officers. In total, 50,000 people made donations. Mrs Wombwell, Mrs Fox and Mrs Head (Christopher Head's mother) each received £26,250, and the remaining £131,250 was put into trust for the men's five children. Sir Billy later made a further donation of £150,000 and this, together with other donations, resulted in the Police Dependants' Trust being formed. John Cunningham, who had identified Roberts' lair, received £300, part of the £1,000 reward offered for his capture.

With a shocking lack of sensitivity, 'Foxtrot One One' was given a complete overhaul and returned to service. Tony Gledhill, who had been awarded the George Cross following a shooting incident two weeks after the murders, went to Catford police station two years later to crew the 'P' Division 'Q' car, 'Papa One One'. He realized that this was the car – registration number GGW 87C – he had last seen at the Forensic Laboratory and, checking the vehicle's log book, saw Geoff Fox's signature as the driver on 12 August 1966. Horrified, he and the crew complained about the car still being in service; several months later, it was grudgingly withdrawn. The blood-spattered Book 85 made its way to what was then referred to as 'the Black Museum' at the Yard and it was there, as a young detective, that I saw it in 1971; a shiver went down my spine.

On 29 June 1988 a memorial stone was erected in Braybrook Street by the Police Memorial Trust; flowers are laid there annually. In 1992 there was a fire at St Thomas' Church and the memorial tablet erected to the memory of David Wombwell was destroyed. Although the damage was so bad that the church had to be demolished, Wombwell's ashes were recovered and were reinterred in the Garden of Remembrance at St Stephen's Church, Shepherd's Bush, and a replacement memorial tablet was erected. The 'Braybrook Suite', containing a wealth of information, was created at Hammersmith police station.

Three good men dead. Three bad men in prison. The lives of their wives, children, parents and loved ones disrupted forever. And for what? That was the question that had vexed the investigating team from the beginning of their enquiry. When Mrs Perry first saw the guns, she had told Roberts, "You'll get fifteen years if you're caught with them!" However, Jack Slipper's interpretation of the scenario was probably more accurate when he said to me, "If they'd stuck their hands up when the guns were found, they probably wouldn't have drawn more than half-a-stretch (six months' imprisonment) apiece." This was not an arrangement which would have suited Roberts; he had stated that he would be prepared to shoot it out rather than return to prison.

★   ★   ★

Duddy died on 8 February 1981 in the hospital at Parkhurst, the high security prison on the Isle of Wight. He and his wife had divorced four years previously; his father had died within hours of Duddy being sentenced, following a fall down the stairs at home.

Following his inexplicably early release in 1991, Witney was murdered at home in Bristol in August 1999. He was bludgeoned to death by his flatmate, a heroin addict who was wielding a hammer.

However, Prisoner No. 231191, Harry Maurice Roberts, was a different kettle of fish.

★   ★   ★

According to a claim by Roberts in a newspaper interview in 2004, he made twenty-two escape attempts during his first ten years in prison. This was probably an exaggeration, although his mother did assist in at least one of the attempts by smuggling into prison a set of bolt cutters concealed in her brassiere. The plan was frustrated after Roberts was 'grassed', in the same way that Witney and Duddy grassed him after the shooting (he said, "they made out it was all my plan"). He spent twenty-one years in high-security prisons.

In 1999 Roberts was transferred to an open prison at Sudbury, Derbyshire. The following year, he commenced unsupervised work at the St Bernard's Animal Sanctuary in Alfreton. He was considered a prime candidate for parole, and in anticipation of his release had already been allocated a flat nearby. But then, on 2 October 2001, he was recalled to a closed prison at Lincoln and placed in solitary confinement. Why? True, he was a murderer with a violent temper, was cunning, vicious and manipulative, with a strong self-pitying streak and a propensity to blame anybody but himself for his misfortunes. Referring to the murders, he said, "Jack [Witney] said, 'Let him have it', and I just reacted automatically." He was boastful, and would later say that he had been a sergeant in the Rifle Brigade (when others said he was a lance-corporal) and that his team had killed forty communist terrorists in Malaya whilst he had personally accounted 'for at least four'. He said that he and Witney had carried out 'dozens' of armed robberies at betting shops and Post Offices, but stressed that Witney was 'the boss'. He bragged that when he was on the run he had stood next to a wanted poster of himself while a police officer gormlessly wandered past. He was not, of course, reformed; he painted pictures of police officers being killed and decorated the pies which he baked with similar effigies. The former armed robber John McVicar claimed that Roberts 'gloated' about his killings, and Roberts was quoted in 1993 as saying, "The police aren't like real people to us. They're strangers. They're the enemy. And you don't feel remorse for killing a stranger." Despite all this, he had done his best to portray himself to the authorities as a model prisoner, because he added, "I do feel sorry for what we did to their families. I do." Jake Arnott had written a novel, based on the shootings, entitled *He Kills Coppers*, but that was hardly Roberts' fault. So what could possibly have gone wrong, to send Roberts back to solitary confinement?

Initially, the (then) Home Secretary, David Blunkett, refused to inform Roberts or his solicitor of the reasons for his continued incarceration, stating that the evidence was too sensitive and refusing to name the person who had supplied the information. It was ruled that the Parole Board should have a special advocate – an independent barrister – to deal with the allegations, rather than Roberts' lawyer. Roberts attempted, unsuccessfully, to have this ruling overturned by both the Court of Appeal and, on 7 July 2005, by the House of Lords.

Rumour followed rumour – it was alleged that he was involved in drug dealing, bringing contraband into prison, mixing with criminals, taking driving lessons in contravention of his licence – and Roberts provided good copy for the press, with whining comments, including, "I'm not Harry Roberts, police killer; I'm Harry Roberts, old-age pensioner," until 17 April 2009 when an injunction in the High Court was lifted and a horrifying scenario emerged.

Joan Cartwright, aged sixty-seven and a deeply religious woman, ran with her husband the St Bernard's Animal Sanctuary and farm and had in the past taken in community service offenders. She received a letter from Roberts stating that he had spent thirty-five years in prison for an unspecified offence, for which he was now full of remorse. His name meant nothing to Mrs Cartwright and, living in this rural retreat, she had no idea of what he had done, nor that the more moronic of so-called football fans would gleefully chant his name to the tune of 'London Bridge is falling down':

> Harry Roberts is our friend, is our friend, is our friend,
> Harry Roberts is our friend, he kills coppers.
> Let him out to kill some more, kill some more, kill some more
>   ...

"We are liberal, community-minded people and we thought it a wonderful opportunity to help someone," said Mrs Cartwright, and Roberts started working three, then five days per week at the farm. But when her husband discovered precisely who Roberts was – and what he had done – and informed her, she was horrified. Roberts quickly realized that the couple were aware of his background, and a far more sinister figure began to emerge. Mrs Cartwright stated that Roberts now started to glory in his past and as he did so, his personality changed; he started to make demands, display a violent temper and bring some questionable-looking characters back to the farm. These people handed him money; he purchased a Volvo and told the dealer that the car would be in Mrs Cartwright's name. She was by now too terrified of him to refuse, as she was when he demanded that she add him to her insurance policy. He told her that he had 'prison officers in his pocket' and that if anybody were to contact the prison about him, he would get to hear of it. This, Mrs Cartwright could well believe; several of the prison officers whom she saw in his presence appeared to defer to him. On several occasions, Mrs Cartwright stated, Roberts had told her, "Everyone who has ever crossed me, is dead." After six months' placement at the sanctuary, Roberts could only remain if it could be proved he was being paid; and Mrs Cartwright stated that Roberts forced her husband to falsify his accounts to suggest that he had been paid.

The Cartwrights' son James mentioned that he was going to the bank, and Roberts said he would accompany him. Whilst he was there, Roberts wanted to open a bank account, giving James' address; James was too intimidated to argue. Terrified though the family were of Roberts, they felt enough was enough, and details of Roberts' behaviour were discreetly passed to the Prison Service. Unfortunately, the Prison Service then told Roberts that serious allegations had been made about him which sent him into a fury. He telephoned Mrs Cartwright, telling her he would ensure that whoever had made the allegations would be 'torn limb from limb'. And for the next four years Mrs Cartwright descended into what she described as 'a spiral of fear'.

Five nights per week, Roberts would telephone her, sometimes cloyingly loving, sometimes threatening, always manipulating, telling her he would 'send round one of his friends to take her for a drive' and demanding that she write to him on a regular basis. He insisted that she visit him in prison, and believing that if she did not it would unmask her as his accuser, she did so.

Roberts was pursuing a parole hearing and wanted a statement from Mr Cartwright giving him a glowing character reference; not unnaturally, Cartwright refused. A few days later, Bella, one of Mrs Cartwright's horses, had to be put down, after she was discovered to have been hit with tremendous force on the back of her leg; this was sufficient to induce Mr Cartwright to sign the statement. A family cat had to also be put down after it was electrocuted; shortly afterwards, Roberts telephoned Mrs Cartwright and unexpectedly asked after the cat's health. On being told the cause of its demise, Roberts replied that it was very easy to electrocute a cat; all one had to do was tie it to a battery. Then one of the Cartwright's horses was attacked and lost an eye, and a peacock was strangled.

Worst of all was what occurred on 7 November 2005, the day before Mrs Cartwright and her son were due to give evidence against Roberts at a parole hearing. Intruders had attacked another of their horses and had practically severed her head, then hanged her from a tree. The horse's body had been horrifically mutilated.

Panic alarms had been installed in the Cartwright's house, but still the incidents continued. Prowlers were seen. The brake pipes on a car belonging to James Cartwright's wife were cut. Roberts had often enthused to Mrs Cartwright about the benefits of kidnapping a victim; James saw one of the persons who had visited Roberts at the sanctuary lurking outside his thirteen-year-old daughter's school. Roberts was aware that Mrs Cartwright was in the habit of visiting an auction house in Nottingham on Saturday mornings; on one visit, she recognized one of Roberts' associates waiting on the auction house steps with a group of men. By the time the police arrived, the men had left in a Transit van.

In a letter to Roberts, dated 12 December 2006, the Parole Board refused to recommend his release, stating:

> While in open conditions, you demonstrated that you are untrustworthy, utterly egocentric and highly manipulative. In your evidence at the hearing, it was plain that you had no appreciation of why your dishonest and devious conduct might be regarded by others as giving rise to serious concerns about the risks that you pose.

In August 2007 Roberts' cell was searched by Derbyshire Police, who took possession of all the documents there; a man alleged to have supplied documents to Roberts was arrested, and correspondence and a computer were seized. The Treasury Solicitor obtained an injunction prohibiting the media from publishing any details contained in these documents.

Roberts has always completely rejected any and all of the allegations made by the Cartwright family as to his alleged misconduct and has denied any knowledge of the depredations of others. It is of small comfort to the family, who believe that they are in constant danger, even now.

Manipulating the system to its fullest extent, Roberts has nevertheless continued to apply for parole. He has, however, received fierce opposition to his applications.

★   ★   ★

Gillian Wombwell did not see the trial at the Old Bailey. The young widow was utterly consumed with grief; as she told me, "I didn't know what was going on for two years after it happened. I was existing in a grey existence." Her children grew up; Daen joined the army and now lives in the USA. Melanie has her own business. "I wasn't angry at the time," recalled Mrs Wombwell, "but over the years, I get angrier and angrier, especially when parole for Roberts comes up."

David Wombwell's father, Kenneth, had brought his son up single-handedly following divorce from his wife, and he was remembered by former Police Sergeant 38 'F' Derek Foskett, who had trained and supervised David as a young probationer. Foskett recalled Kenneth Wombwell as being "a very quiet man, very similar to Dave, had not remarried and was the one who had the greater influence on Dave. He was a lovely man and we kept in touch for some time." Referring to her father-in-law, Gillian Wombwell said, "[he] was devastated to lose his only child and never recovered from the trauma. He championed the cause to keep the public safe from Harry Roberts."

Kenneth Wombwell had devoted himself to his grandchildren; they were a very close-knit family, and when he died on the way to church in the late 1990s, it was Gillian who took up the cudgels. Since that time, she has badgered every Home Secretary to keep Roberts behind bars.

In 2009 she attended a parole hearing. For ten minutes she addressed the parole board, reading from a statement prepared by her son, Daen:

> Every member of a democratic society is given the benefit of the doubt and enjoys freedom of movement and choice. However, when they commit murder they forfeit that right, as the Government is required to protect the ordinary member of society from danger. It is the hope of most that when someone goes to prison, they learn and reform. If they try hard at this, they may earn the right to freedom but this should only be awarded if that person can convince the Government beyond any doubt that they will be a safe addition to society.
>
> In the time Harry Roberts has been in prison and even when on parole he has done nothing to indicate that he is safe to

release back to society. He has consistently shown that he will do whatever it takes to get what he wants. The law is nothing more than an inconvenience to him and he lacks the fundamental judgement to know the difference between right and wrong – he can only understand what he wants. Worse, he thinks of himself as some sort of a crime hero and has adopted that persona; it is all he has. It is therefore highly likely that if released he will recommit a crime.

If the Government releases a person of this kind back into society, they are failing the most important thing the electorate charges them with – the protection of everyday persons.

From a personal perspective, we will always be seen to be biased, because of the harm Roberts did to our family. My father will never be given the chance Roberts is asking for, the family will never get to see their father, regain the lost opportunities, enjoy the very thing most children and wives have – which is the experience of having a father or soul mate. Those things are deprived of us because of Roberts and unless you have experienced it, it is impossible to describe the pain of a wound that will never heal. Because of this, I would ask the Government officials who consider his case these two questions:

Is he really someone that should be given the benefit of the doubt? If it was your family, would you want him free to be near them?

The letter is signed Daen Wombwell and is followed by the words, 'son of a murdered father' – who after 42 years still <u>every</u> day remembers and feels what has been lost. There is no parole for me or my family.

The moving contents of this letter were not lost on the Parole Board, who refused to authorize Roberts' release.

They were not lost on Roberts, either. Whilst Mrs Wombwell read out her son's statement, Roberts sat there, arms folded, looking at her and smirking. Why not? He had a small army of lawyers, paid out of the public purse, to do his bidding. Most importantly, he was the centre of attention. Harry Roberts was well-fed, toned from the gym, healthy and confident. It was rather difficult to associate him with the unshaven, dishevelled creature who had crawled out of a hide forty-three years earlier, whimpering plaintively to his captors, "Don't shoot ..."

Does evil only exist as a concept or a perception? Or can a man's personality be so utterly warped and degraded, with no redeeming features whatsoever, that he epitomizes evil?

Ask Prisoner No. 231191.

CHAPTER 7

Hiding Behind the Law

I was having a drink with Jack, an old 'B' Special, in a discreet bar off the Shankill Road in Belfast, and during the course of our ruminations (or *craic* – pronounced 'crack' – as Jack would have described our discourse) he mentioned reminiscently, "Sure, if we'd had our way when the Troubles started, we'd have cracked a few of those Provie bastards over the head with our batons and that would've been the end of it. Fancy another?"

Perhaps Jack's solution to ending 'the Troubles' as soon as they began was rather simplistic, but the fact remains that when tension flared up in the Province in 1969 the Irish Republican Army (IRA) was woefully ill-equipped to stage an all-out campaign. The 'B' Specials, who were almost exclusively Protestants (or Loyalists), had been formed in 1920 to supplement the Royal Irish Constabulary and later the Royal Ulster Constabulary (RUC) in the fight against violent nationalism. The IRA and their supporters suffered from the enthusiastically wielded 'B' Specials' batons, but following rioting in Londonderry and Belfast in 1969, when the first 6,000 British troops were called into the Province, an enquiry was conducted by Lord Scarman. As a result, Home Secretary James Callaghan commissioned Lord Hunt (of Everest fame) to advise on the policing situation. Hunt recommended the disbanding of the 'B' Specials, and the day after this was brought into effect, the police were unable to contain the rioting in the Protestant Shankill Road, which developed into a gun battle. A rather naïve senior officer at Scotland Yard suggested the use of horses to curb the demonstrators. "Not at all," replied his RUC counterpart laconically. "They might eat them."

So my friend Jack's uncomplicated plan to deal with civil insurrection died stillborn, the politicians procrastinated, the IRA became stronger, their supporters supplied them with money and munitions and they grew more cunning and daring, so much so that in 1974 they launched a mainland campaign. It was a repeat of their offensive in London and the Home Counties in 1939, with one subtle difference. Thirty-five years previously, when IRA killers were convicted of murder, they were hanged. Now, the death penalty had been rescinded. If they were caught, the terrorists could receive long prison sentences and still be martyrs, without the inconvenience of losing their lives.

There had been a series of bombings at Birmingham, Guildford and Woolwich, with substantial loss of life and damage to property, and Commander Bob Huntley BEM, QPM, was detached from his duties at C1 Department at the Yard and told to take control of the Bomb Squad as a separate unit. Bombs were thrown into the Naval and Military Club in Piccadilly and the Cavalry Club; it can only be assumed that the Special Forces Club was spared because its whereabouts were so shrouded in mystery that not even London taxi drivers knew its location. There was a spate of shootings: the Churchill Hotel was sprayed with bullets, and a stockbroker named Allan Quartermaine was shot dead in his chauffeur-driven car when it stopped at traffic lights. The bullets from the two incidents matched.

After 1974 came to a close, there was no let-up to the atrocities in the New Year. The bombings and shootings continued, and on the night of 27 January 1975 there were seven separate explosions across London in which eighty-five pounds of high explosive were used. Then everything went quiet. It was as though the terrorists had used up their entire stock of munitions. In fact, on 11 February the IRA called for an indefinite truce with the British Government so that discussions could take place on the future of the Province. It is entirely possible that this was a ploy to enable the terrorists in London – or Active Service Units (ASU) as they were known – to rearm. But who were they? How many of them were there? Where was their base? Did they have more than one location?

No one knew. It would take a tragedy to uncover the first of their bases.

★   ★   ★

In spite of the terrorist attacks, crime in London – of the common or garden variety – still went on. There had been a spate of daytime housebreakings in and around the West Kensington area, so four plain clothes officers from Hammersmith police station were deployed to carry out surveillance in that area at ten o'clock in the morning of 26 February 1975. The officers – Temporary Detective Constables (TDCs) Derek Wilson and Kenneth Matthews and Police Constables 255 'F' Adrian Blackledge and 419 'F' Les White – were in radio communication with each other and the station.

By mid-morning Wilson and Matthews were patrolling Charleville Road, and, one street away to the south, Blackledge went to the area of Fairholme Road because a number of burglaries had been reported there. His partner White had gone north to the roof of Barton Court in Barons Court Road, from where he had an overview of the area. Blackledge walked along Fairholme Road to the junction with Challoner Street, and from a staircase in Challoner Court he was able to keep observation on the length of Fairholme Road. At one o'clock Blackledge noticed a man walking along Challoner Street and turning right into Fairholme Road.

The man was aged twenty-five to thirty, heavily built, with a slightly tanned complexion, straight, light brown collar-length hair and wearing a light, close-check fawn jacket, fawn trousers, a blue, round-necked T-shirt and brown shoes. But though the man's appearance was unremarkable, his behaviour was odd; as he walked along the north footway towards the junction with Vereker Road, he stopped, looked both ways along Fairholme Road, crossed the road, stopped again and looked up and down the road once more. Then he started to walk towards the junction with Vereker Road again before he stopped, turned and retraced his steps along Fairholme Road; and as he reached the junction with Challoner Street, he turned right, walked towards the junction with Perham Road and turned right into that thoroughfare. Because the man was acting in such a shifty, suspicious manner, Blackledge decided to follow him. Entering Perham Road, Blackledge saw the man, who was about fifty yards ahead of him, turn into Vereker Road. Blackledge hurried up to the junction but when he looked down Vereker Road there was no sign of his quarry, and he assumed that the man had turned left into Fairholme Road. Blackledge ran to the junction and looked left, just in time to hear a door slam behind him; he turned towards the source of the noise and fixed his gaze on the door of 39 Fairholme Road. There was no trace of the suspect in the street, therefore it was reasonable to assume it was No. 39 that he had entered. He radioed his partner White, who met him at the junction. Both officers sat on the step of the first house, 43 Fairholme Road, to see if the man would emerge from No. 39; their presence attracted the attention of the occupier of the house, who asked them what they were doing; the officers identified themselves and told her they were looking for a burglary suspect.

After half an hour the two officers got up and walked the length of Fairholme Road, looking in basement areas for signs of a break-in, but without success. At 1.40 they were in Challoner Street, and

White – with hindsight, rather unwisely – went to get some lunch; but Blackledge, who having seen the man's bizarre behaviour sensed he was on to something, returned to his original first-floor observation post to see if the suspect would emerge from the house.

Within ten minutes he did. Blackledge saw the man walk towards him, turn left into Challoner street, then right into Charleville Road and then into North End Road. With Blackledge following, the man stopped at a bus stop. There Blackledge approached him and produced his warrant card, saying, "Excuse me, guv, police from Hammersmith."

"What's that?" asked the man, who spoke with an Irish accent and was studying the warrant card. "What does that mean? That doesn't mean anything to me." Blackledge let him read his warrant card, whereupon the man replied, "OK, all right."

"Where have you just been?" asked Blackledge.

"Round the corner – why?"

"I want to know where you have just been," persisted Blackledge.

"I don't think you've got any right to ask me," replied the man, adding, "Besides, how do I know who you are?"

Rapidly tiring of this evasiveness, Blackledge replied, "I'm a police officer, you've seen my identification and I've got every right to ask you questions if I think you're acting suspiciously." Noticing by now that the man was extremely nervous, he added firmly, "If you like, I'll get on my radio and get a uniformed officer here."

"No, that's all right," he replied. "You're obviously a copper."

"Right," said Blackledge. "Where have you been?"

"A friend's place."

"Where is that?"

"Just round the corner."

"Yes, but where?"

"Fairholme Road," answered the man, "but I don't know the number. I know it, but just as – you know ..." His answer tailed off, and Blackledge thought that he meant he knew the address by sight.

Blackledge asked the man his details, and received the reply that he was William Rogers (in fact, Rogers was his mother's maiden name) of 213 North End Road, W14. "Have you got anything in your pockets to verify who you are?" asked Blackledge, and stepping back, the man replied, "No."

"Why are you so nervous?" asked Blackledge. "What have you got to hide?"

"Nothing," replied the man.

"All right, empty your pockets," said Blackledge. As he later told me, "I thought, this bloke must have something on him."

"All right, let's go back to my friend's flat, if that will satisfy you," was the reply, and the man started to walk off along North End Road towards the junction with Charleville Road. Blackledge caught up with him, took hold of his left arm and said, "You are either going to be searched here, or back at the police station." The man then pulled out a wad of brown bank notes which he said were Irish £5 notes, but that was not in itself really odd because there was a large Irish community in the area, many of them in the building trade and used to being paid in cash.

What was suspicious was the man's generally shifty, evasive behaviour. He also produced a key on a ring which he stated was for his front door. Pointing to the man's right inside breast pocket, Blackledge asked, "Have you got anything inside your inside pocket?" But it was from his left inside pocket that he produced a brown, fold-over wallet.

Blackledge attempted to call the station on his radio, without success, and the man then made a sudden dash across North End Road. Blackledge gave chase and caught up with him near the junction with Charleville Road, but the man evaded him and continued running until he turned left into Castletown Road. Blackledge was calling for assistance on his radio, since his suspicions were half-confirmed that he was dealing with a daytime burglar. But he was wrong.

The man's name was William Joseph Quinn, he was a member of an Active Service Unit and about as dangerous as they come.

★ ★ ★

The man who was known to his compatriots as 'Yankee Joe' (and also Liam Quinn) was born in the Sunset district of San Francisco in 1949 and became a devoted supporter of the Republican movement in Ireland. His parents – his mother was a school clerk, his father a motor mechanic – were not politically minded and were unaware of their son's growing fixation with Northern Ireland. But after Quinn dropped out of high school he learnt Gaelic, read books on Irish history and on the evening news watched the civil rights marches which were being held against an ever more troubled background in the Province. He helped set up the San Francisco chapter of Irish Northern Aid (Noraid). He gave up his job as a postal worker in California in 1971 and travelled to Ireland; with his American passport and a lack of previous convictions, he had no trouble entering the country and even less in becoming a member of the IRA. He adopted an Irish accent and in 1975 replaced terrorist Brendan Dowd as an ASU member and moved in with two fellow terrorists at 39 Fairholme Road. The first, Harry Duggan, had been born in Kilburn; in 1973 his parents were untruthfully told that he had been 'killed in action in the north' and that he had been buried in Feakle, Co. Clare. The other, Hugh Doherty, had tried to emigrate to Canada as a carpenter in the early 1970s, but the Canadian authorities had refused him a visa, possibly on the grounds that his brother Pat was vice-president of Sinn Féin.

Quinn's terrorist credentials were sound. Prior to moving in, his fingerprints had been linked with the use of four explosive devices. The first was on 18 January 1974, when a bomb concealed in a hollowed-out copy of the Bible was sent to the London address of Bishop Gerard William Tickle, the Roman Catholic Bishop to the British Armed Forces; fortunately, the device was defused. The next two recipients of letter bombs were not so fortunate. John Huxley Buzzard (later His Honour Judge Buzzard), then Senior Treasury Counsel prosecuting in a number of high-profile cases, was at home on 30 January when a parcel was delivered to his Surrey address. As he unwrapped the package, it partially exploded, causing the loss of two fingertips on his left hand and lacerations to his face, hands and wrist. Five days later, a letter was sent to Sir Max Aitken, chairman of the *Daily Express*, but after it was half opened by his secretary, suspicions were roused, and a security guard was called. As he picked up the package, this device also partly exploded, and the guard lost most of the fingers of his left hand. On 27 January 1975 a bomb contained in a black bag which had been found on the steps of the Charcoburger Grill in Heath Street, London, was successfully defused, unlike the seven other devices which were detonated in London on the same evening.

In addition, Quinn was linked through association with his colleagues to two other explosive devices, one in the foyer of Aldershot Railway Station, the other in the entrance to the King's Arms public house, Warminster. Fortunately, both were defused.

These were the qualifications of the man who was now fleeing along Charleville Road towards the junction with Gledstanes Road, with PC Blackledge in hot pursuit. Both men ran past TDCs Wilson and Matthews, who joined in the pursuit. It was then that a fourth man entered the chase.

★   ★   ★

Twenty-one-year-old Police Constable Stephen Andrew Tibble had just finished tinkering with his 125cc Honda motorcycle at the rear of the police married quarters in Auriol Road, West Kensington, where he lived with his wife Kathryn in the ground-floor flat. Doug MacDonald was a probationary police constable at Fulham police station who lived on the top floor of the flats, and he and his wife left the building as Tibble completed work on his Honda. "I've got it going!" said Tibble exultantly, and the Macdonalds smiled and walked away towards North End Road. Tibble rode off on the motorcycle to report for duty at Fulham.

It was as Tibble was driving along that he saw the running men and joined in the chase. Wilson heard the sound of the motorcycle's engine and stepped out into the road, waving his warrant card and shouting for the driver, who was dressed in jeans and an anorak, to give him a lift. Although Tibble paused, it is difficult to say whether he heard what Wilson said or whether he thought that he would do better by himself, but he accelerated past the officers and Quinn and reached the junction. Tibble then dismounted and barred Quinn's way, crouching low with his arms outstretched, obviously intending to grab hold of him; but Quinn drew out a Browning pistol and at practically point-blank range shot Tibble twice in the chest, a third bullet nicking another part of his body and ending up in a nearby doorway.

It was suggested that other shots rang out – possibly intended for his pursuers, but no one was hurt (and Blackledge was not aware of any further shots) – and Quinn turned north into Gledstanes Road towards Comeragh Road, which would provide access to Talgarth Road, the busy thoroughfare of the A4, and Barons Court Underground Station. A nearby resident, Mrs Tania Lee, had heard the shots, saw Tibble crash face-first onto the pavement, telephoned for the police and an ambulance and ran into the street carrying a blanket which she placed under Tibble's head. The fatally injured young man took off his motorcycle helmet and Blackledge heard him say, "Oh, please God, help me – I'm a police officer," and then, as Blackledge told me, "His eyes rolled back." Wilson arrived on the scene and used his radio to inform Hammersmith police station of what had happened, then mounted Tibble's discarded motorcycle and took up the pursuit of Quinn; however, unused to a Japanese motorcycle, he experienced grave difficulty in pushing the machine to its full potential. He saw the fugitive turn left into Comeragh Road, then right into Palliser Road and head directly towards the Underground Station. Wilson was giving a commentary on his personal radio, but was experiencing a number of difficulties with transmission and reception. The radio was on the Hammersmith police frequency but the location was right on the borders with the frequency used by Fulham police station, so signals were at their weakest. The signals were breaking up, nobody was taking proper control of the communications at the police station, many officers were transmitting at the same time and when Wilson informed the other officers that Quinn was heading for Barons Court Underground Station, it was thought that he had actually entered the station premises.

Police Constable 184 'B' Peter Westley was the RT operator on Kensington's area car, 'Bravo Two', and because he was an authorized shot, he was recalled to the police station, issued with a Webley revolver and sent with another authorized shot and a dog handler into Earl's Court Underground Station. "We made sure the current had been switched off and then we set off along the tunnel towards Barons Court; we had to be careful because we knew an armed team from Barons Court was coming towards us."

Recounting this episode to me thirty-six years later, Westley discovered for the first time – as undoubtedly many other officers who were there at the time did – that the killer had never entered the Underground Station; Wilson later lost Quinn, after he ran into a block of flats off Talgarth Road and out the other side.

Meanwhile, TDC Matthews also made a telephone call for assistance, and an ambulance and PC White arrived. Blackledge, who had been tending Tibble, now got into the area car, 'Foxtrot One', to help chase the suspect. Now, thirty-six years since that traumatic incident, the order of events are somewhat hazy in Blackledge's memory. Blackledge had returned to the scene, and a detective inspector arrived and asked him to provide a description of the gunman to a group of officers; having done so, Blackledge asked on the radio for a senior officer to meet him at 39 Fairholme Road. A uniformed inspector arrived and Blackledge told him, "This is the premises he went into and came out from." There were two rooms in the basement; one was unlocked, and as he entered it Blackledge realized he had been in the room before. Some time previously, he had been checking premises as part of an anti-burglary campaign and it had been his practice, when he found a property which was insecure, to leave a note with his name and police station in order that crime prevention could be discussed. Now, entering the room, he saw his original note tucked into the corner of a mirror. "It gave me an odd feeling," he told me. However, the door to the other room was locked; it would not be opened until later, and then under the provisions of a search warrant.

Tibble, meanwhile, had been rushed to Charing Cross Hospital, Fulham Palace Road, which had opened two years previously on the site of the old Fulham Hospital. He was immediately operated on but he had lost a great deal of blood, one of the bullets severing his aorta. His young wife Kathryn had been brought by police car from the bank where she worked in Brentford, but within two hours of admittance to the hospital, poor, brave Stephen Tibble was dead. Richard Swarbrick was then a detective constable at Hammersmith and it was his unhappy task to be the exhibits officer at the post-mortem. Tony Holt, who was then the detective inspector at Fulham, described Tibble to me as being "one of the nicest young men that I came across during my service, with ambitions for the CID." These aspirations were now never to be fulfilled; Tibble, who had graduated top of his class at Hendon with 80 marks out of a possible 100, had served just 199 days in the Metropolitan Police.

Doug Macdonald had gone to his bank when he heard the wailing two-tones of police cars. "Your lot are busy today," commented a cashier, and as MacDonald emerged into the street he saw the Fulham area car, 'Foxtrot One', at a road junction. He walked over and asked "What's up?" The driver recognized him and said, "Hello, Doug – it appears a PC's been shot."

MacDonald had no idea who it was until later when a Press reporter knocked on his front door and asked, "PC MacDonald? Did you know Stephen Tibble?" It was only by the reporter's use of the past tense that MacDonald realized his near-neighbour had not just been shot, but was now dead.

★   ★   ★

The search of 39 Fairholme Road revealed an interesting treasure trove of intelligence and evidence. There was no trace of the tenants of two of the flats in the building, but the landlord, David Ahmed, described Harry Duggan (whom he knew as Michael Wilson) as renting the basement flat and Hugh Doherty (who had adopted the alias John Anderson) as using one of the other rooms. They had been joined a few weeks previously by 'William Rogers', better known to his associates as William Joseph Quinn.

There were sufficient explosives in the rooms to manufacture half a dozen bombs, together with detonators, timers and wires. There were documents, books, maps and plans for fresh attacks on property and persons. Best of all, there were fingerprints, a lot of them. Quinn's fingerprints were found on a road map, a plate, a knife, a mug and an ashtray; but at that time Quinn's fingerprints were not on file anywhere, so the identity of the maker of these prints remained a mystery to the police.

★   ★   ★

The inquest opened briefly on 4 March 1975 and was adjourned for a month, but not before the coroner, Dr John Burton, heard an outline of the circumstances of the incident from the officer leading the murder aspect of the investigation, Detective Chief Superintendent Robert Wilson, who also told him:

> I would like to bring to your notice the brave conduct of PC Tibble who, obviously seeing the man was armed, endeavoured to stop him, and likewise the three officers who went in pursuit of the suspect, having seen one of their colleagues shot.

The coroner agreed that there was no doubt that Tibble was standing right in front of the gunman, trying to stop him, and added, "Quite clearly from the evidence and what we have seen, he knew what he was doing and he knew it was his duty."

★   ★   ★

Stephen Tibble's funeral was held at Mortlake Crematorium on Monday, 10 March 1975, and the forty-minute service was conducted by the Reverend S. E. Barrington; he had married Stephen and Kathryn two years previously. Stephen's parents, Mr and Mrs D. M. D. Tibble, were in attendance, as were members of 3rd Osterley Sea Scouts, whose leader Stephen had been, plus members of his cricket club from Ockham, Surrey. The club's president, Julian Boyle, described him as 'Mr Sunshine'.

Twenty-year-old Kathryn Tibble had asked that the service should be open to whoever wished to attend; and many did. Seven of Stephen's colleagues accompanied the hearse – Police Constables Gerry Gallagher, Morgan O'Grady, Owen Griffin, Neil McAlpine, Peter Cormack and Roger Joyce – led by Police Sergeant Bill Payne. The six constables – "all six feet two, or taller", as Morgan O'Grady told me – carried the coffin, draped in the Service flag, into the chapel where it rested on the catafalque. The Commissioner, Sir Robert Mark GBE, QPM, read the lesson from 1 Corinthians, verse 15 and also made a moving tribute, ending with the words, "Stephen Tibble shall not be forgotten. We and the public he served so selflessly are forever in his debt." The congregation sang traditional hymns: 'The

Lord's my shepherd', 'Abide with me', 'Jerusalem' and 'O God our help in ages past'.

Sir Robert was not the only senior officer there; chief constables attended, as well as 500 other police officers. Chief Superintendent Fred Sargeant from Fulham thanked the officers who had arrived from far and wide – Merseyside, Carlisle and Yorkshire – and masses of floral tributes filled the chapel.

Nor did appreciation of Stephen Tibble's short life stop there; a charity football match between Chelsea and Fulham was held on 14 April to raise money for the Police Dependants' Trust, and there was a gala night at the Hammersmith Palais. The Chief Constable of the RUC, Sir Jamie Flanagan CBE (highly regarded by his men as a 'Copper's Copper' and the first Catholic to be head of Ulster's police force), sent a cheque for £1,000 on behalf of the RUC, and a great deal of money was raised for Kathryn, who received a widow's pension of £17.83 per week.

Adrian Blackledge had been badly shocked and severely traumatized by the sight of a murder committed in front of his eyes; nevertheless, on the day following the shooting he went to a studio at Putney Park Lane, SW15, where at Blackledge's instruction, an artist, Mr Worsley, drew a picture of the gunman which Blackledge declared to be "an excellent likeness". But after a couple of tough months assisting the murder investigation, Blackledge very sensibly took leave and was recuperating at his parents' house in Chorley, Lancashire, when in the early hours of Wednesday, 14 May he received a telephone call from Deputy Assistant Commissioner Ernie Bond OBE, QPM. A very tough former member of the wartime Special Air Service, Bond was also a compassionate man, who was adored by his officers, and now he mysteriously told Blackledge, "I want you to go to Dublin, where you'll be met." And so, later that morning, Blackledge was driven to Manchester Airport by his parents, where for the first time in his life he boarded an aeroplane; upon arrival in Dublin, he was met by Detective Chief Superintendent Rollo Watts of Special Branch, a dapper man with a moustache.

Watts took Blackledge to the police headquarters in Dublin, where he explained that a man had been detained by the *Garda Siochána na hÉireann* (literally, 'Guardians of the Peace') who, it was suspected, could have been responsible for the murder of Tibble. He stated that the man would be appearing that day at the Special Criminal Court and that arrangements were being made for Blackledge to see the suspect in the company of others, with a view to possible identification. Blackledge was unaware why the man had been arrested; in fact, he had been charged with membership of the IRA. "Mr Watts impressed upon me that I was under no obligation whatsoever to effect any identification, and that if I did not see any person whom I recognized I was to say so and not endeavour in any way to effect what could be considered a doubtful identification," said Blackledge.

At noon, Blackledge walked into court and instantly recognized the man whom he had known as 'Rogers'; he informed Watts of his positive identification and both men left the court. When he returned a few moments later a witness had just finished giving evidence, and Blackledge heard the judge say, "William Joseph Quinn, you have heard this officer's evidence; have you any questions you wish to put to him?"

Quinn did have some questions; and, as Blackledge later said, as soon as Quinn started speaking, "The accent I heard him use in the court room was an unmistakably American accent and quite different from the Irish accent which I had heard him speak with, to me."

However, this difference in accents in no way shook Blackledge's recognition of the man whom he had seen shoot Stephen Tibble, and he and Watts left the court. He would not see Quinn again for another thirteen years.

A decision was made not to attempt extradition proceedings, which might well prove lengthy, difficult and, possibly, ultimately unsuccessful. Believing that following his release from the twelve-month prison sentence which he received, Quinn would return to the mainland where links might be made with his associates (and where he could also be arrested for the murder of PC Tibble with the minimum of fuss), Quinn was left to serve his sentence in Portlaoise Prison. But on 2 January 1976 Quinn was released – and vanished.

Meanwhile, with their hideout at Fairholme Road well and truly compromised, Doherty and Duggan split up, Doherty moving in with fellow terrorist Eddie Butler at 61 Crouch Hill, Islington, and Duggan sharing a flat with Joe O'Connell at 99 Milton Grove, Hackney. It was at the latter address that an IRA 'Death List' was later found, containing 325 names of prominent politicians, peers, military leaders, police and businessmen listed for execution. Included in the list were Margaret Thatcher, Edward Heath, James Callaghan, William Whitelaw, Denis Healey, Sir Keith Joseph, Roy Jenkins and Michael Heseltine. The ASU would continue their terrorist activities – and the police were still unaware of their identities – until 6 December 1975, when following a shoot-out with the police, the four men took an elderly couple hostage in their flat at

22b Balcombe Street for six days. This heroic band cravenly surrendered after misinformation suggested that the Special Air Service was about to take a decisive role in the proceedings (which of necessity would <u>not</u> have included peaceful negotiations), and the following year at the Old Bailey all were sentenced to concurrent terms of life imprisonment. The gun used to murder PC Tibble was found, with a great deal of other terrorist paraphernalia, at Balcombe Street.

By now, quite a lot was known about Quinn, including the fact that he came from San Francisco, and it was thought that at some time in the future he would return there. In 1979, he did.

Quinn's presence was not detected immediately, but by 1981 the relationship between Prime Minister Margaret Thatcher and US President Ronald Reagan had led to a far more sympathetic American attitude to Britain's campaign against the IRA. The Director of Public Prosecutions issued an arrest warrant in respect of the bombings and the murder of PC Tibble. A tip-off sent Federal Bureau of Investigation (FBI) officers to his uncle's stationery store in Daly City, California, where Quinn was working. Some covert purchases of notepaper and typing paper were made, and when fingerprints were lifted from them they matched those of Quinn, both on file and also on the wrapper of one of the letter-bombs. Scotland Yard was alerted and Detective Inspectors Alec Edwards – a former Flying Squad officer who had previously worked on the 'Bertie' Smalls Supergrass case – and Alan Lewis, a Bomb Squad officer of long standing, flew out to San Francisco. They took no part in the arrest on 30 September 1981 which was the result of a provisional arrest warrant issued by a United States magistrate acting on behalf of the United Kingdom, but a long legal battle ensued.

Quinn argued that the offences were 'of a political nature', but on 29 September 1982 the magistrate rejected Quinn's defence and issued a Certificate of Extraditability and Order of Commitment to the Secretary of State. In turn, Quinn filed a petition with the district court for a writ of habeas corpus for the United States Marshals to release him. US District Judge Robert P. Aguilar accepted that there was a political uprising in Northern Ireland and ordered Quinn's release, but Judge Mary Schroeder of the 9th Circuit Court blocked his release, following the US Government's appeal on behalf of the British Government.

In February 1986 Circuit Judges Duniway, Fletcher and Reinhardt decided that Quinn should be extradited for the murder of PC Tibble, but sent the case back to the San Francisco federal district court to determine if the statute of limitations had run out in respect of the terrorist bombing charges. Eventually, it was decided to drop the terrorist charges – it also meant that upon his return to the United Kingdom, Quinn could not be further charged with those offences – but the fact that Quinn was extradited at all was due to the magnificent work of Assistant District Attorney Mark N. Zanides who, as Alan Lewis later told me, "really pushed for the British Government, all the way through."

After spending five years in San Francisco County Jail, Quinn made a last-ditch stand to convince the authorities that Tibble's murder was a political offence and therefore not covered by the extradition treaty. However, the US Supreme Court refused to hear the case, and a week later, on 21 October 1986, a Royal Air Force jet landed at Brize Norton and Detective Chief Inspectors Edwards and Lewis, together with William Joseph Quinn, disembarked and stepped into a police helicopter which took them to Paddington Green high security police station. Quinn was the first member of the IRA to be successfully extradited from the United States to the United Kingdom.

"Quinn was a total professional," Lewis told me. "He would have a smile and a chat but never gave anything away."

The bundle of documents which pointed to Quinn's complicity in the terrorist outrages was huge, but when I saw Alec Edwards take Quinn into Lambeth Magistrates' Court to commit him to the Old Bailey just for the murder of Stephen Tibble, the committal documents were very slim indeed. At his five-day trial in February 1988, Quinn pleaded not guilty to the murder of PC Tibble, claiming mistaken identity. The defence, led by Michael Mansfield QC, agreed that the man in the Dublin courtroom was Quinn, but disputed that it was he who had shot Tibble. It was suggested that Blackledge (by now a detective sergeant working from Chelsea police station) was under pressure to identify somebody for the offence – who just happened to be Quinn. The jury deliberated for two hours and forty minutes before convicting him, and the trial judge, Mr Justice Rose, told him:

> It was an appalling, cold-blooded killing, untinged by any remorse on your part and motivated no doubt by the terrorist activities on which at that time you were engaged. You shot repeatedly and at point-blank range at a man who was in fact a police officer, though you could not have known he was other than an ordinary member of the public.

In case anyone in the packed courtroom at the Old Bailey had any doubts regarding Quinn's lack of remorse, the man who had spent years cowering behind a team of legal experts, backed by Irish sympathizers and furiously attempting to exploit every legal loophole, now grinned contemptuously as he was sentenced to life imprisonment. It had taken thirteen years, almost to the day, for justice to be done, although many police officers and the loved ones of PC Tibble did not view it in that light. Quinn was repatriated under the Good Friday Agreement and had served eleven years before being released on 9 April 1999 from Portlaoise Prison, fifty miles west of Dublin.

A memorial was erected in Charleville Road where Stephen Tibble was murdered, and on 18 June 1976 he was posthumously awarded the Queen's Police Medal for gallantry.

A sober footnote was provided by former Detective Sergeant Dave 'Sandy' Sanderson, who instructed a Beat Crimes Course at Peel House in 1975. A tough veteran of the Kenya Rifles, Sandy believed in making his lectures as realistic as possible, and one of his lessons was on the subject of stopping and searching suspects. To this end, he would secrete forged currency, cannabis, and a stolen credit card in his clothing in order to see how adroit his pupils were in discovering the suspicious items and how intelligent their questioning of him was. "I remember Stephen Tibble," he told me. "Very bright and always asking the right questions." But the one item the students never found was a small derringer pistol – and Tibble was no exception. And as soon as the student had completed the search, Sandy would whip out the pistol, point it at them and say, "Bang, bang – you're dead!"

"I thought about that after I heard he'd been murdered," Sandy told me. "I felt awful." It was an understandable emotion, although Sandy's remorse at his role-play was certainly more profound than Quinn's, which was non-existent.

⋆   ⋆   ⋆

Derek Wilson was deservedly awarded a commissioner's high commendation for the chase on Tibble's motorcycle. However, the last word must go to Adrian Blackledge, who was also commended for his part in chasing Quinn and who retired with the rank of detective inspector after thirty years' service. He told me, "Every year on 26 February at two o'clock, I stop and think about what happened. It has never left me."

CHAPTER 8

Carnage – the Harrods Bombing

When an habitué of the Special Forces Club described Harrods to me as being 'the Knightsbridge Souk' it did make me chuckle; although since the former owner, the controversial and colourful Mohamed Al-Fayed, stepped down, it is just possible that expulsions of pent-up breath, signalling sighs of relief (including those from members of the Royal Family), have been heard throughout London. But that is neither here nor there; arguably, Harrods remains London's most prestigious store.

★   ★   ★

Charles Henry Harrod, a draper and wholesale grocer, first opened his shop in Knightsbridge in 1849. Following a fire which gutted the store thirty-four years later, work commenced to rebuild the premises at its present five-acre site in the Brompton Road, and it was completed in 1905.

Before and since the fire of 1883, the name of Harrods has been synonymous with luxury goods and large, opulent surroundings. Over the years, the great and the good have flocked to the store: Oscar Wilde, Lillie Langtry, Noël Coward, Laurence Olivier and Vivien Leigh and members of the Royal Family. Harrods has over 1,000,000 square feet of selling space (Selfridges in Oxford Street has only half that) to house its 330 departments, and it caters for every requirement – jewellery, sporting equipment, food and drink, furniture, bridal trousseaus and pets. This last possibly included an Egyptian cobra, to guard a pair of ruby, sapphire and diamond encrusted sandals, valued at £62,000 in 2007. There are thirty-two restaurants catering for a miscellany of tastes, a bank, financial services, tailors and a food and wine delivery service. There is also a dress code, designed to keep the riff-raff out and enforced by courteous uniformed security officers. For those who can afford it, Harrods' motto, *Omnia Omnibus Ubique* ('All Things for All People Everywhere') has a ring of authenticity about it.

The staff of 5,000 from fifty different countries cater for customers who, on peak days, can number 300,000 – very much

as they did in the run-up to Christmas, on Saturday, 17
December 1983.

★   ★   ★

On that morning, with the store full of Christmas shoppers, a
blue Austin 1300 GT saloon, registration number KFP 252K
and with a 'Capital Radio' logo across the upper part of the
windscreen and a black vinyl roof, was parked outside Harrods in
Hans Crescent. Since that thoroughfare is a one-way street and
the car was parked the wrong way round, facing the Brompton
Road, it was surprising that, whether or not anybody noticed it,
nobody commented. This was a pity, because the IRA mainland
offensive was at its height and the car's boot was packed with
approximately 25lb of Frangex (a commercial nitroglycerine-
based high explosive), set to be detonated with a timer.

At 12.44 a call was received at the Samaritans' organization
from a soft-spoken man with an Irish accent. In fact, he spoke
so quietly that the operator made three attempts to write down
the message, which was that there were bombs at Harrods, two
inside the store and one in a car outside. The caller stated that
should he telephone again, he would authenticate the call by
using the codeword 'Wonder'. This call was immediately passed
on to Scotland Yard, who informed Chelsea police station and
the store. Pat Hastings, a store detective with the company since
1964, had taken over from the telephone operator when the call
came in and she alerted the management. Frank Nichols, the
chief security officer, and the general manager, Aleck Craddock,
decided not to evacuate the premises, believing that if they did
so, the rush of customers – who at that time numbered 50,000
– might well emerge straight into the blast of any bomb outside
the store. They were right. In fact, there were no explosive
devices inside the store; it was the usual IRA trick designed to
cause maximum panic. It was also a classic manoeuvre to
ensure that there were as many police officers as possible in the
vicinity outside the premises, searching for the bomb, when it
detonated.

Jim Diplock had been the manager of uniform security at
Harrods since 1973 and had a system to deal with this type of
emergency. He sent out a coded call for all the security officers to
come immediately to his office in the basement and handed out
keys for them to search various areas of the store where explosive
devices might be placed; when the search was complete, they
were to report back.

Meanwhile, at Chelsea police station, Chief Inspector Peter Francis was the senior uniformed officer on duty and he was in his office on the top floor, in plain clothes, dealing with paperwork. It was the practice for one of the two chief inspectors to go in on a Saturday morning, check the books and prisoners and then go home at about two o'clock in the afternoon and be 'on call' for the rest of the weekend.

Francis received a telephone call from the duty officer, Inspector Stephen John Dodd, to say that a coded message had been received stating that there was a car bomb in Hans Crescent, outside Harrods. In fact, Chelsea police station had already received twenty-two false alarm calls that day, but this message, Dodd believed, was a genuine one. He had checked with Special Branch and C13 – the Anti-terrorist Squad – and discovered that although the code was authentic, it was an old one. While it was still used in Northern Ireland, code words had not been used on the mainland since 1976.

As well as being colleagues, the two men were good friends, and Dodd was a man to be looked up to, quite literally, because he was six feet seven inches tall. Born in 1949 in Isleworth, Middlesex, Dodd had served as a police cadet, entered the Metropolitan Police immediately afterwards in 1968 and had served a tough apprenticeship as a police constable on 'N' Division. Just how tough that period was is reflected by the injury he sustained during the arrest of a dangerous criminal who had discharged a firearm with intent to resist arrest. Dodd was highly commended for his outstanding courage and devotion to duty by both the commissioner and the judge at the Old Bailey and was awarded £20 from the Bow Street Reward Fund. Promoted to sergeant four months later, Dodd served on 'Y' and 'Z' Divisions before promotion to Inspector brought him to Chelsea in June 1981. Married in 1970, he had three children, Anthony, aged eleven, Melanie, nine, and Susan, seven.

"Steve asked if I wanted to go with him in the car," remembered Francis, "but my life was undoubtedly saved because I was in plain clothes. I asked him to take someone else but to get another car ready, as I had to change into uniform. Instead of me he took Noel Lane, a young sergeant who I had welcomed to Chelsea only a few weeks previously."

Police Sergeant 88 'B' Noel Joseph Lane was born in Reigate in 1955. Previously a technician, he joined the Metropolitan Police in 1977, married eighteen months later, and after working as a constable on the streets of 'L' Division had been promoted to sergeant with just over six years' service and been posted to Chelsea on 3 October 1983.

Because of the approach of Christmas, it had been decided that a police sergeant and nine constables should patrol the immediate vicinity of Harrods during opening hours to deal with pedestrian and vehicular traffic, reported crimes and any other problems which might arise; and now Dodd instructed the group by radio to start searching the area of Hans Crescent to try to locate the bomb. With other officers converging on the scene, there were now almost thirty police officers in the vicinity.

Chief Inspector Francis rushed to the scene in a car driven by a sergeant. In Hans Crescent was Woman Police Constable 481 'B' Jane Philippa Arbuthnot, who was twenty-two and had been born in Rowland's Castle, Hampshire. Formerly a clerk/typist, she was single and shared a flat with her friend Philippa Carlton-Kelly. Jane had joined the Metropolitan Police in 1981, and the whole of her two and a half years' service had been spent at Chelsea. "Jane was a great all-round girl," recalled Police Sergeant Mick Thwaites. "Well-spoken, ambitious and at home in Chelsea. Her father was a retired naval officer and her grandfather a former Chief Constable of Oxfordshire Constabulary."

Jane had gone to the store and seen Pat Hastings, with whom she was friendly; Pat had given her and Police Sergeant John Stanger Harrods' security radios. They had left Harrods via No. 5 door – opposite the suspect vehicle.

As Francis arrived at Harrods, he got out of the car and was walking quickly towards Hans Crescent when at 1.21 the small explosive charge in the detonator, activated by a timer, exploded into the main charge of 25lb of explosive in the vehicle's boot, right next to the petrol tank, which detonated.

There was an initial blue flash, but because it lasted milliseconds, nobody saw it. Then came the blast wave, travelling at supersonic speed, which was so great that it shook London within a five-mile radius and was heard distinctly at distances even further away; it travelled outwards and upwards, spraying razor-sharp fragments of the car body into the air, and was instantly followed by an orange flash. This was the effect of the air rushing back into the vacuum created by the blast where it mixed with the combustible, super-hot gases and instantaneously caught fire, turning into a huge fireball sixty feet in diameter. The flying debris, including metal, glass and masonry, travelling at colossal speed, tore into police officers and passers-by and shattered shop windows. The resultant shards of window glass themselves became weapons, tearing into everything and everyone in their path.

There had been four police officers in the blue Hillman Hunter which had driven into Hans Crescent from Sloane Street and had drawn up opposite the Austin. The driver was Police Sergeant William Kane – he had taken the initial call from the Samaritans – and Police Constable Paul Brogan was in the rear off-side seat. In the front passenger seat was Inspector Dodd, behind him was Noel Lane; both men got out of the nearside of the vehicle. Dodd walked up Hans Crescent to speak to the sergeant in charge of the initial group of constables. Lane walked between the bomb-car and another vehicle. An onlooker saw a police officer – it was obviously Lane – bending down by the Austin, when 'there was a ball of orange flame and the whole car was lifted up.' Parts of the car, including the bonnet, were later found on the sixth-floor balcony of a building, eighty feet above ground level and fifty yards further down the street. Four storeys of Harrods facing Hans Crescent were damaged, and shoppers panicked as broken glass cascaded down on them; in their terror to get away from the scene, they impeded the progress of the police and the ambulance service. Eight of Harrods' green and gold semi-circular window canopies hung in tatters. Two dozen cars in the immediate vicinity were damaged by the flying debris – some burst into flames – although a Rolls-Royce, parked next to the suspect vehicle, sustained only broken windows. The blast sucked the windscreen right out of the Rolls, although it was a tribute to the makers that afterwards the car started first time.

Chief Inspector Francis ran round the corner to see the remains of the suspect vehicle, which were lying upside down on top of a police officer still clutching his radio; that was Noel Lane, and he had died immediately. The car had in fact been blown in two, and the two sections were two yards apart. Only the wheels were intact. Stephen Dodd had suffered appalling injuries to his head after a projectile – part of the bomb-car's engine – struck him. The police car in which he had arrived was on fire; Sergeant Kane had been hit by glass and had a piece of shrapnel in the side of his left eye; and Police Constable Paul Brogan had received a wound in his right ankle which required stitches.

Police Sergeant Andrew Melham and Police Constable Martyn Holgate had arrived prior to the explosion and had met up with Jane Arbuthnot, who had gone in one direction to clear the road. A second woman officer, Pamela White, had gone in the other direction. She had been more fortunate; as the bomb detonated, she was behind a Ford Transit van, which took the force of the blast. Physically she was unharmed, but she suffered the most profound trauma thereafter. Jane Arbuthnot had caught projectiles in her neck and body, had been blown across the road and was killed instantly. Sixty-five years had passed since the formation of London's Women Police, and Jane had been the 6,021st member of it. She was the first to be murdered, but she would not be the last.

PC Holgate's thigh was gashed open by shrapnel and Police Constable Jon Gordon, a dog handler with eight years' service, lost his right leg, his nose (which was found and successfully sewn back on) and his right thumb; in addition, his body was hit by a number of projectiles, and his police dog 'Queenie' had been grievously wounded. "I gave authority for an armed SPG [Special Patrol Group] officer to shoot the Alsatian, which was in a terrible state," recalled Peter Francis. It took three shots to put her down. Far more fortunate was Sasha, a Golden Retriever who was being walked by his owner yards away from the blast; the glass and metal that sliced into his throat were successfully removed at St Stephen's Hospital.

Other police officers were also wounded, fourteen in all. Sergeant Andy Melham, who had shrapnel embedded in his liver, was blown into the gutter and suffered a collapsed lung and severe back injuries. Chris Stanger lost a finger – "He had been a captain in the army," recalled Mick Thwaites, "and had survived several tours in Northern Ireland, only to be hurt in central London." WPC Valerie Claire was badly shocked and her neck muscles were strained. PC Neil Fowler was hit by shrapnel in his left ankle and PC Mark Grover sustained a cut to his right hand. PC Peter Weinberg was hit by flying glass in his right eye. PC Mark Thomas sustained a cut above his left eye, shock and deafness, as did PCs Mark Hird and George Hockney.

There were three more fatalities, just ordinary passers-by. Philip Geddes, a journalist for the *Daily Express*'s William Hickey diary column, aged twenty-four, of Tradescant Road, Lambeth, had been in the store with his girlfriend and caught wind of a good story. He sent the girlfriend away, emerged into Hans Crescent and was killed instantly when a projectile hit him in the chest as he stood on the opposite side of the street to the car bomb. Kenneth Gerald Salvesen, aged twenty-eight, an American citizen of Park Mansions, Kensington, was walking towards the bomb-car and was about ten yards away when the detonation occurred. The projectile which struck him in the left eye killed him instantaneously. Caroline Jasmine Kennedy Cochrane-Patrick, aged twenty-five of Adelaide Court, Hill Road, St John's

Wood, was married to the son of a wealthy Scottish landowner; they had a two-year-old son, James. She was the second-closest person to the car at the time of detonation. She was blasted through a shop window and died instantly. In addition, ninety-six other people were wounded.

Pat Hastings had ascended to the first floor in the escalator and was just about to get into the escalator to the second floor when the bomb exploded. "I was deafened," she told me. Jim Diplock was still in his office in the basement when the explosion shook the store. "I immediately grabbed hold of a First-Aid box," he told me, "because I knew the worst casualties would be from broken glass." Diplock walked outside into the street, which was enveloped in "a haze of brown smoke". The pavements were littered with broken glass from the shop windows – "two or three inches deep," recalled Diplock. "It was like walking on ice."

In describing events like this, it is almost impossible to deal comprehensively and chronologically with all the trauma, death and destruction. Diplock saw Police Sergeant Stanger, who was bleeding badly. Other police officers were arriving to assist. "There were two doctors from the Brompton Hospital who had been out shopping – they helped," remembered Diplock. "I saw an American air hostess, staggering – she was bleeding badly from the stomach." (This was Renee White, a thirty-three-year-old Delta Airlines stewardess from Atlanta, Georgia, who had sustained life-threatening injuries and who was admitted to the intensive care unit at the Westminster Hospital.) "And I saw two women with glass which was embedded in their legs so deep no blood was coming out. There was a dog handler; his dog was peeing itself."

Finally, quietly and sadly, Diplock told me, "I saw Jane Arbuthnot. She was in a terrible state."

One passer-by, cut by flying glass, saw a man with his arm hanging off; another had lost a hand. An Air Malta pilot, Captain Godwin Miceli, was just twenty-five feet away from the car when the bomb exploded and was lifted from his feet and blown against a plate-glass window. "A poor man selling chestnuts on the corner was in a terrible state," he said. "His legs were hanging off."

A huge pall of smoke hung over the scene; Peter Ryan, then a constable, was miles away policing Arsenal football ground (Watford won 3–1), and remembered seeing the smoke ascending, but did not realize the significance of it until the news filtered through later.

Stephanie Smith was on attachment to C13 (the Anti-terrorist Squad) at the time, and she and a companion had initially decided to visit Harrods for a shopping trip but then changed their minds and headed for the Army and Navy Stores in Victoria Street. "On our way there we heard this loud and hollow sound, looked at each other and just said, 'That's a bomb'."

They immediately returned to Scotland Yard. "Innocent people had been killed and badly injured. When we learned that fellow police officers had also been killed, things seemed to step up a notch," Stephanie told me. "Without anyone saying anything, we just seemed to work extra hard. I remember feeling that we were working for them."

Detective Constable Jeff Maund was in the reserve room at C13 when the bomb exploded. He was now in his third year of service with the branch and had attended many bomb scenes. "I … heard a loud crump-type sound and even a slight resonating in the windows. No one needed to be told that a bomb had just gone off and that it was close," he told me. "I grabbed my exhibit bag and other bits of equipment and ran to the lifts." A former Chelsea officer, Maund drove his team in the C13 van to the scene.

Former Chief Inspector Alan Clarke MBE was off-duty at home when he was informed by his chief superintendent of what had happened at Harrods. Clarke was the chief instructor at the Dog Section, his job included the training of explosive detection dogs and he had worked with the Royal Ulster Constabulary in Northern Ireland on several occasions. He was informed that Jon Gordon and his dog had both been badly injured and was tasked to go to Nine Elms police station, which was the Dog Section's operational headquarters and where the search dogs were based. Clarke's task was to liaise with any other units who might require assistance from the Dog Section and make enquiries about the welfare of the dog handlers who had been employed around the area of Harrods. However, Clarke decided to go straight to the scene, where he spoke to the dog handlers. "I also ascertained the situation of PC Gordon's dog, 'Queenie', whose body was lying near to where the car had exploded," Clarke recalled. "We eventually buried her at the Dog Training Establishment." As he left the scene, an attempt was being made to lift the remains of the Austin 1300 off the body of Noel Lane.

'Queenie' was also seen by Munna Malik, a tailor, who used clothes from his shop to cover the dead and dying. "I felt sick when I saw a whimpering dog with an entire hind leg blown off," he said. "The experience will haunt me for life."

The Anti-terrorist Squad arrived within ten minutes of the explosion. They were fortunate to be led by Commander William

Hucklesby QPM, FRGS, who by then was forty-seven years of age and in his twenty-seventh year of service. He spent a total of ten years with the Anti-Terrorist Squad – as detective superintendent, detective chief superintendent and now, commander – and he was the quintessential investigator. He had served on the Flying Squad and the Fraud Squad and had been in the forefront of many high-profile investigations; he had been commended time and again for superb police work. Affectionately known as 'Posh Bill' ("I must say he was and is the nicest senior officer one could ever work for," Chris Burke told me, adding caustically, "unlike some of the arseholes who thought they were too good to go to the toilet!"), Hucklesby was worshipped by his staff. Burke's sentiments were confirmed by Detective Constable Jeff Maund. "'Posh Bill' was an absolute gent; even to this day at the retired CID Association functions, he remembers you and by your first name," Maund told me. "He was a good boss and supported his team throughout – also took care of the politics and let us do our jobs."

Initially, the squad was informed that there were sixteen people dead and forty-nine injured. Clearly, their informant had been confused by the mannequins strewn about in the shop windows. A control vehicle was set up at the rendezvous point and a log of events started. The detective inspector in charge of the scene, the explosives officer and the exhibits officer (all of whom would be in radio contact with the van) stood 100 metres outside the scene of the bomb blast and waited for the chaos to die down. These were the priorities: dead left; injured out; cordons up; and then stand off until the area was professionally cleared by an explosives officer.

Meanwhile, the walking wounded were treated at the scene. Some of the injured (plus thousands of shoppers) were evacuated through the doors in Brompton Road; it was the only exit where vehicles were not parked, thus avoiding or at least reducing the danger of a possible second or third bomb.

Ambulance crews are trained in this type of eventuality to stop approximately 100 yards from the scene of an explosion and wait to be briefed by the first police officer on the scene. However, in reality (as in this case), they often go straight into the scene and rescue the injured; this is highly understandable because the saving of human life must be an absolute priority. But this course of action, laudable though it may be, is not without its drawbacks; if another device should then explode, the ambulance itself would fragment and become a collection of projectiles, flying through the air, killing and maiming passers-by. In addition, small items of what may be essential evidence – wires, batteries, bulbs etc – may become trapped in the vehicle's tyres. This was the case with the ambulance that took Inspector Dodd to hospital; part of the bomb-car was later found underneath the ambulance.

Ambulances, police and army vehicles ferried the more seriously wounded to the four local hospitals, which had been put on emergency alert. Mattresses were provided for some of the injured at the entrance to the Accident and Emergency Department at St Stephen's Hospital, Chelsea; after they ran out of bandages and gauze, further supplies had to be rushed in from surrounding hospitals. Not only that, the South London Transfusion Centre at Tooting quickly used up its reserves of 160 pints of blood in treating the injured, and a further 600 pints had to be brought in. But the response at St Stephen's was magnificent. Ten minutes after the bomb exploded, the hospital had marshalled a staff of 250; the workforce was called from different departments in the hospital, from the residences, from their homes. Staff from other hospitals offered their services. Theatre Sister Thelma Peters had been shopping in Sloane Square when she heard the sound of the explosion; driving straight to the hospital, she was in time to assist in the first operation. Dr Mary Harrington toured the hospital, discharging patients who were considered well enough to allow their beds to be used for the incoming wounded; several of the patients literally leapt out of bed and insisted on being discharged as soon as they discovered what had happened. Within the first hour, twenty-two of the thirty-nine injured who had been admitted had been treated. Inspector Stephen Dodd was one of those who remained. His head wounds were appalling.

"Amazingly and totally to the credit of the local uniform officers and other emergency services, all the injured persons had been moved from the vicinity," Jeff Maund told me. "The devastation made an immediate impact, canopies torn and fluttering, alarms going off but in a strange way, quiet. It was rather like walking on to the deck of the *Marie Celeste*." As he surveyed the scene, he said, "I could see Jane Arbuthnot lying on the pavement on the corner with Basil Street where she had been struck down." With a different perspective to Jim Diplock's, Maund stated, "She looked quite peaceful and there were no clear outward signs as to what had killed her."

After the overriding consideration of saving human life, the necessity of gathering every single scrap of evidence was paramount. Detective Inspector Chris Burke decided to sweep a 'common approach' path from the outer cordon right into the centre of the bombed area. In doing so, every piece of evidence on the path could be swept up, bagged, identified and sealed for onward transmission, in due course, to the Forensic Science Laboratory. Thereafter, the taped-off 'common approach' path could be walked along without fear of losing or contaminating any evidence.

However, before this vital step could be taken, the sombre scene was slightly lightened by a dash of unconscious humour; it was provided by the Deputy Assistant Commissioner (Crime), David Powis OBE, QPM, a man whose previous short career in the CID had been over a long time ago. He was regarded by CID officers either as a buffoon or a very dangerous adversary, egged on by his bunch of uniform sycophants, and able to ruin many a promising detective's career on a whim. Now, he arrived at the scene and insisted on inspecting the site. This had been normal practice for Powis at the scene of a number of terrorist explosions, and on this occasion Chris Burke, who had assumed total control of the scene with the authority to prevent anybody entering it, tried in vain to stop him. Burke told him it was not safe and that a secondary device could well be present; when he added that Powis could be killed, he was only expressing the hopes and aspirations of over 3,000 CID officers. But as Burke told me, Powis pushed past him, roaring, "At least people will know my name!" This, however, was false modesty; there was no question that the entire personnel of the Criminal Investigation Department could ever forget it.

As Powis crunched his way through the broken glass, he made some pompous and illogical statements for the benefit of the press ("not even wearing flak jackets would have saved them") before poking the remaining cars in the area with his umbrella. Seeing Noel Lane's body partially underneath the car and also Stephen Dodd's inspector's cap nearby, he immediately came to the conclusion that it was Inspector Dodd who had died under the vehicle. He then imparted this inaccurate news to an American television company, who duly broadcast this nonsense as fact.

So there was nothing remotely funny about his behaviour; the amusement came – and it is a matter of debate whether this happened at Harrods or some other bomb scene – when an officer, possibly at the end of his career and almost certainly destined not to rise any further through the rank structure, demanded that Powis hand over his shoes for forensic examination – and got them. Once again, Powis had lived up to his most repeatable nickname, 'Crazy Horse'.

Cordons had been set up and manned by police constables; nevertheless, the cordons had to be extended to 150 yards, because inquisitive people were peering around street corners and from shop doorways. If a secondary device had exploded, these onlookers would have been in mortal danger because, amazingly, blast waves actually travel round corners.

With the 'common approach' path in place, Jeff Maund entered the sterile area with John Horne, the explosives officer, whose job it was to clear the scene of any unexploded or secondary devices. "John always brought a sense of calm professionalism to bomb scenes," Maund told me, although on this occasion Horne's composed exterior was being tested to its limits; he knew that his wife had been shopping in the immediate area, just as he knew a woman's body had been found at the scene. After he saw the lifeless body of Caroline Cochrane-Patrick, still lying in the shop window, he realized from her clothing that it could not be his wife; nevertheless, it took several hours before it was established that she was not amongst the injured.

There was a second moment of trauma, not only for Horne but for everybody else in the vicinity. Maund was listening in to a sophisticated piece of equipment designed to detect radio waves used to initiate a secondary device by means of remote control. When a radio signal was received, the equipment would set off a high-pitched whine and hopefully jam the incoming signal. Suddenly the warning signal sounded. "RUN!" roared Horne, and the young woman divisional surgeon, one of those on the 'common approach' path, hitched up her skirts and did just that. "We took off like frightened bloody rabbits," Chris Burke told me. "'Posh Bill' was faster than me and it was the only time a DI from the Anti-terrorist Branch was seen 'slip-streaming' its commander!"

In fact, there was no secondary device; the signal received had been from a radio receiver/transmitter on a roof, several streets away. It was a release of tension in a very fraught, tense situation; and by the time the area was found to be safe, over four hours had passed.

With the 'common approach' path now reopened, the divisional surgeon, accompanied by a detective constable to act as scribe and an exhibits officer, was able to view the bodies and officially pronounce life extinct. However, at that time the identities of the three civilian victims were not known. One – or indeed, all – of them could have been terrorists, caught in a premature detonation of the bomb. Therefore, nylon bags were put over their hands to stop traces of explosives disappearing, also over their heads to ensure that no debris dropped out of their hair after the bodies were picked up.

Sergeant Thwaites was led by Commander Hucklesby along the sterile corridor to crawl under the wrecked bomb-car and, with the aid of a 'seek and search' torch, to endeavour to identify Noel Lane. But due to his horrific burns it was impossible to do so, and the best Thwaites could do was to identify the charred epaulette on his shoulder with the insignia 88 'B'. (Incredibly, not one bone in Lane's body had been broken; his death had been due to the tremendous heat generated by the blast.) For the same reason, the following morning, the pathologist, Dr Ian West, refused to accept Thwaites' identification; quite rightly, too. Any person could have pulled on Lane's jacket before running out of the police station, and therefore proper identification would have to be made, using fingerprints and dental records. The rest of the bodies had been taken to the mortuary, where post mortems and identification were carried out and X-rays were taken. Shrapnel and debris taken from the bodies by the pathologist was handed to the exhibits officer and carefully bagged and preserved. The same applied to the body of 'Queenie', and the blankets which had covered all of the bodies were similarly safeguarded.

Sergeant Mick Thwaites, who miraculously was unscathed, had directed all of the remaining members of his relief to use the telephone box (this was before the days of mobile phones) on the corner of Walton Street to telephone their families to let them know they were uninjured; but in looking after the welfare of his officers, he regrettably neglected to do so himself.

The Commissioner, Sir Kenneth Newman GBE, QPM, who had been Chief Constable of the Royal Ulster Constabulary and therefore was no stranger to the IRA, arrived at the scene with the Prime Minister, Margaret Thatcher, and her husband, Denis, and they were shown the carnage in Hans Crescent by Chief Inspector Francis, now appointed Press Liaison Officer, "with glass and light bulbs falling around us, everywhere," as he recalled. "She, I thought, was magnificent and genuinely in tears for those killed."

"The emotion was clear on the face of Maggie Thatcher when she visited the scene and spoke with us," Jeff Maund told me. The Lab liaison officer, Detective Sergeant Dave 'Sandy' Sanderson, had been given the melancholy task of supervising the removal and the continuity of evidence in respect of one of the dead police officers. He felt a hand on his shoulder and heard a familiar voice say, "Thank you for all you do." He turned to see it was Mrs Thatcher. She later visited the injured at St Stephen's hospital, and at Scotland Yard sent out a furious, unequivocal message: "I've called this a crime against humanity. Now, I say it's a crime against Christmas."

The area was split into zones, and owing to the time of day, with darkness looming, the immediate bomb scene (designated Zone 1A) was dealt with immediately. Detective Inspector Chris Burke explained to me that this was "to ensure that we had a good chance of obtaining explosive traces before the weather elements had a chance to destroy them. After that was done, any of the other zones could be cleared according to their respective priority problems. For instance, Zone 5 had to be cleared to allow arterial traffic to continue its daily flow. I then sealed off Hans Crescent with scaffolding which allowed my team to work uninhibited."

It took until ten o'clock that night before the last body was removed and it was time for the team to go home. But before they left, the scene was photographed, all of the relevant areas were covered with tarpaulin sheets and the drains were blocked, in case it rained overnight, with the strong possibility that tiny, vital pieces of evidence would be washed away. The blood in the gutters stayed where it was.

But first, it was time for a drink, to unwind and (most importantly) to talk about the shocking events which the team had witnessed. Then the officers went home to confront their demons. "We all confessed to having a weep or a cry," Chris Burke told me. The following day was Jeff Maund's birthday, which he celebrated in the early hours by weeping into a glass of whisky.

Many of the officers involved, both uniform and CID, were later advised to take psychiatric counselling, and wisely some did. Others did not, and a number of them, months later, suffered utterly debilitating nervous breakdowns. One died, some thought by his own hand. He was an officer 'on loan' to C13, and Chris Burke is still bitter at that officer's divisional commander (whom he describes as 'contemptible'), who refused to sanction compassionate leave for him.

★   ★   ★

The next day, the search for evidence recommenced. An army vehicle checked the area again for radio-controlled devices before the team entered the scene and got to work. The 'common approach' path had deliberately been made wide and it would be needed. Nine of the vehicles in Hans Crescent affected by the blast were taken away for forensic examination, and the Fire Brigade used rising steps to search for evidence along the ledges of buildings, on roof tops and inside the shattered windows. Occupants of these buildings were refused permission to replace their broken windows until these searches had been completed. It was imperative that if the evidence was there, it should be seized and appear in an exhibits book.

All of the debris was collected into dustbins (each having a bin liner to maintain the integrity of the contents), which were clearly marked by the exhibits officers according to the zone from which they emanated; therefore, twenty-six dustbins from one particular zone became one exhibit. All of these dustbins (and sometimes builders' skips as well) were taken to the Forensic Science Laboratory under police escort. The brushes and shovels used to deposit the debris in the bins were sterilized by the Forensic Laboratory to negate possible claims by defence lawyers of cross-contamination. Furthermore, and for the same reason, no officer was allowed to go from one scene to another during the same day. In addition, no officer who had had contact with any of the explosive exhibits would be permitted to swab a suspect, for fear, once again, of accusations of cross-contamination.

The log of events scrupulously recorded every occurrence. The comings and goings of the explosives officer and every police officer were logged, as was the appearance of members of the Fire Brigade, forensic scientists, building inspectors, surveyors and representatives of the gas and electricity companies, as well as people in charge of additional lighting and heavy lifting machinery. In many cases, the emergence and re-emergence of many of these people was of no evidential importance whatsoever. However, miss just one of them out on the log and the officer concerned would, in months or years to come, be subjected to screeching denunciations of incompetence (or worse) from the lips of one of the more predictable left-wing lawyers who line up to defend terrorists. It matters not that the omission is not of the slightest importance to the case; what does matter is that the lawyer (who is fully aware that his client is as guilty as sin) is able to weaken the prosecution's case to such an extent that a credulous jury will acquit.

In order for a prosecution brought under the provisions of the Explosive Substances Act 1883 to succeed, it is necessary for a scientist to prove both the existence of an explosive substance and that it was responsible for the explosion. Therefore it was imperative that the seat of the explosion was cleared and examined at the first opportunity before the elements had a chance to erase it. Previously, it had been the practice to 'swab' the scene, but scientists would much rather examine the actual exhibit than a swab. And that was why, outside Harrods, the kerbstones which were thought to have contained traces of explosive were dug up; it also explained the presence of Kensington and Chelsea's Borough Surveyor.

So the kerbstones, 180 dustbins, seven building skips and nine vehicles made their way to the Forensic Science Laboratory for a lengthy and painstaking examination.

In the meantime, the Home Secretary authorized extra police to patrol in London: 320 extra uniformed officers, 200 CID and Special Branch officers, and four extra Special Patrol Group units totalling 120 officers, sixty-four dog handlers and thirty Traffic Patrol units.

★   ★   ★

At the same time as the Harrods' warning was issued, there had been another bomb alert, this time to the C&A Store in Oxford Street. It was a hoax call, which diverted police and ambulance personnel away from Harrods, as did another caller with an Irish accent who informed the operator that there was a bomb in one of Debenhams' stores. This was Gary Coomber, a twenty-six-year-old London Transport cleaner from Stanmore, Middlesex, who appeared at Harrow Magistrates' Court and was sentenced to three months' imprisonment. Coomber was one of four people arrested for hoax bomb calls; another was Jeremy Seymour-Eyles, a seventeen-year-old catering student from Twickenham, who thought it necessary on Christmas Day to inform the emergency services that there was a bomb planted near Harrods. He was sent to a detention centre for three months. They were the tip of the bomb hoaxers' iceberg. In the week following the outrage 800 false calls were made. Pat Hastings did not leave the store until eleven o'clock on the night of the bombing. Afterwards, when she was manning the switchboard, she would receive sick telephone calls. She told me, "The caller would say, 'Talk dirty to me or I'll blow up your colleagues.' There were quite a few of them. On one occasion, I had to keep the caller talking until the police could trace the call, and they caught him."

★   ★   ★

In a classic, hypocritical transference-of-blame statement, the IRA Army Council admitted that its members had planted the bomb, stating:

> The Irish Republican Army have been operational in Britain throughout last week. Our volunteers planted the bomb outside Woolwich barracks and in the car outside Harrods store. The Harrods operation was not authorized by the Irish Republican Army. We have taken immediate steps to ensure that there will be no repetition of this type of operation again. The volunteers involved gave a forty minutes specific warning, which should have been adequate. But due to the inefficiency or failure of the Metropolitan Police, who boasted of foreknowledge of IRA activity, this warning did not result in an evacuation. We regret the civilian casualties, even though our expression of sympathy will be dismissed. Finally, we remind the British Government that as long as they maintain control of any part of Ireland, then the Irish Republican Army will continue to operate in Britain until the Irish people are left in peace to decide their own future.

Twelve hours before the Harrods bombing, Noraid, the US organization which has raised funds for Irish terrorists, paid a fee of £1,000 for an illuminated sign in Times Square, New York which read, 'Season's greetings to Irish Prisoners of War.' The US ambassador in London condemned the bombing as being "an insult to civilised people, everywhere." Sinn Féin's president, Gerry Adams, expressed 'regret' at the killings but within days considered legal proceedings against Granada Television's *World in Action* programme, which alleged that he was the mainspring of the Provisional IRA. The leader of the opposition, Neil Kinnock, visited the injured in Westminster Hospital and angrily attacked the IRA's sentiments of regret. "Their statement that they regret the bombing will not bring back the dead," he stated, adding, "Nor make better the people I have seen." When asked about a call from the GLC leader, Ken Livingstone, for the Government to seek discussions with the IRA, a furious Neil Kinnock replied, "In a free society, Mr Livingstone is entitled to his opinion." He added, forcefully, "It is not an opinion that I share."

Two of the nine children under the age of sixteen who were injured were ten-year-old Periman Parmar and his five-year-old brother Rajan, who had visited Father Christmas in Harrods. They were detained in St Thomas' Hospital to receive treatment for the cuts they had sustained from flying debris, as were their mother and aunt. The following Monday, they were amongst the many who were visited by the Prince and Princess of Wales. The Princess joked with Rajan, and the Prince commiserated with the parents of an injured American geologist, Mark McDonald, telling them, "I apologize on behalf of London. It was terrible." The pale-faced Prince spoke from the heart; it was just four years since his great-uncle, Lord Louis Mountbatten, had been murdered by the IRA. Robert Brown, a twenty-nine-year-old stockbroker, was one of six victims in the Westminster Hospital being treated for his injuries: a broken arm, a three-inch gash on his forehead and four shrapnel wounds. A year later he would remark, "Having survived that day, I now feel part of a special family."

And on Christmas Eve Inspector Stephen Dodd died from the appalling injuries he had received. He had been twice operated upon, and although the surgeons battled to save him, his kidneys failed. Superintendent Hames had to authorize the switching off of his life support machine. "Steve was my relief inspector and was a great guy who helped me a lot," recalled Mick Thwaites. "I needed it, as I was a detective out of water on a relief, having just been made sergeant."

Donations had started pouring in, and on 19 December the *Sun* newspaper launched an appeal for the families of the victims with their own donation of £5,000, which was swollen on the first day alone with donations totalling £976.10p; two days later, balloon seller Derek James, who had survived the blast, collected £1,276 for the fund and handed over another £1,246 directly to Chelsea police station. By Christmas Eve, £28,000 had been deposited at Chelsea police station for the families of the fourteen officers injured and the three who had been killed; four small boys emptied the contents of their money boxes on the counter in the front office; the total amounted to £4.16½p. Harrods started a trust fund with £50,000 for the families of the victims, and an unnamed businessman pledged a reward of £250,000 for information leading to the murderers. A lump sum of £29,493 was paid to Jane's parents, and £51,092 and £59,092 to the widows of Lane and Dodd, respectively.

Generous offers of assistance came into Chelsea police station; half a dozen people offered holidays for the families of the dead or wounded officers, and other offers of assistance included two of kidney donations.

★   ★   ★

The media furiously condemned the IRA. 'These IRA Bastards' were denounced by the *News of the World*, and there was a rush of anti-Irish feeling, unfair to the vast majority of the decent Ulster people but given the circumstances, perhaps understandable. The mainland had been plagued with attacks by the IRA since 1974; there were 'cease-fires' from time to time, although this was usually a cynical ploy to allow the various 'Active Service Units' to regroup and acquire more munitions. The IRA had learnt from their mistakes and were becoming more cunning and ruthless. At least ten additional women were recruited by *Cumann na mBann* (the IRA's women's organization), and the terror campaign was stepped up. On 10 October 1981 Chelsea Barracks had been bombed, killing two, and on 26 October Ken Howarth GM, a bomb disposal expert, was killed whilst trying to defuse a bomb in a Wimpy Bar in Oxford Street. Four days later, a bomb exploded at the home of the Attorney General, Sir Michael Havers.

On 20 July 1982 a bomb exploded as mounted guards of the Blues and Royals rode through Hyde Park; two guardsmen were killed and seventeen civilians were injured. Hours later, a bomb exploded at the bandstand in Regents Park, killing six bandsmen of the Royal Green Jackets and injuring twenty-four civilians; three others later died of their injuries.

Now came this latest atrocity, just before Christmas; and the public were sick and tired of it. When a 1961 Norman Wisdom film was shown on television, the scene in which he sang 'When Irish Eyes are Smiling' was cut, as was the scene in which a tourist asked the way to Harrods. Although the IRA had grandly announced a pre-Christmas bombing campaign in order to terrorize Londoners, it backfired. The general public refused to be cowed, and Harrods re-opened two days later, courteously apologizing for the temporary closure which had been beyond their control. Five days before Christmas, 150 tons of Christmas puddings had been sold by the store, a 20 per cent increase over the previous year. The January sale netted the store £7.24 million, and by 29 January Harrods would become the first European store whose turnover exceeded £200 million in a fiscal year. Prior to Christmas, Denis Thatcher, displaying the fortitude which had resulted in his award of a military MBE and two Mentions in Dispatches during World War Two, was one of the first shoppers at the re-opened store. "No damned Irish murderer is going to stop me going shopping at Harrods," he growled. Jane Arbuthnot's family – her mother Susan, father John (known to all as 'Jake'), sister Sally and brothers Richard and Charles – made a point of going to Harrods to purchase black scarves and ties. "My daughter has not been killed for people to stay away – that's important," said Mrs Arbuthnot. "The last thing we want is for these IRA people bringing London to a halt. The Germans didn't manage it; neither will the Irish." Perhaps matters were best summed up by Mrs Maureen Bryant from North London who said, "I'm not really a Harrods person. I'm here because the bloody IRA wanted to scare us off – wish I'd come years ago. Scared? How could one be, with all these marvellous people doing their best to turn a horrible tragedy, vicious damage, into something that's already history?" Her Majesty the Queen sent a message of sympathy as did His Holiness the Pope, who said it was, "a brutal act of cynical and mindless hatred".

★   ★   ★

The investigation was now well under way. The Yard had found an expert who could reconstruct a bomb, using the fragments available, so that its components could be identified and traced. Incredibly, on one occasion he was actually able to trace the nails used inside a bomb to the manufacturers and then to the retail shops where they had been sold. The Anti-terrorist Squad was working on the assumption that two cars were involved, one taking the parking space and holding it until the car packed with explosives could be put in place. Therefore, the parking meters in Hans Crescent were opened and every coin was subjected to fingerprint analysis. The chain of owners of the Austin 1300 were traced, interviewed and eliminated from the enquiry, until the last known buyer could be identified. The vehicle had been bought from an Irish car dealer in Maida Vale on 22 November 1983, and the purchaser, wearing gloves, had paid £270 cash. The dealer was said to be 'in fear of his life', although public sympathy for him was somewhat diluted after it was reported that following the bombing in Hyde Park, the man's sister who lived in the flat next door was heard to shout, "Up the IRA!"

There was little to fingerprint in what remained of the car, but a print was lifted from the coil in the engine. It belonged to a previous owner and was therefore of no evidential value, but its discovery demonstrated that the investigating team would leave no stone unturned. Jim Diplock had called together all of the green-coated Harrods doormen to see if any of them had seen the car being parked. One of them had. Diplock told me, "I said to him, 'How many men got out of it?'" The answer was: "None – it was just one woman."

One convicted IRA terrorist was arrested in Manchester on Wednesday, 21 December with his girlfriend. He had been released eleven months previously after serving a sentence for his part in the 1975 Birmingham bombing campaign in which twenty-two people died. He was later taken to London for further questioning and his girlfriend was released after being interviewed. She told friends, "All they wanted to know was what I was doing on Saturday." The former terrorist was later released, as were four more suspects who were arrested in London.

★ ★ ★

"Mick Hames was the superintendent at Kensington and came over to assist and then remained at Chelsea," Mick Thwaites told me. "He and I took it upon ourselves to be the link with the next of kin and had some very emotional times with our dead colleagues' family members."

Meanwhile, Philip Geddes was buried at Barrow-in-Furness, Cumbria, and at St Andrew's Church, West Kilbride, Jasmine Kennedy Cochrane-Patrick was laid to rest. She had spent three months working in London as a trainee stockbroker and had hoped to find a job in Glasgow the following year. She and her husband Nigel had purchased Wyndhurst House at Portencross, near Largs, earlier that year in order to be nearer the land which her husband farmed. Now, this idyllic lifestyle was at an end. The Reverend Arthur Fletcher castigated the IRA and said, in part:

> Today, we cannot speak of Jasmine's death without the realization that it was the result of the evil, indiscriminate and murderous tactics of a group of people who care nothing for the feelings, the principles or the values of those whom they seek to impress. Their cause grows weaker, not stronger as they hope, whenever they launch an attack of this kind. We cry out against, condemn and call accursed in the sight of God, our creator and theirs, the inhuman violent crimes they commit in a cause which they pretend has to do with freedom.

Noel Lane was cremated at the Croydon Crematorium on Friday, 23 December. The service was conducted by Father John Daly, the parish priest of St Dominic's, Waddon, and there was a reading from Corinthians by Commander J. A. Perrett. This was followed five days later by a Requiem Mass, held at St Joseph's Church, Redhill.

Jane Arbuthnot's funeral at St Luke's Church, Chelsea, on Friday, 30 December attracted 1,000 mourners. The cortège was preceded by the Lord Bishop of Kensington, the Right Reverend Mark Santer and the Rector of St Luke's, the Reverend Derek Watson. Two of the six police-constable pallbearers, who carried the coffin draped in the Force flag and adorned with a cross made up from white lilies of the valley, were Mark Grover and Peter Weinberg, who had been injured in the explosion but demanded to be returned to duty two days after the incident. And Sergeant Mick Thwaites gave a moving address to the congregation. It is well worth quoting part of it:

> Jane's style was that of not 'what can I take from?' but 'what can I give?' to life. In the two years, nine months that she was in the Police Service, she gave laughter, fun and enjoyment to others whilst maintaining efficiency and professionalism. Chelsea has seen many changes in life styles. Fads have come, styles have come but Chelsea remains Chelsea, especially in the eyes of the many thousands of visitors to the area. One of the styles was Jane's bicycle. She got it to enable her, in her own words, to 'zap around the ground'. It enabled her to be seen to be approached and to be talked to. Her approach to the job was 'the work has got to be done, so let's get on and do it.' Even if it meant losing some of her refreshment time or having to work longer than her normal tour of duty. And so we come to that Saturday. Like all of us, Jane enjoyed her private life, but work still had to be done. She had altered her duties so that she could do her job and still enjoy her evening. In answer to an emergency call, Jane and others despite being in the middle of their lunch immediately went to Harrods in the knowledge that they would be searching for a bomb. The story of that bomb is now part of our history. The life of a young person who was doing the job she loved and caring for people whom she served was instantly and tragically ended. All of us in the Police Force but especially those of us at Chelsea are proud to have known her and served with her.

Stephen Dodd's funeral service on 5 January was held at the same church as Jane's, and over 100 wreaths were received from friends, colleagues and Police Forces from all over the country. His wife Maureen and their children were comforted by the officers from Chelsea. Maureen, a former police woman, and Stephen had separated but they remained good friends and had agreed that the family should be reunited over Christmas. And the senior officer who had previously worked at Chelsea, Chief Superintendent Gordon Lloyd, paid tribute to his former inspector: "His dedication to duty could not be surpassed – he would ask no one to do what he could not or would not do himself. And this quality was clearly apparent on the fateful day of Saturday, 17 December 1983 – the day of the car bomb explosion outside Harrods when he was to be fatally injured." The Assistant Commissioner 'D' Department, Geoffrey Dear QPM, read a lesson from the twenty-first book of Revelation, and Cornelius' *Requiem Aeternam* was sung by the Metropolitan Police Choir.

Just over a month later, on Monday, 30 January 1984 at twelve noon, a memorial service was held at Westminster Abbey for the six murdered victims of the IRA. The families of the police officers and their colleagues were there, of course. Karen Salvesen, the widow of Kenneth Gerald Salvesen, arrived from California, together with her father-in-law Gerald, who had to catch her during the service to stop her from collapsing. Her four-year-old son had remained behind in America. The husband of Caroline Jasmine Kennedy Cochrane-Patrick, together with their small son, two-year-old James, and her mother, Mrs Armour, were present, as were the relatives of Philip Geddes. He was so well thought of that annual prizes in his honour are awarded to aspiring journalists attending Oxford University, and every year a Philip Geddes Memorial Lecture on the theme of the future of journalism is given by a leading journalist. The Band of the Metropolitan Police played music by Purcell, Sullivan, Beethoven, Handel, Schubert, Barsotti, Albinoni and Elgar. The Prime Minister and the Commissioner were present to read lessons from the Scriptures – the former read Revelation 21, verses 1–7, the latter Micah 6, verses 6–8 – and were part of the throng of 2,000 mourners who attended, by ticket only, to pay their respects.

The confirmed vegetarian and extremely liberal-minded Dean of Westminster, the Very Reverend Edward Carpenter, offered up prayers which he thought appropriate:

So we do pray for the perpetrators of violence that through His grace and forgiveness they may, with us, seek and find a more excellent way of reconciliation, the way of justice, the way of peace.

Given the circumstances of the service, this venerable gentleman's sanctimonious twaddle was entirely misplaced and was not well received by the police officers in the congregation, many of them openly weeping, all of them still smarting from the slaughter of their contemporaries.

There was a concert in aid of what had become known as 'The Knightsbridge Disaster Fund' in March 1984 at St Luke's Church, with the BBC Symphony Chorus and the Chalk Farm Band with guest soloists, and two months later the Chelsea Police Social and Athletic Club held a charity ball at the Carlton Tower Hotel. Both events boosted the funds for the families of their murdered colleagues.

★   ★   ★

Meanwhile, the Anti-terrorist Squad was still working flat out. Everything of forensic interest had been submitted for examination, statements were still being taken and those statements in existence were being checked and re-checked. Actions were being issued and cross-referenced with those which had been completed, and fresh actions often emerged as a result: 5,577 of them, together with 3,060 telephone calls, mainly from members of the public.

Special Branch and the intelligence agencies were adding their input to the investigation, as were security organizations in Northern Ireland. The Royal Ulster Constabulary's Special Branch – E4A, who dealt with surveillance and setting up observation posts, and E4B, who dealt with technical surveillance and installing bugging and tracking equipment – also assisted. The Army's Force Research Unit (FRU) had been set up in 1980 and its members were drawn from the military, mainly the Parachute Regiment, Special Forces and the Intelligence Corps. Their role was to recruit informants from within the terrorist groups and they worked closely with the Special Air Service and the 14 Intelligence Company. Although these operations were geared to striking at the terrorist groups operating in Ulster, information came in which might not necessarily benefit them but which would prove useful to the authorities on the mainland. The same applied to the police in Eire, the *Garda Siochána na hÉireann*, and on 15 January 1985 they proved to be especially helpful.

★   ★   ★

The IRA's Army Council were deeply concerned; the bomb at Harrods had claimed the life of one American citizen and injured several others; Noraid was attracting poor publicity in the USA, and the feeling was that the bombers were getting out of control, choosing targets which would alienate Irish-Americans sympathetic to the Republican cause. Therefore, when the Army Council decided to send their quartermaster, Natalino Vella of Knockmore Avenue, Tallaght, Dublin, to 'find out why Harrods had been bombed', Special Branch in Dublin heard of it and informed Scotland Yard. When Vella boarded a flight to London, a seventeen-strong surveillance team were waiting at Heathrow, ready to see whom he would meet.

Two of the most dangerous IRA terrorists were Paul Kavanagh and Thomas Quigley. They worked independently from other groups, so if one member of a cell was arrested, they would be less likely to be compromised. They had access to arms dumps which had been buried in dustbins, one in Salcey Forest in Northamptonshire and the other in Annesley Forest in Nottinghamshire. The men were constantly on the move, leaving and returning to England as and when necessary. Vella's instructions were to check whether or not those arms dumps were secure and to tell Kavanagh to get out of England.

Vella met up with Paul Kavanagh the following day in London, and the surveillance team followed the two men, plus two others, all of whom were in a white Rover saloon. This vehicle had been sighted in the Knightsbridge area, prior to the Harrods bombing. The driver of the Rover used anti-surveillance procedures, but without success; the presence of the surveillance team went undetected. The car made two stops, one in Annesley Forest and another in Salcey Forest. On both occasions, two of the car's occupants got out and walked into the forest, returning some forty-five minutes later. The car drove off but was then lost by the police. It was later found abandoned at Duffield, Derbyshire; it had traces of explosives inside. On 18 January Vella flew back to Dublin. On 25 January the arms dumps were discovered. They contained an Aladdin's cave of evidence: an Armalite rifle, an Army & Navy revolver, a Smith & Wesson revolver, a Luger pistol, an Uzi sub-machine gun and three hand grenades, plus ammunition and explosives. There were wires, pliers which had been used to cut the wire, details of vehicles used and keys to getaway cars. There were memo-park switches (similar to those used in European parking meters but modified to provide a long-term delay between the planting of a device and its detonation), mercury tilt switches, detonators, batteries – and fingerprints.

Many of these items would later be forensically linked to past atrocities, and in March 1984 Paul Kavanagh was arrested in

Belfast and brought to London. He appeared at Lambeth Magistrates' Court, together with Thomas Quigley, under heavy police guard. Both were accused of conspiracy with others to cause explosions in 1981. Quigley was also accused of causing four explosions in 1981, of three murders and an attempted murder.

Kavanagh was additionally charged with conspiring with others to cause explosions between 6 October 1983 and 25 January 1984; this period encompassed the Harrods bombing, although he was not charged with the murders. In addition, he was charged with four other explosives and arms charges which related to the arms dumps in Northamptonshire and Nottinghamshire.

On 18 June 1984 Vella was arrested at Heathrow as he stepped off a plane from Dublin; he had quite a lot to say to the Anti-terrorist Squad officers.

At the Old Bailey on 7 March 1985 Kavanagh and Quigley were both convicted of conspiracy to cause explosions and were sentenced to life imprisonment with a recommendation that they serve thirty-five years. Vella, who pleaded guilty, was sentenced to fifteen years' imprisonment; he also alleged that Kavanagh was the person responsible for the Harrods bombing, but Kavanagh was never charged with or convicted of the offence.

Whilst serving his sentence on the mainland, Kavanagh married Martina Anderson in 1989. A former beauty queen from Derry, she had been sentenced to life imprisonment in 1985 for involvement in a bombing campaign. By March 1997 both men had successfully campaigned to be allowed to serve their sentences in Ireland. They were released in 1999 under the provisions of the Good Friday agreement, having served less than half of their thirty-five-year tariff. Kavanagh's wife had been released a year earlier.

Oh, yes. Remember the woman who parked the bomb-car in Hans Crescent? The whole of the investigating team knew her identity – as I do – but her successful prosecution depended upon a sufficiency of evidence, which they did not possess.

* * *

The inquest at Westminster Coroners' Court had been opened on 21 December 1983 by the Coroner, Dr Paul Knapman, and after a very brief hearing it was adjourned. Almost a year later, there was a full hearing, and dog-handler PC Jon Gordon walked into court on his artificial legs. He was married, with a three-year-old son, and his wife Sheila had been seven and a half months pregnant as she kept an anxious vigil by his bedside at Westminster Hospital. Seven months later, after he had lost a leg in the initial blast and received fifty pints of blood in transfusions, Gordon's other leg had to be amputated.

He told the coroner that although 'Queenie' had not been trained to sniff out explosives, she had sensed danger moments before the explosion. "The hair on the back of her neck was standing up; a sure sign that she sensed something. I couldn't figure out then what she was trying to tell me, but I now know. She was trying to save my life." Gordon had undoubtedly survived because of the high standard of physical fitness he had always maintained. Shortly after the inquest he returned to work, on light duties.

The pathologist, Dr Ian West, gave mercifully very brief details of the frightful injuries sustained by five of the victims. However, at the insistence of Mrs Debe Armour, a Moslem convert and the mother of Caroline Jasmine Kennedy Cochrane-Patrick, Dr West catalogued in full the horrific injuries sustained by her daughter. These injuries, so bad that case-hardened bomb disposal expert Peter Gurney MBE, GM & Bar, had been reduced to tears, were duly recounted in graphic detail, including the fact that her left hand was not found until two days later. Mrs Armour, who at the memorial service at Westminster Abbey had pinned a large colour photograph of her daughter to her dress ("I was afraid no one would realize I am her mother"), asked the pathologist to speak slowly, so that she could record every detail in longhand. She also requested permission (which was granted) to view the police photographs of her daughter's corpse. Praising Allah for her daughter's life, Mrs Armour later stated that she wished to sue the IRA for damages over her daughter's murder. It is not clear if she was ever successful.

Verdicts of unlawful killing were returned on all six victims, and the coroner praised the police officers who rushed to the scene of the bomb, saying:

> Three of those killed were police officers doing their duty. When there is a bomb scare, somebody has to investigate, while members of the public – quite correctly – run away. Those responsible for investigating are the police. They wear the dark blue uniform. They cannot and do not shrink from their duty. We should not forget that.

On 24 September 1985 the Police Memorial Trust ensured that the three police officers who gave their lives would not be forgotten. In Hans Crescent HRH Princess Alexandra drew aside a velvet curtain, revealing a four-foot-six blue granite plinth bearing their names. Speeches were made by Michael Winner, the Chairman of the Trust, Lord Whitelaw and the Commissioner. PC Jon Gordon got up from his wheelchair and laid a wreath, together with flowers to 'Queenie' with the message, 'I didn't forget you, Babes.'

★   ★   ★

Jon Gordon hadn't forgotten 'Queenie', but it appeared – wrongly, as it turned out – that the hierarchy at Scotland Yard had overlooked the dead officers, at least as far as public recognition was concerned.

Immediately following the murder of their daughter, Jane Arbuthnot's parents were visited by Assistant Commissioner Geoffrey Dear QPM, DL (later knighted, and now Baron Dear of Willersey). Mick Thwaites was present and recalled Dear saying, 'that Jane and the others killed would get a medal for bravery, as they had responded to a coded message from the IRA and paid with their lives.' Dear knew what he was talking about with regard to brave actions; just four years previously, aged forty-two, he had been awarded the Queen's Commendation for Brave Conduct for the arrest of an armed, mentally unstable man who had barricaded himself and his infant son in a house, following a shooting incident. But if they were Dear's actual words, well meant though they were, they were a little imprudent, it being one matter to recommend someone for an award but quite another to prophesy the actual granting of it. The years went by and nothing happened. A furious Woman Detective Constable Jacquie Hames of TO12 Department (the wife of Superintendent Mick Hames and a noted presenter of BBC TV's *Crimewatch*) wrote to the Metropolitan Police's newspaper, *The Job*, demanding to know why the bravery of those officers had not been recognized. The letter, published in the 9 December 1988 issue, elicited a supine response from a Chief Superintendent H. Beresford-Peirse, who replied, in part:

> I understand that the question of commendations was considered by the then senior officers at Chelsea and on 'B' District. Five years later it would be difficult and possibly distressing to some people to pass judgement on individual officers and to make recommendations for commendations or bravery awards.

Although, perhaps unfairly, many serving officers regarded *The Job* newspaper as a piece of sycophantic trash, Detective Sergeant Mick Thwaites was not unduly surprised when his letter (far more abrasive than WDC Hames' had been, but just as direct) in reply to these simpering comments was not published. He refused to give up, and after repeated telephone calls to *The Job* (and over six months after WDC Hames' letter) he succeeded in getting an interview with the Assistant Commissioner (Personnel & Training), Paul Condon (later Sir Paul Condon and Commissioner of the Metropolitan Police, 1993–2000, later still Baron Condon QPM, DL, FRSA), who was extremely sympathetic. In fact, the reason why the dead officers had not received posthumous gallantry awards was not due to the senior officers at the Yard, who had backed the recommendation all the way; it came from the highest levels in the Government, who believed that 'the officers had only been doing their duty.' The mandarins in Whitehall should have hung their heads in collective shame.

But Mick Thwaites' unrelenting efforts resulted, seven months later, in Jon Gordon receiving a commissioner's high commendation and the three officers, posthumous awards for their courage and dedication at the scene of the bombing. The ceremony took place at Scotland Yard on 17 December 1989. It had taken exactly six years for the selfless acts of four very brave members of the Metropolitan Police to be recognized.

By contrast, on 3 August 1984 'Queenie' had been posthumously awarded a well-deserved Margaret Wheatley Medal, the RSPCA's highest award. 'Queenie's' qualities of intelligence and courage were recognized rather sooner than her handler's courage and dedication. However, the medal had not relied on governmental backing for its investiture.

CHAPTER 9

Spare a Copper

L ibya in North Africa covers an area of approximately 700,000 square miles, and to the north is the Mediterranean Sea from where, 2,200 years ago, the Phoenicians sailed in for trading purposes. The country was later split into three traditional areas: Tripolitania, Fezzan and Cyrenaica, and the capital, Tripoli, is where approximately a quarter of the country's six million inhabitants once lived. In 1951 the former Emir of Cyrenaica, King Idris I, proclaimed Libya's independence as a sovereign state. The United States of America and Britain were welcome in the country, the former having a large air base there and the latter being involved in engineering projects and the supply of arms. An added incentive to these friendly relations was that in 1959 significant supplies of oil had been discovered. This transformed Libya from being one of the world's poorest nations to one of the ten richest oil-producing countries.

However, envious eyes studied King Idris' rapidly accumulating wealth, and following the humiliating defeat of Libya and other Arab nations by Israel in the Six-Day War of 1967, a group of dissatisfied army officers took advantage of the eighty-year-old King's absence (he was receiving medical treatment in Turkey) to stage a bloodless *coup d'état* on 1 September 1969. The sovereign kingdom of Libya was no more; phoenix-like, the Libyan Arab Republic rose in its place. The leader of the coup was a twenty-seven-year-old army officer by the name of Colonel Muammar Abu Minyar al-Gaddafi. His name would soon become synonymous with terrorist-backed organizations and the world wide assassination of anyone considered to be his enemy; at the same time, he was accumulating enormous wealth from Libya's oil.

He was also considered to be as mad as a March Hare.

★ ★ ★

On Tuesday, 17 April 1984, approximately 1,500 miles from Libya to the north-west, a demonstration was due to be held outside the Libyan Embassy at 5 St James' Square, London, by a group of seventy-five Libyan dissidents styled the Libyan National Salvation Front, many of whom had travelled down from Manchester. They were protesting about the execution of two students in Tripoli who had paid the ultimate price after unwisely criticizing Colonel Gaddafi. The occupants of the embassy – it was also known as 'The People's Bureau of the Socialist People's Libyan Arab Jamahiriya' (their choice of apostrophes, not mine) – were aware that the demonstration was going to be held and organized a protest of their own, staffed by Gaddafi supporters. The Metropolitan Police were informed and barriers were set up, some outside the embassy on the north side of the square and some opposite to the embassy to retain the dissidents. The battle lines were drawn up, and many of the anti-Gaddafi protesters, fearing reprisals, sensibly covered their faces. In theory, the two opposing factions would scream insults at each other for a couple of hours until they either ran out of breath or grew bored with the whole thing, before retiring, honour satisfied.

But matters were not as cut and dried as they seemed. As Mark Austin reported in his excellent television documentary, *Real Crime: Yvonne Fletcher – Justice Betrayed*, the British Ambassador in Tripoli had been instructed by the Libyans to get the demonstration stopped; not unnaturally, he refused, but reported the matter to the Foreign and Commonwealth Office in London. However, the Foreign Office had received two visits from Libyan diplomats, also demanding that the protest be stopped. And according to a police source, when the barriers were put up in front of the embassy, a Libyan national, Salah Ibrahim Mabrook, tried to stop them from doing so, saying, "We have guns here, today. There is going to be fighting. We are not going to have responsibility for you, or the barriers."

A detachment of approximately thirty police officers from 'C' Division – from Bow Street, Gerald Road and West End Central – had arrived to police the demonstration. And one of them was Woman Police Constable 341 'C' Yvonne Joyce Fletcher.

★ ★ ★

Although the height regulation of a minimum of five feet four for women officers was abolished in 1990, WPC Fletcher slipped under the radar when she joined the Metropolitan Police in 1977. At one quarter of an inch under five feet three, she had already been rejected by two other Police Forces. Born in 1958 in Mere,

Wiltshire, just to the north-west of Shaftesbury, Yvonne was a bright girl at her comprehensive school, achieving ten GCE 'O' Levels and one 'A' Level before leaving at the age of eighteen and a half. She spent three months working as a mother's help before arriving at Bow Street police station. "Yvonne was on 'A' Relief at Bow Street," recalled former Police Constable Pete Rogers. "As with reliefs in those days, the camaraderie was very good indeed. Yvonne was friendly, conscientious and a popular member of the relief. She was always smiling and a genuinely nice person. Yvonne, although small in height, was always at the forefront when dealing with incidents. She was young in service and very keen to learn. She was happy in her work and in her private life. Everything seemed to be coming together for her. She had a boyfriend who was also on the relief, a little maisonette in Harrow, and everything seemed perfectly normal and happy for her." And Colin Osborn remembered her when he was a detective constable at Bow Street from 1976–8. "She was in and out of the CID office quite a lot and she was the sort of person that didn't have an enemy in the world."

That opinion was backed up by former Police Constable 285 'C' Laurie Young, who was one of the officers working in plain clothes with an inspector on a 'Toms [prostitutes] Patrol' together with approximately fifteen women officers, some in uniform, others in plain clothes, who patrolled the streets arresting prostitutes and identifying, keeping observation on and then arresting their pimps. One of the women officers was Yvonne Fletcher, and Young remembers her as "being afraid of nothing. She had such an infectious laugh – the Toms loved her. She treated them fairly and if, for example, the Toms knew of a young girl being exploited, they'd tip Yvonne off, which would lead to the arrest of a pimp."

At the briefing for the Libyan Embassy demonstration the officers had been told that it was possible that during the protest people might come out of the embassy and attack the demonstrators. But as they made their way to the square, the atmosphere was relaxed among the officers, with plenty of laughing and joking.

Inspector Alex Fish remembers that the protesters had arrived by coach, and before the demonstration commenced he was tasked to send an officer to 'keep an eye' on the vehicles, which were parked south of the square, in Pall Mall. He saw two women officers and told them that one would have to go to the coaches; but as he told me, "Yvonne Fletcher was adamant she did not want to go and wanted to stay where the action was likely to be.

I said to Yvonne, 'You might as well fill this gap, where I am' and walked off."

And Pete Rogers remembered, "On our arrival in the square, I recall thinking there were far more DPG officers than normal. As you know, these were the armed Diplomatic Protection Group. They seemed to be all over the place."

Jim Farrell was part of the 'E' Division District Support Unit 'Echo 30', who had been initially told to stand in front of the anti-Gaddafi protesters and fill the gaps between Yvonne and the other officers. "Literally, just before we took up this post, a group of pro-Gaddafi supporters came round the corner and we were re-tasked to deal with them," Farrell told me. "Just after this, the fatal shots rang out."

The demonstration was at its height, with loud music being played from the embassy, undoubtedly intended to drown out the shouting of the dissidents, when at 10.18 Linda Kells, who was working at 3 St James' Square, was one of the witnesses who saw windows on the first floor of the embassy slide open and two Sterling sub-machine guns open fire. Eleven protesters were hit and five of them were injured quite badly. Yvonne was shot in the back.

"I was about five or ten yards or so from Yvonne," remembered Pete Rogers. "I suddenly heard what seemed like firecrackers going off. I looked up and saw a little smoke from a window which I think was on the first floor of the Bureau. It all seemed in an instant as I then saw in the corner of my eye Yvonne falling to the ground. I began to move towards her and could hear screaming from the demonstrators. Yvonne was on her back and seemed to be rolling from side to side as I and other officers reached her. There were two officers at her side and, they were talking to her. She was conscious and it was obvious she was in pain. I knelt beside her legs on one side of her."

"Her robust and typical 'can-do' attitude was commendable," said Alex Fish, "but it cost her her life, and saved mine. Seeing the barrel of the machine gun appear out of a window in the Embassy and within a split second empty its entire magazine into the crowd, was frightening," said Alex Fish. "How other officers were not hit is beyond me, and as I stated, if I had talked to Yvonne or stood by her for a fraction longer, I doubt I would be alive. Lived with that one for a long time."

"I honestly can't remember how long we were there but the Square had been cleared and a decision was made that despite the dangers of moving an injured person, there was more danger in us all remaining there, exposed," Pete Rogers told me.

It was a difficult judgement to make, but in the circumstances it had to be the only sensible choice. "We really did not know if they would fire again," said Alex Fish, who utilized his man-management skills to employ some very young officers, literally frozen to the spot by this horrific incident, to clear the Square by shouting "the loudest 'fuck off!' I have ever uttered." Yvonne's boyfriend was struggling to get to her as the Square was being cleared.

"I do remember our Sergeant Howard Turner saying, 'Hats off, lads; we're going to get her out of here'," recalled Pete Rogers. "We then carried Yvonne out of the Square, leaving our hats with hers, in the Square. The hats became a sort of focal point for photographers, as I recall seeing pictures of them lying there on the road. It was all a bit surreal after that. I was in a bit of a daze, quite frankly. Yvonne had been taken off in an ambulance, and I was standing around as all the various back-up units were arriving. It's strange the things you recall, but I remember a certain senior officer rushing past me, shouting, 'Get your bloody hat on, son.' Before I could explain, he was gone. I then recall another man, whom I later found was a senior officer and was in plain clothes. I don't know why, but I think he was in the Anti-terrorist Squad. He approached – I think there was five of us – and said, 'Gents, were you in the Square?' Someone said, 'Yes.' He then ordered a uniformed police officer, I think Traffic, to 'look after us and take us back to Bow Street.' I have always recalled the difference between those two senior officers. One in a panic, saying things without thinking; the other, professional, calm, alert, caring and in control. As we got back to Bow Street, it was chaotic. There were armed officers outside, people, presumably demonstrators, being taken in."

One of the demonstrators who had been arrested was Salah Ibrahim Mabrook. He had been arrested prior to Yvonne's murder and later denied any prior knowledge of the shooting, saying that he thought that the embassy was going to be attacked by a Palestinian group.

Meanwhile, Police Constable John Murray accompanied Yvonne first to Charles II Street, then in the ambulance, which raced to Westminster Hospital. She complained that her stomach was hurting, and Murray asked the ambulance attendant for a pair of scissors. He cut her skirt at the waistband, and this appeared to bring her some relief.

Colin Osborn was attached to the Anti-terrorist Squad and was with one of the first of the support units to arrive at the square. With Wally Boreham and John Kathro, he went to Bow Street to commence taking statements from the shell-shocked police witnesses. He told me, sombrely, "The atmosphere that we found is still with me today." Bob Thorn had been a detective constable at C13 at New Scotland Yard and was sitting at his desk when the call came through. He, together with an experienced colleague, Detective Sergeant Don Webb, was tasked to go immediately to Westminster Hospital to take possession of any evidential items. By the time they arrived, Yvonne was already in the operating theatre. "It was not long before a surgeon came to see us," Thorn recalls. "He was crying as he told us our colleague was dead, there was nothing they could do for her. He went on to tell us that the bullet had entered her body and ricocheted off of bones in her body, tearing through several of her organs. The bullet had exited her torso, gone through her arm and out the other side." The bullet had not been recovered, and Thorn told me, "He was really very emotional, with tears running down his face as he spoke to us."

Thorn and Webb took possession of Yvonne's clothing and then went to find the ambulance which had conveyed her to the hospital. They were approached by the driver, who had found a bullet head in the back of the ambulance; it had fallen from her arm into her uniform jacket sleeve and had dropped into the ambulance as she was lifted out of it.

That morning, PC Laurie Young had been attending Bow Street Magistrates' Court and he was approached by one of the gaolers, who said, "She's dead, you know, Laurie."

Young was bemused. "What're you talking about?"

"Little Yvonne Fletcher; she's dead."

"God all-bloody mighty," whispered Young. Shockwaves were beginning to spread, firstly across 'C' Division, then the Metropolitan Police and finally, the whole world.

⋆   ⋆   ⋆

All of the specialist units of the Metropolitan Police were called in: D11 (the Firearms Unit), technical support and negotiators. Incredibly, there was a squabble between D11 and the DPG as to who would have primacy at St James' Square. It became apparent that no hostages were involved, and the two units worked together. With the embassy ringed by armed police, the Special Air Service (SAS) arrived. D11 officers showed the SAS team around the exterior of the building in order to formulate a plan of how to storm the Bureau, should the need arise. Meanwhile, the Anti-terrorist Squad had taken overall control of the investigation under Commander William Hucklesby. Alec Edwards (then a detective inspector) was in charge of a team – it was made up of C13 personnel, uniformed officers and divisional CID officers, on loan – to carry out a sweep of the area. It involved a finger-tip search, looking for bullets; and as he told me, "some of the spent bullets were found in the side of a building, two storeys up, situated on the far side of the square." In addition, COBRA was set up at Downing Street. The acronym stands for Cabinet Office Briefing Room 'A', and it is formed to deal with a civil emergency, with the most appropriate heads of departments attending. In a crisis of this magnitude, the Prime Minister – at this time, Margaret Thatcher – would certainly have attended, but unfortunately she was out of the country. Therefore responsibility for dealing with the situation fell to the Home Secretary, Leon Brittan.

While the SAS were formulating a plan to storm the embassy – one theory was that they were going to effect entry underneath the building, through the sewers – Gaddafi reacted predictably, effectively putting the British Embassy in Tripoli under siege, encircling the building with soldiers, preventing the staff from leaving and stating that the Bureau in London had been stormed and that those in the building had fired in self-defence.

On the second day of the siege, communications had been set up to permit dialogue with the embassy staff. "Well, all I can say is, it's nothing to do with us," said a spokesman. "We're innocent ... that's all." But that was thought not to be the case, because apart from telephone communications being installed, a separate unit of technical support officers had surreptitiously drilled several listening probes into the embassy and a number of heated exchanges between the staff were recorded. Despite the spokesman's denial, it was certainly something to do with them, because the gunman's name was spoken, again and again.

But this was a siege unlike any other. There were no hostages. There were no threats of reprisals if the staff's stipulations were not met and there were no deadlines imposed, because there were no demands. All that was claimed was diplomatic immunity under the terms of the Vienna Convention in respect of diplomatic relations.

In a television interview thought by many to be almost insufferably pompous, Leon Brittan said, "I was conscious all the time of a tremendous responsibility, of course. Yes. It was probably the greatest single crisis-type responsibility that I had in my career as Home Secretary." On 27 April 1984 Brittan attended Yvonne's funeral at Salisbury Cathedral, approximately fifteen miles from where Yvonne's parents lived. Also present was the Commissioner, Sir Kenneth Newman GBE, QPM, together with all of the 350 officers and staff from Bow Street. A large contingent of police officers from across the country plus 2,000 other well-wishers and mourners attended the service.

Leon Brittan would later say, "I felt that this was one of those occasions when you have to suppress personal feelings of outrage, because they're natural human feelings that everyone was likely to have, against the consideration of what really is in the national interest to do."

And so, to the outrage of the country in general and the Metropolitan Police in particular, the occupants of the Bureau walked free on the same day as Yvonne's funeral. First, eighteen bags were returned to Libya under diplomatic privilege without being searched. Were the murder weapons concealed in those bags? Almost certainly. And it was also because of diplomatic privilege that none of the staff were stopped, searched or questioned. In fairness to Brittan, his hands were tied. The Libyans had exercised their right under the articles of the Vienna Convention which had been established almost exactly twenty-three years previously, the same edict that prevents the authorities from entering an embassy without that country's permission.

However, Matouk Mohammed Matouk and Abdulgader Mohammed Baghdadi, who were in the embassy at the time of the shooting and became two persons whom the police definitely wanted to question, were not diplomats and in consequence could not be afforded diplomatic status. Immediately after the shooting, both of them had slipped out of the back door. There were also Abdulgader Tuhami, an intelligence officer believed to have fired the fatal shot, and Moustafa Mghirbi, the chief intelligence officer believed to have passed on Tripoli's orders to open fire. They returned to Libya, and television coverage at that time revealed a tumultuous hero's welcome. One other man who had returned to Libya was of just as much interest to the investigating officers as the four previously named Libyans. Dr Omar Ahmed Sodani was an accredited diplomat who was not in the embassy at the time of the shooting. He had been arrested for obstructing police prior to the shooting because, together with Salah Ibrahim Mabrook, he had attempted to stop the police erecting barriers outside the embassy. At Bow Street he claimed diplomatic immunity, and by the time this was established and he was released without charge, Yvonne was dead. Sodani was one of the diplomats released – in his case on 26 April, the day before the majority of the others. It was stated that upon his return to

Libya he had been hanged on Gaddafi's orders. If that was the case, Dr Sodani subsequently made the most amazing recovery since Lazarus. Almost a year to the day later, Sodani and his wife were expelled from Belgium, after the Justice Minister had described him as "a public danger". He had entered Belgium on 8 March that year and had registered as a medical student, calling himself Ehmeida Omar Mohammad. He and his wife were escorted by police officers to be placed on a flight to Libya, via Paris. The Belgian authorities were aware that Sodani had been expelled from Britain following the murder of Yvonne Fletcher. The *Los Angeles Times* stated that Sodani had been identified as a suspect in Yvonne's murder, and the *Chicago Tribune* went a little further by describing him as 'the man regarded as the prime suspect.'

But Sodani had quickly eschewed the position of medical student in favour of diplomatic status, and under the auspices of the Vienna Convention safely returned to his native land. He would later work in East Germany – and also in Libya.

* * *

The SAS stood down and returned to the Stirling Lines in Hereford as quietly as they had arrived. A former SAS officer involved in the operation was quoted as saying, "Yeah, fuck it. We should have gone in there and killed them." These were sentiments shared by almost the entire population of the country. Diplomatic relations with Libya were severed on 23 April, and a meticulous investigation commenced in order to gather together every available scrap of evidence. The now-empty embassy was searched, revealing high levels of firearms residue on two of the first floor window sills which suggested the presence of two gunmen, also a number of fingerprints. And from the spread of the discharged bullets, it appeared that the gunmen had fired in two different directions. When bomb disposal expert Peter Gurney entered the building on 30 April, he was looking for improvised explosive devices (IEDs). What he did find, by a radiator underneath one of the two windows on the first floor, was a 9mm cartridge case, suggesting that whoever had been responsible for cleaning up during the eleven days of stand-off before expulsion had not been as diligent as they might have hoped.

Conspiracy theories and wild stories abounded. 'Experts' lined up to show how the bullet could not possibly have been fired from the first floor of the Bureau and to demonstrate the various angles at which bullets could or could not enter a human body.

Best of all was the suggestion that Yvonne had been killed by an anti-Gaddafi organization funded by the CIA, and that the fatal shot had been fired from the sixth floor penthouse at 3 St James' Square, next door to the Bureau.

The murder of a colleague, plus the way the suspects had been dealt with, infuriated the Metropolitan Police in general and the officers at Bow Street police station in particular. Worse than their impotent fury was a feeling of complete and utter demoralization. "The murder of Yvonne Fletcher was dreadful and has left its mark on me," former police officer Stephanie Kirkcaldy told me in 2011. "Even now, her death saddens me. Her life was taken in such a sudden and deliberate way. We were the same age, she had served about six months longer than myself, she was ... doing a job she loved and had so much life in front of her. Just like me. The person who committed this crime walked away, a free man. When her death is spoken about, I often wonder what she would have been doing now."

★   ★   ★

This was when Michael Winner stepped into the breach and organized the Police Memorial Trust, and the first memorial, made of granite and Portland stone, was a commemoration to Yvonne Fletcher, whose death had moved Winner so deeply. It was erected in St James' Square and unveiled on 1 February 1985 by Prime Minister Margaret Thatcher, with these words:

> For Yvonne Fletcher, the morning of Tuesday, 17 April began like any other. Her task that day was to police a demonstration, one of some 400 demonstrations held in London each year. It was, everyone thought, a routine task, which would probably be over by noon.
>
> But shortly after ten o'clock the normal life of this London square was shattered by a hail of bullets, and Yvonne lay fatally wounded on duty in the heart of London.
>
> Today, the square has resumed its peaceful way. But memories of those terrible events are still vivid in our minds. We have come here to remember Yvonne Fletcher, privately in our own thoughts, and publicly by this ceremony. Her death was a grievous loss – to her family, to the Metropolitan Police, and to all of us.
>
> This simple memorial, erected by the Police Memorial Trust, will be a reminder to Londoners and to visitors alike of the debt that we owe to Yvonne Fletcher and all her colleagues

in the police. Without them, the law could not be upheld. Without them, indeed, there would be no law, and no liberty.

We have become used to seeing our policemen and women respond magnificently to any challenge. We must never take their professionalism for granted.

Too often especially recently, we hear that our police have been killed or wounded on duty. This has got to stop, and every single citizen has a duty to help make it stop.

Our police uphold the law without regard to their own feelings and their own safety, never knowing what the day may bring. The greater the risk, the greater their courage. The greater their courage, the greater our loss.

We also remember today their families, on whose support and affection they rely. We honour their courage and their sense of duty.

To some, the word duty may seem rather cold. But it is not – because you cannot carry out your duty without thinking of your fellow men; and you cannot know your duty unless you know and love what is right.

Today as I unveil this memorial to Yvonne Fletcher, let us also pay tribute to the other brave men and women police officers who have been killed or injured, calling to mind as we do so the words of Abraham Lincoln:

"Let us have faith that right makes might; and in that faith let us to the end dare to do our duty as we understand it."

On the twentieth anniversary of Yvonne's murder, Alex Fish attended the annual ceremony at St James' Square and gave a lift in his car to the Force chaplain. He told me, "That was the first occasion I felt able to tell anyone about having put Yvonne on the spot where she was to die. He, in turn, told Yvonne's parents that day. I don't know how they received that information as I did not have the opportunity to speak to them. Regardless, it felt like I had finally come to terms with that decision."

This was indicative of the self-blame which many officers felt, quite unfairly; but it obviously had a cathartic effect for Fish, whilst other officers are still suffering to come to terms with the events of that day: 'Why her? Why not me? What could I have done to have prevented it?'

★   ★   ★

Gaddafi still continued to embrace and fund terrorist groups, including the IRA and the Red Army Faction, and he referred to the atrocious attacks on the airports at Rome and Vienna, in which nineteen people were killed and 140 injured, as "heroic acts". After the bombing of La Belle Discotheque in Berlin on 5 April 1986, which killed three people and injured 229, it was discovered that the attack had been planned in the Libyan Embassy in East Berlin. Ten days later, US President Ronald Reagan launched 'Operation El Dorado Canyon', a punitive raid against Libya, and Margaret Thatcher assisted by permitting the bombing raid to be launched from USAF bases in England. Gaddafi was forewarned by the Maltese Prime Minister and managed to escape in time.

Gaddafi's revenge was appalling. He personally ordered (according to Libya's former Justice Minister, Mustafa Abdel-Jalil, in February 2011), the mid-air explosion which destroyed 'The Clipper Maid of the Seas' – otherwise known as Pan Am Flight 103. Four days before Christmas 1988, the transatlantic flight took off from London Heathrow Airport, destined for John F. Kennedy International Airport, New York. The explosion killed the crew of sixteen and 243 passengers; debris from the aircraft accounted for another eleven fatalities in the southern Scottish town of Lockerbie. UN Sanctions against Libya were imposed.

A lengthy investigation was carried out before Abdelbaset al-Megrahi, a Libyan intelligence officer, was named in an arrest warrant on 13 November 1991. Over seven more years were to pass before al-Megrahi was handed over to officials in Holland, on 5 April 1999.

Suddenly, diplomatic relations between England and Libya were restored, and on 7 July 1999, Robin Cook, the Secretary of State for Foreign and Commonwealth Affairs, informed Parliament that the Libyan government accepted "general responsibility" for Yvonne Fletcher's death and had offered compensation; £250,000 was finally paid to Yvonne's family. The Libyans agreed to co-operate in a joint investigation. The following day, Scotland Yard announced its intention to 'reopen the investigation', although, in reality, the enquiry had never closed.

On 24 May 2002 an investigating team including Assistant Commissioner Alan Fry travelled to Libya to interview Abdulgader Tuhami, who was considered to possess "vital information" in respect of the investigation. Access to him was denied. One month later, Metropolitan Police officials met with members of the Libyan Government to discuss the investigation. Two years passed, and during this time the UN sanctions were lifted.

After it was announced that Prime Minister Tony Blair was going to travel to Libya for the purpose of talks with Gaddafi, the

Metropolitan Police Federation angrily stated on 10 February 2004 that Libya had "blood on its hands" over Yvonne's death and demanded that her killer should be handed over, prior to any talks with the Prime Minister.

Two weeks later, Libya responded just as heatedly, when the new Prime Minister, Shukri Ghanem, stated that his country was not responsible either for Yvonne Fletcher's murder or the Lockerbie bombing. The reason why Libya had made the admission and paid compensation, he said, was to bring peace and an end to international sanctions. Sensing lucrative trade talks disappearing in front of his very eyes, Gaddafi swiftly repudiated the statement. It is not clear if it was Prime Minister Ghanem's imprudent remarks which led to his dismissal in 2006.

But it apparently seemed to the British Government good sense to enter into trade negotiations with a country whose unstable leader had a proven track record of wholesale murder, violence and betrayal. This was the man (known as 'The Guide' and 'The Brother Leader') who in 1972 had endeavoured to get China to sell him a nuclear bomb; when they refused, he tried the same request with Pakistan in 1977. It was the same man who filmed dissidents being publicly executed and then broadcast (and re-broadcast) the event on state television channels. It was Gaddafi who abolished the teaching of foreign languages in schools – the same schools, along with factories and Government offices, which were subject to surveillance. Libya was considered to be the most censored country in the Middle East, and Amnesty International believe that between 1980 and 1987 twenty-five assassinations were carried out, world wide, on Gaddafi's orders. To give some credence to this claim, Gaddafi was quoted as saying in 1982, "It is the Libyan people's responsibility to liquidate such scums who are distorting Libya's image abroad."

A chilling, if ungrammatical, statement from the leader of a country which did indeed have "blood on its hands".

However, a grinning Tony Blair did meet Gaddafi and effusively shook hands with him, and just over one month later, on 25 March 2004, Jack Straw, the Foreign Secretary, announced that the police would travel to Libya in an attempt to find Yvonne's killers. On 3 April they did so but the investigation got no further. Two more years went by. In 2006 letters were exchanged between the British and Libyan Governments, and in an act of pusillanimous betrayal the Foreign Office cravenly agreed to abandon any attempt to try the murderers of Yvonne Fletcher in England and stated that any proceedings could take place in Libya. The deal was rubber-stamped by Jack Straw. In

December of that year, Metropolitan Police officers flew to Libya to interview potential witnesses, with a palpable lack of success.

Six weeks prior to another prime ministerial trip to Libya in 2007, a further report into the case, which had been requested from an independent source by the Metropolitan Police, was completed. The contents were only revealed when it was leaked to the *Daily Telegraph* two years later. The report stated that Matouk Mohammed Matouk and Abdulgader Baghdadi could be prosecuted for conspiracy to murder; the finger had been pointed at them by an important witness who stated that the two men had been on the first floor of the embassy where the shooting took place – an area which was controlled by the revolutionary committee (of which both men were members) – on the morning of the murder. They had gone downstairs to initiate the counter-demonstration with the pro-Gaddafi supporters, telling them where to stand to avoid getting shot and to run away after the shooting began. The report also stated that there had been a prearranged plan, instigated in advance from Tripoli, to cause death or grievous bodily harm to the demonstrators.

When these revelations appeared in the *Daily Telegraph*, a white-faced Crown Prosecution Service stuttered that they yet had to receive a completed file.

On the same day that Blair visited Gaddafi a trade deal was struck, whereby British Petroleum signed a £450 million deal with Libya. If Blair did mention the possibility of handing over to the authorities the suspects for Yvonne Fletcher's murder, his plea fell on deaf ears.

On 20 August 2009, Abdelbaset al-Megrahi, the Lockerbie bomber said to be suffering from terminal cancer, was unequivocally released from his Scottish prison after serving eight and a half years of his life sentence and returned home, to the hysterical delight of his fellow countrymen. A furious United States of America demanded to know if the promise of oil deals influenced his release, something strenuously denied by the Scottish authorities.

There appeared a glimmer of hope for the family of Yvonne Fletcher and her colleagues; was there now the chance of a quid pro quo agreement to exchange the suspects in Libya, in return for al-Megrahi? Well … no, there wasn't. Many of the inhabitants of Middle Eastern countries, no matter how much they might display a veneer of culture or good manners, do not recognize the spirit of compromise and the good old English ethos of 'fair play' – they regard it as a sign of weakness. Usually, they are right to do so. And why should they make concessions?

Hadn't they arranged a deal with the good old British Government, to say that any trial would take place in Libya?

Three weeks after al-Megrahi's release, *The Sunday Times* revealed the details of the 2006 deal. The Foreign Office rather airily claimed that the Fletcher family had known of this arrangement, which had been agreed in an exchange of ambassadors' letters; but the family denied this, saying that they knew that any trial might take place in Libya but not that the towel had been thrown in with regards to a prosecution in England. The cudgels were taken up by the family's MP, Daniel Kawczynski, who believed that the Foreign Office had tried to mislead him and the Fletcher family.

Not so, according to the Foreign Office, who have stated that they are "committed to the investigation and often raise the matter with the Libyan Government." On 5 August 2010, they, together with a police delegation, went, at the invitation of the Libyan Government, to discuss the ways of "moving the investigation forward to the satisfaction of both governments." The investigation was not moved forward by one inch.

'Something is rotten in the state of Denmark,' said Shakespeare's Hamlet, but on this occasion it was another country which was emitting a rather unpleasant odour.

★   ★   ★

Back in Tripoli, those close confidants of Gaddafi, Matouk and Baghdadi, had fallen on their feet. Not for them the trembling fear of wondering if they were going to receive, in police parlance, 'a six o'clock knock' – to stand trial at home or abroad, for conspiracy to murder. No, they settled comfortably into their new jobs, Matouk as Minister of Public Administration and Baghdadi in charge of the Revolutionary Committee.

But in February 2011, civil unrest began to spread like wildfire throughout the Middle East. First Egypt, then Tunisia, both Libya's neighbours. By 21 February, the unrest had spread to Libya, and pitched battles broke out between the rebels and the government. The United Nations imposed a 'no-fly zone'. Despite British bombers hammering Tripoli night after night, Britain unctuously stated that they had no desire to topple Gaddafi from his throne; that was a matter for the Libyan people. However, when the rebels took possession of the oil refinery at the seaport of Ras Lanuf, it was wondered who would be heading a new government ... if the rebels were successful, of course. There was, of course, absolutely no question of the coalition countries supplying arms to anti-Gaddafi rebels, good gracious, no. However, mused the (then) UK Defence Secretary, Dr Liam Fox, "it means they will pretty much be in control of Libya's oil exports. That will produce a very different dynamic and a different equilibrium inside Libya."

And then, on 14 March 2011, the rebels captured a man who had been hiding in a farmhouse. At fifty-nine years of age, he was head of Al Ejanalghoria – Gaddafi's militia in Benghazi – and his name is Dr Omar Ahmed Sodani. He denied any complicity in Yvonne Fletcher's murder. However, he stated that he did hear three names mentioned: "Two were students, both named Salah, and the third person was a diplomat – Abdulgader. I do not know what has happened to them ..."

★   ★   ★

The prosecutor at the international court was granted arrest warrants in respect of Gaddafi and others for the murder and persecution of the Libyan people who participated in the uprising. However, with his usual rhetoric, Gaddafi defiantly stated, "We are in our country and we insist on staying until death," adding heroically, "Let them even use nuclear bombs."

In the event, a nuclear strike was not thought necessary. On 20 October 2011, in his home town of Sirte and discovered, suitably enough, crawling out of a sewerage pipe, Gaddafi was executed by an over-enthusiastic young Libyan rebel. Of course, opinions originally varied as to what had actually transpired; one report said he had been wounded, another that he had been shot in the legs as he tried to escape, and yet a third suggested that Gaddafi had been caught in cross-fire. In fact, he was shot twice at close-quarters, although just before his summary execution, Gaddafi was heard to plaintively ask, "Don't you know right from wrong?" Coming from the lips of someone who had been specializing in mass-murder for over forty years, those remarks were considered to be a bit rich.

Gaddafi's demise was greeted with differences of opinion. Some felt that justice had been cheated because he had not stood trial for his crimes. Others – myself included – merely felt that a decade of left-wing defence lawyers had been robbed of the chance to tender their monumental fees.

So – what of Yvonne Fletcher's murderers? Well, the name of Abdulmagid Salah Ameri, a former Libyan diplomat, popped-up as a relative newcomer to the list of suspects. The following day, the new Libyan Government, the National Transitional Council

(NTC), declared that he would not be extradited, and the day after that, he was reported to be dead. Well, well. What about one of the originally-named suspects, Abdulgader Mohammed Baghdadi? Apparently, he is dead as well. Crikey. And the other, Matouk Mohammed Matouk? He is alive, say Libyan sources, but he will not be extradited. Now, what about the other alleged shootist, Abdulgader Tuhami, or the intelligence officer, Moustafa Mghirbi, both of whom the police wish to question? If they are alive, they seem to be keeping a low profile.

In July 2011, the British Government invited the NTC to occupy the embassy in London. The Foreign Secretary, William Hague, stated that Britain would unfreeze assets worth £91 million to the Arabian Gulf Oil Company, now effectively owned by the NTC. However, the process of releasing the assets by the UN Security Council was slow, due to legal and technical reasons, and it was not until 16 December 2011 that the sanctions were lifted, permitting the release of some £96 billion to the Libyans.

In December 2011 Libya's Interior Minister, Fawzy Abdel Aal, agreed to the 'early return' of British police officers to continue the investigation of Yvonne Fletcher's case. Will they? Try not to get yourself into a state, Matouk, or you, Omar, Abdulgader or Moustafa; it might never happen. Because it appears to many cynical members of the Metropolitan Police that trade deals, involving oil, are more important than human life.

At the time of writing – January 2012 – there is now an official police force in Libya which must maintain stability so that important reforms can take place. However, the militia groups who helped oust Gaddafi have taken the law into their own hands, setting up roadblocks and carrying out arrests; so the country is still in a state of upheaval.

However, perhaps something will be done to secure Yvonne's murderers; but don't hold your breath. I suppose it depends on how much pressure the British government brings to bear; perhaps there are politicians who believe in their heart of hearts that Yvonne Fletcher was 'only a police officer'. And given that members of the British Government are prone to uttering *gaffes* of gasp-producing enormity, it may be that one day, one of them will say so.

Although hopefully not within earshot of any member of the Metropolitan Police; or Michael Winner.

CHAPTER 10

A Matter of Disrespect

Having just read through the first draft of this chapter, I appreciate that there are matters and practices contained in it which, to the reader who is not conversant with the 'Gangsta' ethos, may well make it so utterly unbelievable as to appear a work of fiction. Implausible it may seem, but sadly it is true – and this is how such a shattering breakdown in law and order came about.

Following the end of World War Two, the British Government needed to address the country's labour shortage, and to this end Commonwealth immigrants, including those from the West Indies, started arriving in 1948. They settled in Nottingham, Birmingham and west and south London; and that, of course, is a matter of record.

However, what is not generally known – but is nevertheless quite true – is that the Jamaican authorities saw this as a heaven-sent opportunity to rid themselves of some of the most repellent and hardened criminals who inhabited the jail in the capital, Kingston. At that time, luminaries such as Noël Coward, Ian Fleming and Errol Flynn were purchasing properties on the island and expected to find a paradise full of sunshine, rum and inhabitants with beaming smiles; which they did. This was partly because many of the decent islanders had left, to emigrate to a dull, austerity- and smog-ridden faraway country, together with the delights of queues and ration books; and some of the most depraved criminals in the world had travelled with them.

As the years went by, the offspring of these criminals drifted into crime and spawned and then abandoned their own children, who without proper parental guidance perpetuated the whole dismal cycle again and again. And in consequence, the 1980s and 90s saw the emergence of the 'Gangsta', who was readily identifiable. Usually he was the product of a single-parent family and because of self-inflicted lack of schooling was grossly uneducated, illiterate and inarticulate. Whatever he wanted, he took, and eschewing stealth, he usually did so by threats or actual violence. Delinquents like this would quickly spiral out of control, inflicting violence and terrorizing housing estates, and would soon be brought to the attention of the social services, the police and the courts. Normally, they were initially dealt with leniently – a gross mistake, because the budding Gangsta saw this as a sign of weakness, as indeed it was. Their prey would be anyone who could be bullied, and as they saw the way their cowering victims reacted to them, so their confidence grew. As the years passed and they moved in and out of youth custody, being ordered to carry out community work (which they seldom did), they behaved as they pleased; the police were the enemy, but if a Gangsta were arrested, he would claim that he had been beaten up and fitted up; and of course, the race card was played at every possible opportunity.

In the twilight world of the Gangsta, 'respect' was everything, something to be demanded and accepted as a natural right. Not to be esteemed was to be 'disrespected' or 'dissed', and this was an intolerable situation, because if a slight was not rectified and avenged with considerable interest, the affronted Gangsta's days were numbered; his peers were likely to assume he also used unacceptable terms such as 'sorry', 'please' and 'excuse me' and would brand him a 'pussy' – a reference to female genitalia. Being thus stigmatized would in turn lead to humiliation and expulsion from the Gangsta fold.

So with many of their victims too afraid to testify against them, the Gangstas swaggered around the streets, dressed in expensive but ill-fitting clothing and festooned in jewellery, drove expensive cars, inevitably neither taxed, insured or registered to them, and continued to inflict mindless and irrational violence, deal in drugs, rip off fellow drug dealers and casually rob and steal as the mood took them. That was bad enough; what was worse was that the Gangstas were acquiring firearms and they were not afraid to use them.

★   ★   ★

Police officers are murdered in the course of their duties for a variety of reasons, usually because the perpetrator is about to be arrested and wishes to avoid capture; this has been in evidence time and time again throughout these pages. But the following case is rather different. The police officer concerned was not a steely eyed crime-buster; he was a decent man in his forties, doing his duty as a community policeman by gallantly attempting to prevent two inquisitive, possible witnesses from getting themselves shot, and telling them to get back into the safety of their house, because the man who had lived opposite to them had been shot dead. As the police officer turned towards the murderous trio who had been responsible he presented no immediate threat to them, but they shot him fatally in the chest. His killers then swaggered off, roaring with laughter and triumphantly firing their weapons in the air; in fact, one of the bullets arced in a parabola and was later found in Wandsworth, two miles away.

There was an intensive, professional police investigation, and within a month there were three arrests. Ten weeks later, the murder charges against the three men were dropped. It was considered there was insufficient evidence. The perpetrators of the killings went on to commit further, very serious offences. It took almost thirteen years before there was a conviction for the murders. That lacklustre organization, the Crown Prosecution Service (CPS), had sanctioned the release of the suspects, and it is little wonder that embittered police officers said that the initials CPS stood for 'Criminals' Protection Service.' This is what happened.

★   ★   ★

Patrick Dunne was born in 1949 at Shoreham-by-Sea, West Sussex; he was the first of three sons of Mr and Mrs A. Dunne. After the birth of their second child the family moved to London, and following the arrival of their third child they settled in Carshalton. Patrick attended a secondary modern school there and left having achieved ten GCE 'O' levels. Initially, he worked for the local borough engineer, but the job was not to his liking; instead, he decided he wanted to teach, was accepted by Northern Counties College at Newcastle-upon-Tyne and commenced his studies in September 1968. He read mathematics, music and English, and following the successful completion of his BA degree he joined Deane High School, Bolton, teaching mathematics to all year groups. By 1981 he was head of the fifth year but was beginning to feel a little jaded with teaching; after his father died in 1986, Patrick, a single man, decided to move back to London in order to support his mother. He resumed his teaching career in Woking, but then decided to join the Metropolitan Police. Patrick informed his selection board:

> My reasons for joining the Metropolitan Police are varied. The police do a useful job that on the whole is valued by society. I would find it satisfying to contribute to that work. I am apprehensive about the less pleasant aspects of the job but hope I will be able to cope satisfactorily with these.

He was now forty years of age – the police age limit had effectively been abolished – and after his initial training he was posted to Clapham police station on 4 June 1990, as Police Constable 750 'LM'. A year later, he was selected to be a home beat officer, a position he held at the time of his death.

★   ★   ★

Kwame Vaderpuye used a variety of names: William Kwame Danso was one, but he was also known as William Asiedou Danso, Odatel Kwafon and Ralph Vanderpuye. He was a little uncertain as to his date of birth, which he gave variously as 29 July 1961 or 18 August 1962. It is tolerably certain that he was born in Accra, Ghana – his sister, Gifty Tettehmartey, later provided some useful family history – and it was from Ghana that he arrived in the United Kingdom on 5 April 1978. To prevent any further confusion, he will be referred to as Kwame Danso, which was how he was known to most of his associates.

On 20 February 1980, for overstaying his permitted time in the country, he was fined £20 and recommended for deportation; it is clear that he resisted this order, because it was not until over three years later, on 7 April 1983, that he was removed to Ghana under the name of Vanderpuye. However, by 1984 he was back, and when he was convicted of possession of a small amount of cannabis on 12 March 1985 and fined £40, it was in the name of Danso.

In 1986 he married, and during the next seven years this most unhappy alliance resulted in his wife suffering violence at his hands, Danso participating in drugs deals and four children being born. Deborah, his wife, was pregnant with their fifth child when they separated. Danso was living in a London Borough of Lambeth council house, divided into three flats, at 31 Cato Road, Clapham, and had a number of girlfriends. His estranged wife and children moved into accommodation elsewhere in Clapham which was later described as being 'not fit for occupation'.

Danso dealt in drugs, although he was certainly not considered to be a major supplier; he also ran a security company, styled 'Drapeseal', and one of his contracts was with The Academy, a concert hall in Stockwell Road, Brixton, where he worked 'on the door'. A second was at Street Communications, situated at 23 Leigham Court Road, Streatham, SW6. This was a telecommunication retail company, which sold mobile phones as well as selling and fitting car radios and alarms. It comprised a shop front and a service and installation area at the rear. The

company was part-owned by Eugene Djaba (of whom we shall
hear much more, later); Danso, a tall, powerfully built man, was
employed at the shop on a part-time basis in a security capacity,
primarily to prevent shoplifting. Danso's background and lifestyle
suggest that he was not a particularly loveable character, although
this assertion would have been disputed by several of Danso's
paramours, English, African and Croatian. However, Danso was
almost adorable compared with Gary Nelson.

★   ★   ★

Gary Lloyd Nelson – known as 'Tyson' for reasons which will
become obvious, not least that he facially resembled the boxer of
the same name – now enters the equation. At the time of these
events, he was twenty–three years of age, five feet eleven tall,
stocky, black, with very short hair and high, protruding cheek
bones.

Born on 5 October 1970, Nelson lived at Fieldview,
Wandsworth. He attended Chelsea Juvenile Court just after his
thirteenth birthday for taking a pedal cycle without the consent
of the owner; he was conditionally discharged for twelve months.
Less than two years later, he was ushered into Balham Juvenile
Court after having punched someone in the face in Woolworths;
for the offence of actual bodily harm he was told to carry out 100
hours unpaid community service. However, it is unlikely that
much of the work was carried out; within two months of that
court appearance he appeared at the Inner London Crown Court
charged with robbery and possessing an offensive weapon; he was
sentenced to a total of six months' youth custody. Nelson had
hardly been released from his incarceration when on 7 March
1986 he assaulted two police officers who went to interview him
at his home about an offence. It took nine months for him to be
sentenced at Balham Juvenile Court, where he received eighteen
weeks' youth custody for the assaults and, inexplicably, was fined
just £100 for theft from the person.

Again it appears that no sooner had he been released than he
was arrested again. Following his appearance at Kingston Crown
Court on 30 September 1987, at the age of sixteen, for theft from
the person, possessing an offensive weapon, possessing controlled
drugs, handling stolen goods and an indictable common assault,
he was sentenced to a total of four and a half years' youth
custody. At Chelmsford Magistrates' Court he was then
sentenced to twenty-eight days' imprisonment for actual bodily
harm; he had punched and kicked a fellow prisoner in the

prison's exercise yard. At Kingston Crown Court on 4 March 1992, for handling stolen goods he was, incredibly, ordered to carry out 120 hours of unpaid community service work; and for reckless driving and no insurance he was fined and disqualified from driving for fourteen days. These last two motoring offences may seem pretty small beer compared to the catalogue of serious crimes he had carried out in the previous nine years, but as this chapter progresses it will become clear that car-related offences would assist in bringing about Nelson's downfall.

★　★　★

That there was bad blood between Nelson and Danso was never in dispute. In his role as a security man, Danso had previously stopped Nelson from entering the Brixton Academy Club, and in Nelson's eyes this was a piece of jaw-dropping insolence by which he felt he had been 'disrespected'. In fact, following this confrontation, Nelson had entered Street Communications whilst Danso was there and, out of his hearing, said to the part-owner, Djaba, "What's pussy doing here?" It was a highly provocative, insulting remark and it was an indication that Nelson had neither forgotten nor forgiven Danso's actions at the Academy Club.

On Tuesday, 19 October 1993, Nelson returned to the shop. Danso was not present but another security guard, Ian Bourne – he was known as 'Rambo' – was, and as Nelson went to enter the private area behind the counter, Bourne stopped him. There was an argument and a struggle and Nelson repeatedly asked, "What you going to do about it?" He put his hand inside his jacket as an indication that he was carrying a weapon – as indeed he was. At that moment, Djaba, who had heard raised voices, came into the shop and saw the struggle. Bourne told him, "He's not meant to come through."

Djaba defused the situation, calmed 'Tyson' down and took him through the shop to the garage where a red Peugeot 205 belonging to Nelson's girlfriend was having an immobilizer fitted. There was some general conversation about the work which was being carried out, and as the two men sat in the car Djaba asked what would have happened in the confrontation with Bourne had he, Djaba, not intervened. Nelson replied that he would have "shot Bourne in the belly" and to reinforce his statement produced a self-loading pistol from under his jacket. "It carries twenty rounds," remarked Nelson. Shortly afterwards, Anthony Patrick Francis arrived, a friend of Nelson's and four years older than him, and the two men left the shop premises. Francis – known as 'Tony' – was born in 1965 and was six feet tall, slim build, with short black hair, the top slightly higher than the sides, which were shaved. He had a gold front tooth and sometimes sported facial stubble. Francis had a number of offences recorded, including theft from the person and assaulting the police, none of which had been thought serious enough to merit his imprisonment. Exactly two months previously, he had been cautioned at Tooting police station for using threatening behaviour.

The following day, Wednesday, 20 October, Danso was working at Street Communications. During the morning, Tony Francis arrived at the shop in his burgundy-coloured Triumph Stag, in order to have repairs carried out on it. Danso asked Djaba to return home to collect some photographs of Francis which Danso had taken at a funeral. He did so, Danso handed them to Francis, who appeared to be pleased with them, and Francis left shortly afterwards.

At about three o'clock that afternoon one of Danso's oldest friends, thirty-seven-year-old Henry Ernest Uwekuotou Wood, arrived at the shop. He had worked for Danso at The Academy and he had come to collect £25 which he was owed for security work there.

Two hours later, Francis returned to the shop to pick up his car and intimated that he wished to speak to Djaba. Within ten minutes a man known only as 'Blue' entered the shop with a companion. Precisely why he did so is not known, but he was not welcome at the premises, and Kwame Danso was aware of this, because he stepped forward, obviously intending to eject him. It was at that moment that Francis re-entered the shop premises and instantly became furious upon seeing 'Blue', advancing towards him saying, "I don't like you, I'm going to do you something." Danso got between Francis and 'Blue' and his companion, telling them that it was disrespectful to fight in the shop, and ushered the two men to the door. As he did so, Francis went into the office and a witness heard him make a telephone call, saying, "I'm at Street Comma, there's a dude down here giving me grief, hurry up and bring his things."

Five minutes later, Nelson arrived. By now, Francis had armed himself with a small bat, smaller than a baseball bat and probably a rounders or softball bat, and Blue's entourage had increased to three or four companions. A great deal of verbal abuse was hurled by both sides, with Danso in the middle endeavouring to keep the two factions apart. Blue threw a dustbin cover at Francis, and

Danso tried to get Blue to move to the other side of the road, shouting at him, "Go, go, go!" To Francis, Danso said, "Don't let him wind you up." At one point, Danso had grabbed Francis in a bear-hug to prevent him fighting, and Francis shouted, "Leave me alone, leave me alone."

It is clear that Francis was furious, because he screamed on at least three occasions, "You lot disrespect me!" at Blue and his associates; the disturbance was noticed by Raymond Sevan Ibrahim, a fifty-six-year-old shoemaker, who was driving past the scene at the time and saw four black men run across the road from Street Communications. Blue and his companions got into a dark green VW Golf and drove off; Danso released Francis and he and Nelson left the scene, with Francis still in possession of the rounders bat.

Francis had left behind his keys, glasses, mobile phone and briefcase in the shop. Michelle Elisabeth Williams, who worked at the shop, was a friend of Francis and had been expecting a lift home from him; Djaba asked her to take the property with her, so that Francis could collect it from her later on. At six o'clock, the disturbance finished, the shop was locked, Michelle Williams went home, and Danso and Wood left together in Danso's blue Mini.

Francis was still undoubtedly furious at the way in which Blue and Co had treated him with such disrespect; but it is possible that Danso had incurred his displeasure as well. Although the two men had appeared to be on friendly terms earlier in the day when Danso had handed over the photographs to Francis, holding him back and preventing him from fighting Blue, especially since there were onlookers to witness Francis' discomfort, may have caused a rift in the relationship.

Djaba then made three calls to Nelson's mobile phone; the first two were unsuccessful but the third, at 6.35, enabled him to speak on the same call to both Nelson and Francis. He told Francis that Michelle Williams had his property, and then Francis asked Djaba where Danso lived; Djaba replied that he did not know. But Francis persisted, saying, "Is it Clapham, Cato Road?" and Djaba replied, "Yes, something like that."

And then Francis said this: "Kwame's fucked me up, Eugene."

There then followed a conversation between Djaba and Nelson, in which Nelson stated that he would see him the following day. Because of the content of these conversations, Djaba attempted to contact Danso on his mobile phone, without success. At seven o'clock Michelle Williams met Francis, who was alone, driving his Triumph Stag in the Old Kent Road, where she handed over his property to him; but Francis still looked tense and upset.

Meanwhile, having left Street Communications, Danso and Wood drove to the latter's home address so that he could pick up a fresh shirt and tie, after which they arrived at Danso's flat at 31 Cato Road at seven o'clock. They did not go out again, because they had decided to watch Arsenal playing the Belgium team Standard Liège in the European League Cup on television. Both men had something to eat, and Danso smoked some cannabis before settling down to watch the match, which commenced at eight o'clock.

★   ★   ★

Cato Road, Clapham, SW4, is a residential thoroughfare, comprised of Edwardian terraced dwellings, which by 1993 had mostly been divided into two or three flats. It is a narrow street, no more than twenty-five feet wide, and vehicles park on both sides of the road. Vehicular access to the road is from Clapham High Street, and it stretches down to its south-east corner at Kendoa Road. In fact, Cato Road used to exit into Bedford Road, but by 1993 access to Cato Road as a quick cut-through into Clapham High Street had been denied. Had access been possible, one could have driven out of Cato Road, crossed Bedford Road and driven straight into Sandmere Road, which is directly opposite. The relevance of this route will become clear, a little later. The lack of vehicular access would not prevent pedestrians from using that route to and from Bedford Road, nor would it stop someone riding a bicycle. Someone like Police Constable 750 'LM' Patrick Dunne.

★   ★   ★

Just before nine o'clock, PC Dunne, in uniform and wearing a high-visibility yellow jacket, arrived on his bicycle at 28 Cato Road, directly opposite to Danso's address. The visit was in response to a call to Clapham police station from the occupant of the ground floor flat, Marino Ceria, a fifty-year-old Italian wine waiter. Following a trip to Italy, he had earlier that day returned to his flat to find it in a terrible state of disorder and immediately suspected (rightly or wrongly) that his brother, Pier Ceria, fifty-two and unemployed, must be responsible. Ceria wanted a police officer to witness the mess and also provide advice on how he could deal with the situation. In addition, he telephoned his friend Antonio Thomas Leon, a forty-year-old chief art and design technician, and asked him to come over, and Leon arrived at 9.10, some twenty minutes after PC Dunne's arrival. Parking his car in Cato Road, Leon walked back towards No. 28, but as he did so he noticed three black men standing on the pavement outside Danso's address and formed the opinion that 'something was not quite right'. But of more immediate importance was the mess in his friend's flat, and both men sat down with PC Dunne to discuss the problem.

Signor Leon was quite right in his assumption that something was wrong. The man who lived next door to Danso heard a knock on his front window. When he opened the door, a black man asked him, "Is Kwame there?" The neighbour replied that Kwame Danso lived next door. Mark Christopher Goodwin, a thirty-year-old copywriter, was walking along Cato Road, in order to get access to Clapham High Street, when he noticed a black man knocking with his fist very loudly on the door of one of the houses situated between numbers 27 and 35. He also noticed that leaning against the wall of the house was a silver and black bat, which he thought looked smaller than a baseball bat; possibly a bat used for softball. Goodwin also noticed two other black men on the same side of the road, some thirty metres away, who started to walk towards the third man.

Another witness, who was visiting a friend in Cato Road, also saw the bat propped up against the wall; he also heard the man at the door, who was very angry, swearing and using a lot of West Indian slang. He then saw two other men approach the man at the door, one of whom took something from his pocket and slid one hand across the top of the other which resulted in a clicking sound; the other had his hands behind his back, and the witness heard a metallic noise similar to the first. As he entered his friend's house, the witness heard the first of the seventeen shots.

*   *   *

Wood and Danso were watching the football match on television when there was a ring at the front door. Danso got up, said to Wood, "I won't be a minute," and went to answer the door. Wood knew it was Danso's practice to look through the lounge window to see who the caller was, prior to opening the front door; and given the confrontation at Street Communications earlier, this would have been a prudent course of action. In fact, when a friend had arrived at Danso's flat earlier that evening, Danso had done just that before opening the door to him; therefore it is probable that Danso did so on this occasion as well. If he did, it follows that he saw someone that he recognized, who he thought was a friend and therefore no threat to him, and that was the reason why he opened the door.

Wood heard a noise which sounded like a struggle, then the sound of gunshots, Danso screaming, the smell of smoke and then rapid gunfire. It was enough for Wood, who grabbed his coat and ran out of the flat's back door, into the small garden and across the fences separating the properties. A neighbour, a retired man aged sixty-four who lived at number 35 Cato Road, heard the sound of the gunshots, and then a few moments later his German Shepherd dog started barking. The man went into his garden to find the dog with its teeth embedded in the trouser leg of a black man who was in the act of straddling his fence, and called the police. The fence-straddler, who was in such a state of shock that he could hardly speak, answered to the name of Henry Wood.

Upon hearing the gunshots, Marino Ceria left his flat, followed by PC Dunne and Antonio Leon, who heard Dunne utter a number into his radio – obviously his divisional number – followed by the words, "Gunshots fired." As he did so, two black men walked out of the hallway of No. 31 opposite, followed by a third who pointed a firearm directly at PC Dunne, who shouted to the two Italians, "Get in, get in!" As Ceria and Leon turned to re-enter the flat, so the gunman fired, the bullet hitting PC Dunne in the chest. He fell to the ground, fatally wounded.

As Ceria telephoned for an ambulance, so the three men strolled away, firing triumphantly into the air as they did so and laughing loudly. A large number of people heard the shots, but because it was just two weeks away from Guy Fawkes Night, many of them, especially the children, thought they were fireworks. The trio reached the end of Cato Road, crossed the paved section of Kendoa Road and walked across Bedford Road into Sandmere Road, where a car was waiting. They were seen by David Tomlinson, a forty-five-year-old charity director who was working in his study in his home at Tremadoc Road and who had looked out of the window after hearing the shots. The man in front was seen to place a gun inside his jacket, and another of the group was carrying an object which was approximately a foot in length and bore a suspicious resemblance to a rounders bat.

Shortly afterwards, Hilda Ann Harding left Clapham North Underground Station at approximately 9.20 and began to walk home south along Bedford Road. She noticed a police car with its siren wailing being driven into Clapham High Street and moments later she was about to cross Lendal Terrace when a dark coloured car, which she believed was a BMW convertible, tore out of Bedford Road and into Lendal Terrace, in front of her. She could see two black men in the front seats and felt that there was a third person in the back who was not sitting up straight. The car screeched to a halt because the access to Clapham High Street was temporarily blocked by other vehicles, and Miss Harding looked at the registration plate. She believed it read '8 MOB' or '9 MOB' and she duly passed this information on to the police.

Police and the ambulance service were arriving in Cato Road, in response to a number of telephone calls; Police Constable 325 'LM' Richard Stocker found PC Dunne's body in Ceria's hallway and attempted resuscitation, as did Steven Nichols, a paramedic attached to Landor Road Ambulance Station, but without success. At 9.50 that evening PC Dunne was certified dead by Dr Stephen Metcalf at St Thomas' Hospital.

Meanwhile, Danso had crawled into the lounge and telephoned for an ambulance at 9.09. He told the operator he had been shot, but his condition was such that he had great difficulty breathing. He staggered back to the hallway, where he collapsed. Police Constable 730 'LM' McLellan arrived, knelt down and asked him, "Who did this to you?" but Danso groaned and replied, "I can't breathe." Paramedics attended to give assistance, and Danso was conveyed to St Thomas' Hospital; but fifteen minutes after PC Dunne was certified dead, so was Kwame Danso.

Detective Superintendent John Jones, the head of No. 4 Area AMIP (Area Major Investigation Pool), was dining with his wife and friends in Godstone, Surrey, that evening. "Barely had I lifted a forkful of steak towards my mouth," he told me, "than I received a telephone call to tell me a PC had been shot. Ten minutes later, I received a second call, to say he was dead." Jones rushed the twenty miles to the scene in his Reliant Scimitar SS1 sports car, arriving twenty-five minutes later. The Press had already arrived. "What's that awful stink?" asked one of them, and received Jones' laconic reply, "My tyres and brake pads." Jones (or 'JJ' as he was known to his contemporaries) had joined the police in 1960 and had served on the Flying Squad for two tours, totalling seven years. He was a shrewd, well-informed investigator, whose expertise had been recognized with twenty-five commendations, and now, coming to the end of his service, he was utterly determined to leave no stone unturned in catching the murderers of the two men. He assembled a team of fifty detectives, and 'Operation Fordyce' was under way.

* * *

The day following the murders, a post mortem examination was carried out at the mortuary at St Thomas' Hospital by the forensic pathologist, Dr Richard Shepherd. PC Dunne had died from a single gunshot wound to the chest. The bullet had struck Dunne five feet one inch from ground level, penetrating both lungs and disrupting the thoracic aorta which had resulted in extensive internal haemorrhage. There was also an injury to Dunne's right wrist which may or may not have been caused by the same bullet. The bullet had passed right through PC Dunne's body and clothes, and it was discovered on the sheet underneath his body after his clothing was removed for scientific examination.

Kwame Danso had been hit by six bullets, all of which had passed clean through his body; no bullet fragments were recovered from any of the wound tracks. Death, however, had been caused by just one of the bullets, which had entered the front of his abdomen and exited through his buttock, causing fatal injuries to the stomach and bowel arteries.

Two handguns had been used for the murders, and at least seventeen shots had been fired. Two different shoe prints were lifted from Danso's hallway, and an intensive forensic examination was carried out. Witnesses were interviewed and re-interviewed. It was clear from the witnesses that three black men were involved in the murder, one being lighter-skinned than the other two.

On Saturday, 30 October, ten days after the murders, Nelson telephoned Eugene Djaba on two occasions. By now, Djaba had made a long statement to the police concerning the events at Street Communications on the day prior to the killings, and Nelson was aware of this. Although he had not seen the statement, he must have been fully aware of the damage that Djaba could do him: he would have provided police with a suggested motive for Danso's murder and he could also place a firearm in Nelson's possession on that day. During the first call he told Djaba, "I want to see you Eugene, I want to see you today." When Nelson made the second phone call, he told Djaba that he knew he had given names to the police and that he believed the police would arrest him and Tony Francis, based on Djaba's evidence. If that was the case, said Nelson, and the police asked him (Nelson) questions based on Djaba's statement, he would come looking for him.

The investigating team had focussed their attention on the BMW seen by Miss Harding – '8 MOB' or '9 MOB'. The owners of the vehicles bearing these number plates were seen and quickly eliminated from the enquiry; the vehicles themselves were not of the colour or type seen by Miss Harding, and in any event, the owners were able to prove that the vehicles were not in London on that day. Next, the team sought details of all vehicles in which the letters 'MOB' appeared, preceded by a defined set of numbers. Of these, there were only fifty-four, and again most could be excluded because of the vehicle type or colour. Of the very few left, almost all could be excluded from the enquiry because the owners were able to confirm that their vehicles were not in the vicinity of Cato Road on the night of the murder or, indeed, on any other night. All except one.

The registration number closest to the two recollected by Miss Harding was 'A9 MOB'. It was a black BMW 3 series, registered to a Richard Watts. Watts was born in 1959 and was six feet one, of powerful build, and had hair described as wiry and untidy with a small, three-inch ponytail. He had a goatee beard and moustache and was of mixed race (Afro-Caribbean and Asian). Some said he could be taken for a South American, others a tanned white man, but others suggested he resembled a Chinese – hence his nickname, 'Chen'. Watts had a bad criminal record; he had received a supervision order the first time he was convicted of robbery, but five years later, in 1979 (with several more convictions recorded in the meantime), he appeared at the Old Bailey and for two cases of robbery and possession of a firearm with intent to commit an indictable offence was sentenced to Borstal Training. Eighteen months later, he appeared at Croydon Crown Court, again for robbery, and this time he was sentenced to three years' imprisonment. Following his release, he was fined £50 at Camberwell Magistrates' Court for causing actual bodily harm to a police officer, and four months later he appeared at the Inner London Crown Court, where for robbery and burglary he was sentenced to a total of thirty months' imprisonment. He had been released on 10 April 1987, having served just over half of his sentence.

He and Nelson were friends, so friendly in fact that Watts permitted Nelson to borrow his car – 'A9 MOB'. Watts and Nelson were in the car on the day following the murders when it was involved in a minor collision with another vehicle. Nelson was observed driving it on 2 November 1993 in Fieldview, his home address. Not that Nelson relied on Watts for transportation; he had his own green BMW, registration number PPE 810W. When he was stopped by police in Ilford on one occasion, whilst he was driving his own car, he felt compelled to give his name as 'Richard Watts'.

John Jones had served as a detective sergeant in south London, where the name of Nelson kept coming up; he was regarded as a minor but a violent young criminal. Although promotion and various postings had come his way, Jones kept closely in touch with the goings-on in that area and had maintained friendly relations with a number of members of the black community. Even though Nelson was feared in that area of London, some of them contacted Jones. Thanks to Jones' contacts, a surveillance operation had been set up by officers who were part of the 'Operation Fordyce' team, as well as officers from Scotland Yard's SO11 Surveillance Team; some of the officers were armed. Their brief was to control the movements of the occupants of the BMW, registration number A9 MOB. On 23 November 1993 Nelson was driving this car and Watts was the passenger; it would be the date of their arrest.

★   ★   ★

That evening, the vehicle was followed from south London, across the Thames and north to the area of Highbury Vale, N5, where Watts and Nelson met up with the occupants of another vehicle, a black Peugeot. One of the latter was Donville David Gibson, and there was a short conversation between the men before they returned to their respective vehicles and drove off in convoy; with the surveillance units in pursuit, they arrived at Highbury Hill and parked up at the junction with Aubert Park, just south of Arsenal tube station. Gibson got into the BMW, and then the unexpected occurred – as it inevitably tends to do.

Police Sergeant 39 'NH' Stephen Sands and Police Constable 340 'NH' George Thompson, both attached to Holloway police station, were on patrol in plain clothes in an unmarked police car. They were, of course, nothing whatsoever to do with the surveillance operation, being on completely different duties, and, indeed, had no conception that they were in the middle of a surveillance operation, because they and the officers from 'Operation Fordyce' were operating on completely different radio frequencies. But as they turned the corner, they saw Nelson in the driver's seat of the BMW, Watts in the back with a black bag over his shoulder and Gibson, out of the car, who appeared to be urinating against a front garden wall. Matters were not helped by Gibson grinning at the officers. Then Watts got out of the car and he and Gibson walked off up Highbury Hill towards the Underground station. Because of their behaviour the officers decided to have a word with them, and PC Thompson got out of the police car, whereupon both men took to their heels. As Gibson dashed in and out of gardens, so Thompson rugby-tackled him, bringing him crashing to the ground, before spotting that Gibson was holding a small hand gun. In the ensuing struggle, PC Thompson also became aware of the presence of Watts, who was pointing a sawn-off shotgun directly at him. "Give it to him, give it to him!" screamed Gibson, and it was clear that he was not suggesting that Watts should surrender his weapon to PC Thompson, who prudently backed away.

Sergeant Sands had also left the police car and was unaware why his associate had abandoned his struggle with Gibson, until he was two or three yards away from Watts, who levelled the sawn-off at him. "Come on, waste him!" screamed the bloodthirsty little Donville Gibson to Watts, whereupon Sands stopped, put his hands in the air and backed away. Watts and Gibson ran off, and the two officers chased them in their police car, at the same time calling for armed assistance on the radio. Other officers started swiftly converging on the scene.

Two of the surveillance team – Detective Constable Michael Eade from the 'Fordyce' investigation and Detective Sergeant Peter Rowling from SO11 (and armed) – saw Watts and Gibson in Highbury Hill and followed them in their unmarked police car into Aubert Park. They saw a marked police car, its blue light flashing and being driven by Police Constable 225 'NH' David Feaster, arrive and park in Elfort Road, some ten yards from the junction with Aubert Park, in response to the call for assistance.

DS Rowling stopped his car, drew his revolver and moved to the right; DC Eade also got out of the car, moved to the left and advanced towards the two suspects. Watts, who by now was breathing fast, tried to push the holdall he was carrying between the railings of a house, but then changed his mind and pulled it back. As the two officers moved in to arrest the men, Gibson turned and fired three shots in quick succession. "I heard what appeared to be the sound of breaking glass," said DC Eade later, "and I heard a high-pitched whizz to my right." Shouting at PC Feaster to lie down across the seats, DC Eade and DS Rowling continued the chase, and after a few yards, as DC Eade recounted, "I heard another loud bang, which sounded more like a boom, where the earlier shots sounded like a firecracker." This was the sound of the shotgun being fired.

Watts and Gibson were chased into the gardens of 46 Elfort Road, then over a wall into the rear of 152 Highbury Hill. There they were trapped, because the area was immediately contained by DS Rowling and Detective Constable Ray Ridge (another armed SO11 officer), assisted by a Trojan (armed response vehicle) unit and officers from No. 1 Area Territorial Support Group. The garden was now surrounded by five armed officers, and the area was illuminated with Dragon Lights, making the scene as bright as day. Assistance in the form of support dogs and a hostage negotiator was requested, but these were not needed. Before they could arrive, a voice was heard plaintively wailing, "Mr Policeman, I've had enough. I want to surrender." There was a conversation between Watts and the police, in which Watts begged police not to shoot him. After he was assured that this was not the intended course of action, he emerged, followed by Gibson, who squealed, "I'm here, I'm coming out!" and both were arrested. A search of the area revealed a green shotgun cartridge and the sawn-off, which had been stuffed into a dustbin.

Meanwhile, Nelson in the black BMW had been followed until his car was blocked in by a stationary vehicle, whereupon a loaded .25 automatic handgun was tossed out of the driver's window. Nelson, who was alone in the car, got out and raised his hands. As two uniformed officers advanced to arrest him, Nelson ran towards them but was overpowered and arrested.

Initially, Nelson was taken to Islington police station where, upon being formally arrested for the murders of Danso and PC Dunne, he replied, "What the fuck has that got to do with me?" It was whilst he was being booked in that the custody officer, Police Sergeant Edwards, explained that he wished to take possession of Nelson's clothing for forensic examination, a course of action which Nelson expressed reluctance to agree to.

"If you don't go into that room now and take them off, you'll be taken into that room and your clothes will be removed," stated Sergeant Edwards categorically, adding, "That's the end of the conversation."

"Will you enjoy that, are you enjoying it?" responded Nelson hotly, to which Sergeant Edwards replied, "I won't be doing it, mate, so it really doesn't make any odds to me."

That, together with the calmness of Edwards' response, blew Nelson's very short fuse. He no doubt felt that he was being 'dissed' on an unbelievably grand scale. "Watch yourself ... watch yourself, Mr Sergeant, watch yourself," he hissed, then stood up and walked to the surgeon's room, to where he had been directed. And then he stopped. He turned and told Edwards, "You'll cop it like the other one fucking copped it."

The incident did not end there. Nelson was detained overnight, and the following morning, two custody officers checked the prisoners in their cells. Nelson was awake, and as the officers looked into his cell he bellowed, "I'll throw a cup of piss at you, fuck off! I'll take one of you out, again."

In the space of nine hours Nelson had thus twice referred to the murder of PC Dunne, and on the second occasion put himself forward as the murderer. The incident at the cell was not recorded on tape, because the facility to do so did not exist. But the booking-in procedure *was* videotaped because a camera had been set permanently in position to record all aspects of these transactions; and much later, an enhanced version of the audio track was produced for a jury to hear.

Nelson and the other prisoners were interviewed over a period of two days, with Nelson refusing to answer any questions. While this was going on, the prisoners' homes were searched, including the home of Richard Watts at Churchmore Road, Streatham, SW16. In a box behind a mirror a cartridge case was found. It was forensically proved, beyond doubt, that the weapon used to fire this cartridge was the same one which had been used to murder Kwame Danso.

Nelson was formally charged with conspiracy to murder PC Dunne and Kwame Danso and he replied, "That ain't true, it's not true." Remanded in custody to stand his trial, Nelson was not picked out by any of the witnesses; he refused to attend the proceedings.

Nelson was one of three men charged variously with either murder or conspiracy to murder the two men, and the investigating team were busy investigating other offences and strengthening the existing case; but three months later, on the advice of senior Treasury Counsel, the charges were discontinued in respect of all three men, on the grounds of insufficient evidence.

It broke the heart of the investigating team. As John Jones told me, "I was very angry. I didn't sleep properly for ages afterwards."

"Of course we were disappointed at the cessation of the enquiry," Ivan Dunne, Patrick's brother, told me in 2011. "I remember a very senior officer arriving to break the bad news. John Jones ... and the team were devastated."

This raises the question, should proceedings have been discontinued? John Jones and his team obviously thought not, but it goes far, far deeper than that. When a police officer is murdered and no one is convicted for it, it puts an enormous dent in the public's confidence. The public unfairly blame the police, their reasoning being, 'If they can't catch someone who murdered one of their own, what chance have we got?' Apart from that, the morale of the police slumps, and they begin to think, 'Why should we bother to try and catch the perpetrators of this outrage and present compelling evidence, only to have the lawyers let them out?'

No. It was an obtuse decision made by lawyers who like to have every piece of evidence cut and dried; and in the real world it seldom happens like that. In the real world of criminal investigation, experienced detectives make their own luck, they work hard and get results. Over the years, Scotland Yard detectives had acquired reputations second to none for crime-busting; they were variously described as 'being able to pluck a result out of thin air' and 'tough, clever and unorthodox, with a terrier-like ability to shake a case until every prisoner was arrested.' Most famous of all was Detective Chief Inspector Peter Beveridge's investigation into a triple murder in Kent in 1940. No one had witnessed the murders, there was no forensic evidence, no fingerprints and certainly no confession; but a meticulous assembling of all of the circumstantial evidence resulted in the rock-solid conviction of Mrs Florence Ransom.

John Jones was one of this brand of detectives – he had been involved in the investigation of scores of murders – but many felt that the lawyers who reviewed this case did so myopically and that when they presented their findings to the deeply flawed and lacklustre Crown Prosecution Service, who demand a far better than average chance of conviction, they eagerly grabbed their chance and discontinued the case. Some police officers who were involved in the investigation believe that this was the correct decision; others, however, thought it a disgrace.

★ ★ ★

Nevertheless, the investigation continued. The clothing which Nelson reluctantly handed over was submitted for scientific analysis, and firearms residue – a combination of chemical particles found only after a firearm has been discharged – was found on four items. Although firearm discharge residue is not like a fingerprint or DNA evidence, it is categorized by type. Each of the seventeen cartridge cases found at Cato Road was of Winchester make and each produced what was known as 'Type 3' residue when fired; it was 'Type 3' residue which was found on the items of Nelson's clothing.

At the time of the incident, Nelson was living with his mother at Fieldview, Wandsworth. The road stretches from Burntwood Lane in the south up to Magdalen Road. The area is surrounded by cemeteries: Wimbledon, Lambeth and Streatham. And opposite the junction with Fieldview, across the road from Magdalen Road, is Wandsworth cemetery, a two-minute walk from Nelson's home. It was there that an informant told the police that evidence vital to the enquiry would be found. On 19 January 1994 a search was carried out, but the cemetery covers a wide area with almost 2,500 interments, and since the informant had not indicated a precise spot, nothing was found. But on 6 June that year better information was forthcoming, and after forty-five minutes' search with a metal detector in a much smaller area, a metal container was found. Wrapped in a black plastic bag were two handguns; both of them were later proved to have been used in both murders at Cato Road.

The first pistol was a 9mm Browning. It has the capacity to fire thirteen rounds and was once a favoured sidearm of the Special Air Service. It is capable of killing a man at a distance of fifty metres, although when it was used to murder Danso, the range was somewhat closer. Of the seventeen cartridge cases which were found at Cato Road, nine had been fired from this Browning.

The other pistol was an Italian-made 9mm Tanfoglio. These are popular sporting and defensive pistols, widely used across Europe; they are also imported into the USA.

Each of the pistols had been placed in a red Virgin amenity bag; it was discovered that Nelson's mother, Shirley Wright, had flown to Miami with Virgin Atlantic Airways on 10 September 1993 with another member of her family and returned on 24 September – these bags were issued to passengers on that flight. The pistols and the Virgin bags were in turn placed inside Bally shoe bags. After the guns had been discovered, a further search was carried out at Nelson's home in Fieldview; a third Virgin amenity bag was found, as were six pairs of Bally shoes. The black plastic bag in which the pistols were wrapped was found to bear the fingerprint of Nelson's mother.

In August 1994 Eugene Djaba attended an identification parade at Brixton police station, but this was not a parade of people; it was to try to pick out the gun that Nelson had showed him the day before the murder. Ten pistols were shown to Djaba, of which the Tanfoglio was number four. It was this weapon that Djaba picked out, with these words: "I picked out number four as being similar to the gun I saw Gary Nelson with at the back of my shop. Number four was the same type of gun but Nelson's was very new and it didn't have a wooden handle, it had a black rubber-type handle."

What Djaba could not know is that the wooden grips on a Tanfoglio can speedily be exchanged for black rubber grips. And when Nelson informed him that the pistol held twenty rounds, either he was boasting or his numeracy skills had failed him; a Tanfoglio holds sixteen rounds. Eight of the spent cartridges fired from this pistol had been left at Cato Road. It was also the weapon used to murder PC Dunne.

The Tanfoglio's serial number had been filed off – a common occurrence when a gun is going to be used in crime – and a false number punched in its place. The team's enquiries led them in July 1994 to the door of one Sidney Wink, a former police officer, then a firearms dealer and about as crooked as they come. Wink's firearms register revealed that in October 1990 a 9mm Tanfoglio pistol was entered incorrectly and then went missing. The police searched his premises and found eight boxes of marking punches; when comparisons were made, it was discovered that the number 4 punch in one of the boxes had been used twice to punch the bogus number 4 on to the Tanfoglio. There was a further interesting connection; in Nelson's diary was a reference to a man named Alan and a telephone number. Next to the name were the letters GU, and it is more than possible that this was a fairly transparent code for 'gun'; either that, or Nelson had made a creditable attempt to spell the word correctly. Through intelligence connections, it was possible to make a link from 'Alan' to other underworld gun sellers and users, leading to Wink.

Not that Wink would be of any further help to the officers from 'Operation Fordyce'; within seven days of the officers focussing their attention on him, and undoubtedly feeling the net closing in around him, the man also suspected of providing the guns for the £26,000,000 Brink's-Mat robbery in 1983 blew his brains out.

This strengthened the case for the murders against Nelson, and the enquiry team (without the leadership of John Jones, who had retired in October 1994) was also examining other matters; so that when he stood trial at Southwark Crown Court, together with his associates, some of whom featured in the incidents in Highbury Vale, Nelson was also charged with attempting to murder Mohammed Massaquoi at the SW1 Club, Victoria, SW1, on Monday, 12 July 1993. Following an incident of disrespect involving a woman, Massaquoi told the court, Nelson had fired shots at his vehicle in Lewisham High Street. Massaquoi stated that Nelson then approached him a week later at the SW1 Club, saying, "Remember me? I'm the guy that was buzzing shots at you," before pulling a gun from his waistband and shooting him in the legs, thigh and buttocks; a second man also fired a shot at him. Massaquoi's brother had taken him to University College Hospital, where it was discovered that, amazingly, very little physical damage had been caused. A week later, Massaquoi was arrested on a minor charge and upon being taken to a police station and searched, was discovered to be in possession of a small box of spent bullets. Asked to explain these, Massaquoi described the incident and told the officers that having extracted these rounds from his body the surgeon had thoughtfully handed them to him, without informing the police. The police attended the SW1 Club – habitués of the club were advised to wear earplugs on the dance floor which probably explained why nobody heard anything – and took possession of the spent cartridge cases. The cartridge case found in the box behind the mirror in Richard Watts' home was found to have been fired from one of the guns used at the SW1 Club and also at Cato Road. However, Nelson was acquitted of this charge of attempted murder. At the time of giving evidence Massaquoi was similarly in custody, also awaiting trial for attempted murder. Two days after Nelson's acquittal, he was found hanged in his cell. The cause of death was believed to be suicide.

Nelson was also acquitted of the charge of possessing a loaded .25 pistol at Highbury Vale. The officer who saw the pistol thrown from the driver's window of the car which Nelson was driving and of which he was the sole occupant, was unable to say with any certainty that it was Nelson who had discarded it.

However, there was a further charge. Six weeks before the murders, on 2 September 1993, at about 2.50 pm, Nelson was driving his BMW, registration number PPE 810W, in Merton Road, SW18. Travelling behind him in the same direction in a Leyland Sherpa van was a man named Gary Kewell. Nelson repeatedly slowed down as he passed road junctions on the left-hand side and, tiring of this, Kewell overtook him correctly on the offside. Nelson, in turn, overtook Kewell on the inside and, manoeuvring his BMW in front of the van, made a rude gesture with his hand. Kewell stuck his finger up in reply. This, as can be imagined, was too much for Nelson. Kewell told the court that he became nervous when he saw a girl, who was the front-seat passenger in the BMW, reach into the footwell and hand Nelson something. "I thought it was getting a bit silly so I decided to turn right," said Kewell. "Then he [Nelson] leaned out of the window and pointed his right arm at me. I heard a cracking noise and I ducked down behind the dashboard. I felt the thuds of the bullets hitting the van. From the rate of fire, I would have said it was an automatic weapon. I was very shaken." From a distance of twenty feet Nelson fired five shots at Kewell's van, three of which hit it.

Nelson was acquitted of attempting to murder Gary Kewell; however, he was found guilty of possessing a firearm with intent to endanger life and on 16 August 1995 he was sentenced to eight years' imprisonment. His associates, including those who had fired shots at the police officers in Highbury Vale and others who were convicted of kidnap and extortion, were variously sentenced to terms of imprisonment up to and including twelve years.

Within ten days of receiving his sentence, Nelson, who at his trial had adorned himself with jewellery with an estimated value of £50,000, had assaulted three prison officers at the top-security Belmarsh Prison and had six months added to his sentence. Thereafter, his behaviour was constantly disruptive: issuing serious threats against the prison staff, bullying inmates and believed to be involved in the prison drug scene. And yet, in August 1999, having served just half of his sentence, Nelson was released.

Police officers were stunned at this pusillanimous decision by the parole board; all the further evidence in respect of the two murders had been submitted to the Crown Prosecution Service for their consideration, in the hope that this compelling evidence would prompt them to reverse their decision. It did not. In fact, five months prior to Nelson's release, Paul Boateng (now Baron Boateng), then New Labour MP for Brent South and Minister of State at the Home Office, told the House of Commons:

> I have no plans to establish an independent judicial enquiry into the decision not to bring to trial the three men arrested in connection with the murders of PC Patrick Dunne and Mr William Danso ... Following the arrest and charging of the three men, the Crown Prosecution Service sought the opinion of Treasury Counsel, who advised that there was insufficient evidence to proceed with the charges of murder and conspiracy to murder.

It will come as no surprise to learn that prior to his appointments in Her Majesty's Government, Boateng had been a lawyer.

The previous year (and five years after the murders), the inquest into the deaths of PC Dunne and Kwame Danso was heard at Southwark Crown Court. Nelson did not attend but one of his associates, then serving a prison sentence, did. In a swaggering performance in the witness box, he replied, "No way, no way" when the coroner, Selena Lynch, asked him if he had any involvement in the murders. But the tranquillity of the courtroom was shattered when Kwame Danso's widow Deborah confronted the witness and screamed, "Rot in hell!" before storming out of the court in tears. A few moments later she returned to say, "I would like to ask you, why did you do this, why?" and received the answer, "I don't know what you're talking about."

Having heard the circumstances of how the guns were found, Nelson's mother endeavoured to assist the court by stating that the police had collected the bag from her home and planted the guns in it.

The coroner recorded a verdict of unlawful killing in respect of both men, adding that PC Dunne had died in the line of duty. "His killers are nothing but worthless cowards," said the coroner, adding, "and so are they who can, but will not, give them up."

So Nelson was released, and as the years passed his reputation grew in stature; as he had boasted at one of his trials, "I walk heavy. I am a serious person." He travelled widely, including to Cyprus and the United States. It seemed impossible that he would ever be brought to justice for the two murders. But then something happened to change that; it did not come from the police and it certainly did not emanate from the Crown Prosecution Service.

★   ★   ★

The grieving family of Patrick Dunne refused to give up. They had laid Patrick to rest on 12 November 1993 at the Holy Trinity Church, Clapham Common. Hundreds of mourners were inside and outside the church and hundreds more lined the route along the Wandsworth Road, with schoolchildren and shopkeepers turning out to pay their respects. Two cars were required to convey the floral tributes. The service was conducted by the late Reverend John Hackett, there was a reading by the late Police Constable Barry Critchley and eulogies from Patrick Dunne's teacher friend, Fred Tyldsley, his brother Steve Dunne and Superintendent John Reese. Hymns included 'Abide with Me' and 'The Old Rugged Cross', and as the congregation filed from the church, the Metropolitan Police choir sang *Va' pensiero* from Verdi's opera *Nabucco,* a favourite of Patrick Dunne's. This was followed by memorial services, one held in Bolton on 4 December 1993 and others, annually, at the cemetery.

The family knew that the police investigation had been exemplary. Ivan Dunne told me in 2011, "I was always happy with the police, the investigation and the incredible kindness and friendship we received from them, many beyond the call of duty and that continues to this day." But after the proceedings had been discontinued, the two Dunne brothers, Ivan and Stephen, wrote on a regular basis to the commissioner of the Metropolitan Police, asking if any further progress had been made. But nothing had been – in fact, the case, all nine large dockets of it, had, in police parlance, been 'put away'.

But in 2000 the Dunne family's latest letter landed on the desk of a new commissioner, one far different to the vast majority of his predecessors. Sir John Stevens QPM (later Baron Stevens of Kirkwhelpington) was what was known as 'a copper's copper'. Joining the Metropolitan Police as a constable in 1962, Stevens, a career detective, had shot up through the ranks, collecting twenty-seven commendations on the way, and came to public notice when as Deputy Chief Constable of Cambridgeshire he conducted a thorough and extensive enquiry in Northern Ireland into allegations of collusion between terrorist groups and the security forces. Fearless and determined, Stevens was known for taking quick and decisive action, and the Dunnes' letter was forwarded to the commander of what was then called the Homicide and Serious Crime Group, together with a terse Stevens minute: 'Look into this!'

The previous year, Murder Review Groups (MRG) had been set up. Colloquially known as 'Cold Case Review Teams', they prompted the popular television series *New Tricks* and *Waking the Dead*. A less well–known function of the unit was the review of current, ongoing cases to ensure best practice and to assist the Senior Investigating Officers (SIO) as much as possible. The reviews were carried out on a regular basis by the MRG detective superintendent, who was usually in charge of four or five teams, and his staff officer, an experienced detective sergeant. One such officer was Detective Sergeant Dave Ayling, who had joined the AMIP at Barnes police station in 1997. He had been tasked with setting up the review process, and his role was designated as 'Review Sergeant'. He kept computer records of each investigation, informed the detective superintendent when a review was needed and then recorded details of the review. This process concerned unsolved cases, and he would participate in the decision-making as to whether the case should be 'put away' or the investigation continued. Now he was handed the PC Dunne case. It took over a month to read all the correspondence and make notes, and having done so he realized that which had been clear all along: the lines of enquiry by the original investigating team had been correct and the suspects remained the same. He noted that the Treasury Counsel believed the team had come close to solving the case but that a continued prosecution could end in an acquittal. This was before a change in the 'double jeopardy' law and also in the ability to bring in evidence of relevant bad character. Therefore, this was not a 'cold case' matter, in which a fresh investigating team would start from scratch; it was a case which should be continued by an active Murder Investigation Team.

The matter was discussed with the commissioner, and the continuing enquiry was sanctioned. The Serious Crime Directorate (SCD1(4)) was given the task and Team 6 took it on, together with former members of 'Operation Fordyce', who were elated at being given another chance to nail the murderers. The investigation, under the direction of Detective Inspector Steve Richardson, got underway in January 2001. Richardson, who was promoted to detective chief inspector during the investigation (and later to detective superintendent), had come to the SCD from the National Crime Squad; he was very well acquainted with the high-level investigation of serious criminals.

In the five years since the enquiry had been closed there had been developments in the forensic side of investigations, and these included advances in the investigation of mobile phone usage. Nelson had had access to three mobile phones, and in respect of one of them in particular it was clear, through linking the numbers dialled to the names and numbers recorded in Nelson's address book, that he would have made most, although not necessarily all, of the calls. Mobile phones (or cell phones, as Americans refer to them) operate over relatively short distances; they have to transmit and receive signals to and from nearby aerials or cell sites. When a call is made on a mobile phone, data is produced and stored which identifies the cell site or aerial through which the transmission was made. In this way the general location of a mobile phone can be determined when it is used to make a call. In fact, many of the calls made by Nelson were made via the aerial or cell site which served his home in Wandsworth.

Improved technology revealed that at 8.56 on the night when PC Dunne and Danso were shot – just thirteen minutes before the murders – a call was made from that phone to a number used by Richard Watts. It was made from the aerial which provided the best coverage for Cato Road, and the person who made that seven-second call was therefore in or very close to Cato Road. It took months of laborious transcription of thousands of items of data, double-checking the information, to present evidence of maximum value to the case.

In November 2001 appeals and a reconstruction were made on

the BBC television programme *Crimewatch*. This resulted in a former prisoner coming forward. While Nelson had been incarcerated in Wormwood Scrubs Prison in 1994 he got into conversation with this man. A large sum of money – £50,000 – was mentioned (in an entirely different context) and Nelson remarked that this was the same amount that had been placed on his head as a reward for his capture. (Indeed it had been, by the *News of the World* for information leading to the arrest of those responsible for the murders of PC Dunne and Danso.) Asked to explain that comment, Nelson replied, "I shot the copper; the one on the bike."

The investigation was long and tortuous; Nelson was now extremely wealthy and greatly feared, and there was a further setback. Eugene Djaba, the proprietor of Street Communications who could give such damning evidence against Nelson, had stood trial at Wood Green Crown Court with nine other defendants during 1995–6, accused of the fraudulent evasion of VAT and excise duty chargeable on cigarettes to the value of £3,000,000. Towards the end of the trial, Djaba jumped bail and fled to Ghana. He was convicted in his absence and a warrant for his arrest was issued. If he were to return, he could expect a substantial sentence; and Djaba had no intention of returning. What could be done? As yet, nothing at all.

New rules of disclosure to the defence meant that two officers were employed for eighteen months checking all of the documents which resulted from the original investigation, including actions, messages and evidence, plus the newly acquired evidence – over 20,000 such items. These documents had to be assembled into schedules for service on the defence, prior to the prosecution, and a junior counsel was appointed to work full-time for fourteen months doing just that.

In the meantime, a top secret operation against Nelson was underway by the Special Projects Team. This shadowy unit was part of the Serious and Organised Crime Group and dealt proactively with offences of contracts to murder, major drugs supply, multi-dimensional crime gangs (including ethnically composed groups) and large-scale firearms trafficking. Nelson, who was now living at 295 Fishguard's Way, Canning Town, appeared a suitable subject for their attention, and probes were drilled into the flat to enable his conversations to be overheard. On 12 February 2003 police burst into the flat, to find Nelson in bed, wearing body armour. He was in possession of a fully loaded semi-automatic Browning pistol with a red-dot laser guidance device, together with a silencer, twenty-three further bullets for use with the pistol and a stun-gun. The items, which were in a small zip-up bag, were described as 'a hitman's kit'.

On 30 January 2004 Nelson was found guilty of possessing a firearm with intent to endanger life, possessing a firearm and ammunition without a certificate and possessing a prohibited weapon. He was sentenced to life imprisonment.

Nelson was formally arrested for the murders on 18 November 2004 and replied, "It's got nothing to do with me." When he was interviewed, Nelson read from a prepared statement in which he said he knew he had been under surveillance and had been set up before; he also stated that he had nothing to do with the murders and that he had nothing else to say. And when he was asked specific questions about the shootings, he refused to answer them until he was asked about the events at Islington police station, when he had been originally arrested and had made those deeply incriminating comments. He now became quite animated, saying that the police had previously planted evidence on him, and without directly answering the questions said that twenty to thirty officers at the station were calling him "a cop-killer".

The five-week trial took place at Woolwich Crown Court. Armed police patrolled the perimeter of the court. A highly important witness who had to be entered into the Witness Protection Programme had provided utterly crucial evidence linking Nelson with the murder weapons. Despite the most sympathetic and tactful handling, at the last moment she was so terrified of Nelson that her courage deserted her and she refused to give evidence. A warrant was issued for her arrest, but still she adamantly declined to appear for the prosecution.

However, due to a recent change in the law, if it could be proved that a witness was in mortal fear of a defendant, a judge could rule that that person's evidence could be admitted by reading their original statements to the court.

That was what happened in this case; the officers who had been debriefing the witness gave compelling evidence of her fear of Nelson, as did the officers who had escorted her to court, informing the judge that at one stage she had tried to jump from the moving police car. The judge ruled that her statements could be read to the jury in full, and when that decision was announced, as one of the police officers told me, "Nelson went absolutely crazy." Blaming the judge and the police for conspiring against him, he had to be restrained and was led away and refused to attend the rest of the trial, staying instead in his cell at Belmarsh Prison. As his barrister, John Ryder QC, informed the jury, Nelson offered no defence. Eugene Djaba was not present, either. His evidence was given by means of a video link from Ghana.

DCI Richardson and his deputy travelled to Ghana on two occasions in order to find Djaba. Through painstaking enquiries they discovered his whereabouts, and the reason why he had agreed to give evidence – albeit on a video link – was a simple one: Kwame Danso had been his friend.

The former prisoner from Wormwood Scrubs, to whom Nelson had confessed the murder, was present. He had not solicited the reward; instead, he was given a new identity. That Djaba and the former prisoner gave evidence at all was due to the tact and resourcefulness of members of the enquiry team. On 17 February 2006 the jury, comprised of seven men and five women who had received police protection, took twelve hours to find Nelson guilty of both murders. The trial judge, Mr Justice Wilkie, said:

> PC Dunne at that time was performing his public duty at a house opposite. He, too, like Mr Danso, was unarmed and of no immediate threat to Nelson and indeed, his last acts and words were to seek to protect those who were with him in that house by urging them to go inside to safety.

He then sentenced Nelson to two terms of life imprisonment, with a recommendation that he serve at least thirty-five years behind bars. The judge went on to praise the personnel of 'Operation Fordyce', saying, "I would like to congratulate the investigating team on today's verdict which has come about as a result of their dedication and hard work."

The officer in charge of the investigation, DCI Richardson, said, "Nelson has often been called a hitman. But he is not just the person paid to pull the trigger. He is much more than that. Nelson is a major-league, organized criminal who is into extortion, drug smuggling and armed robbery and will use extreme violence in pursuit of his aims. He operated among the top echelons of the criminal world."

Although nothing has ever been proved, Nelson is believed to have carried out a dozen gangland executions. A premiership footballer allegedly owed Nelson £30,000 in drugs debts; it was said that the footballer paid up after Nelson had threatened to end his career by shooting him in the legs.

Reactions to Nelson's conviction varied. John Jones was still bitter that it had taken so long for one of the murderers to be brought to justice, saying that the conviction could have been secured earlier. Some members of the second enquiry team disagree, and ne'er the twain shall meet. But there is no question about the sheer hard work and dedication that both teams of investigators injected into the enquiries. Patrick Dunne's brother Ivan, referring to Nelson, stated, "We have been waiting twelve and a half years. I do not forgive him and I never will. I have hated him and his gang since day one and that will not change. I have lost a brother, my mother has lost a son and we have all lost a good police officer." Five years later, Ivan Dunne's views had not softened with the passage of time. "I get enormous pleasure knowing that every day for him is the same, with no hope of change for the rest of his life," he told me, adding, "I did feel let down by the CPS but now, of course, it could be said that the end justified the means."

However, his brother Stephen, a former Christian pastor, whilst agreeing with the sentence, added, "But personally, to Gary Nelson, even with the effect of his crime on my life, my wife and child – I forgive you, Gary Nelson." These sentiments were echoed by Kwame Danso's sister Gifty Tettehmartey, who said, "Forgiving Nelson has made it possible for me to cope."

For Nelson, in his prison cell, these must surely have been the unkindest cuts of all; to forgive a Gangsta his sins must rate in the highest echelons of disrespect.

The Serious Crime Directorate office in Sutton has been renamed 'Patrick Dunne House' in honour of PC Dunne. In addition, a tree and a plaque commemorating a man 'who died serving the local community' were installed as a tribute from the residents of the Westbury Estate, Clapham.

On 27 November 2007 there was a ceremony at Scotland Yard. The Commissioner, Sir Ian Blair, presented a posthumous commissioner's high commendation for bravery in respect of Patrick Dunne, to his brother Steven. It was a proper tribute to match the plaque unveiled in Cato Road to commemorate his life eleven years earlier. Other members of the enquiry team were commended for their ability and dedication on the case.

DCI Richardson, referring to his investigating team, said, "Our work is not yet complete and we will continue to investigate this case to bring the remaining perpetrators to justice. They must expect that one day, there will be a knock at the door and they too will face justice."

★   ★   ★

And that leads us to the conclusion – or does it? Many of you like matters conveniently tidied up – what happened to a particular person, how a certain matter was resolved, and so on. I know I do. But in this particular story that is not, at the time of writing, possible. There are outstanding threads to the 'Operation Fordyce' enquiry which are still unresolved and are still being investigated. There are also breakthroughs in forensic science waiting to happen; these might include further evidence from the shoe prints found in Danso's hallway. And despite the passage of time, there are still disgruntled people waiting to come forward and point the finger at two other murderers and provide such compelling evidence that even the CPS will have to act on it.

And that is when Patrick Dunne and Kwame Danso will finally have obtained justice.

Bibliography

Beveridge, Peter, *Inside the CID* (Evans Brothers Ltd, 1957)

Braddon, Russell, *The Shepherd's Bush Case* (Taken from *Great Cases of Scotland Yard*, Volume Two, The Reader's Digest Association Ltd, 1978)

Cobb, Belton, *Murdered on Duty* (W. H. Allen, 1961)

Dillon, Martin, *The Enemy Within* (Doubleday, 1994)

Fido, Martin, *The Krays – Unfinished Business* (Carlton Books Ltd, 1999)

Fido, Martin and Skinner, Keith, *The Official Encyclopedia of Scotland Yard* (Virgin Books, 1999)

Frasier, David K., *Murder Cases of the Twentieth Century* (McFarland & Co Inc, 1996)

Gledhill, Tony, *A Gun at my Head* (Historic Military Press, 2006)

Gurney, Peter, *Braver Men Walk Away* (Harper Collins, 1993)

Honeycombe, Gordon, *The Complete Murders of the Black Museum* (Leopard Books, 1995)

Huntley, Bob, *Bomb Squad* (W.H. Allen, 1977)

Jackett, Sam, *Heroes of Scotland Yard* (The Adventurers' Club, 1966)

Jackson, Sir Richard, *Occupied with Crime* (George G. Harrap & Co Ltd, 1967)

Kennison, P. and Swinden, D., *Behind the Blue Lamp* (Coppermill Press, 2003)

Kirby, Dick, *The Squad – A History of the Men and Vehicles of the Flying Squad at New Scotland Yard, 1919–1983* (Unpublished manuscript, Metropolitan Police History Museum, London, 1993)

Kirby, Dick, *Rough Justice – Memoirs of a Flying Squad Detective* (Merlin Unwin Books, 2001)

Kirby, Dick, *The Real Sweeney* (Constable & Robinson, 2005)

Kirby, Dick, *You're Nicked!* (Constable & Robinson, 2007)

Kirby, Dick, *The Sweeney – The First Sixty Years of Scotland Yard's Crimebusting Flying Squad* (Wharncliffe Books, 2011)

Kirby, Dick, *Scotland Yard's Ghost Squad* (Wharncliffe Books, 2011)

Kirby, Dick, *The Brave Blue Line* (Wharncliffe Books, 2011)

Kray, Reg, *Born Fighter* (Century, 1990)

Lawrence, Jane R., *From the Beat to the Palace* (Brewin Books Ltd, 2005)

Massingberd, Hugh (ed.), *The Daily Telegraph Book of Obituaries – A Celebration of Eccentric Lives* (MacMillan Reference Books, 1995)

Millen, Ernest, *Specialist in Crime* (George G. Harrap & Co Ltd, 1972)

Morton, James, *East End Gangland* (Time Warner, 2003)

Moysey, Steven P., *The Road to Balcombe Street* (The Haworth Press, 2008)

Pearson, John, *The Profession of Violence* (Panther Books, 1977)

Read, Leonard with Morton, James, *Nipper* (MacDonald & Co, 1991)

Ryder, Chris, *The RUC – A Force under Fire* (Methuen, 1989)

Scott, Sir Harold, *Scotland Yard* (Andre Deutsch, 1954)

Selwyn, Francis, *Nothing but Revenge* (Penguin Books, 1991)

Slipper, Jack, *Slipper of the Yard* (Sidgwick & Jackson Ltd, 1981)

Thomas, Donald, *Villains' Paradise* (John Murray, 2005)

Trow, M. J., *'Let him have it, Chris'* (Grafton, 1992)

Tullett, Tom, *Inside Interpol* (Frederick Muller Ltd, 1963)

Tullett, Tom, *Strictly Murder* (The Bodley Head, 1979)

Urban, Mark, *Big Boys' Rules* (Faber and Faber, 1992)

Young, Hugh, *My Forty Years at the Yard* (W. H. Allen, 1955)

Index